Coach Skip Bertman walks among his players stretching before the Regional Championship at Texas A&M in 1989.

EVERYTHING MATTERS IN BASEBALL

The **SKIP BERTMAN** Story

EVERYTHING MATTERS IN BASEBALL

The SKIP BERTMAN Story

GLENN GUILBEAU
with Leo Honeycutt

Acadian House
PUBLISHING
LAFAYETTE, LOUISIANA

On the cover: *LSU coach Skip Bertman signals his catcher during a game in the late 1990s. The catcher, in turn, passes on the message to the pitcher. (Photo by Steve Franz / LSU Athletics)*

Library of Congress Control Number: 2022936202

ISBN 10: 1-7352641-4-8
ISBN 13: 978-1-7352641-4-1

♦ Published by Acadian House Publishing, Lafayette, Louisiana
  (Edited by Trent Angers; editorial assistance and research by Madison Louviere)
♦ Interior design and pre-press production by Allison Nassans
♦ Dust jacket design by Jan Bertman, New Orleans, Louisiana
♦ Printed by Sheridan Books, Chelsea, Michigan

Preface

It was Saturday night in Tiger Stadium – Sept. 8, 2018. LSU had just kicked off against Southeastern Louisiana, and I was getting a coffee in the press box. Former LSU pitching coach Dan Canevari came up and asked if I could sit with him and Skip Bertman at one of the tables behind press row.

Within a few minutes, Skip asked me to write the book you are holding in your hands. I was not the first to work on this Bertman biography, but I will be forever grateful to Skip for summoning me from the bullpen to close.

I first met Skip 35 years earlier, in September of 1983, at his original LSU office in the Assembly Center. I had graduated from Missouri that August and had just started covering LSU for *Tiger Rag* magazine in Baton Rouge. Bertman had left the associate head coach job at Miami after the previous season to be LSU's coach.

He still reminds me that I was one of the first to interview him in his office. In that interview and in the last one for this book, on Feb. 9, 2022, Bertman was engaging, captivating, entertaining, funny, and you learned something.

Hopefully, this book is the same way.

I was also Bertman's first scoreboard operator at Alex Box Stadium for his LSU home opener on Feb. 22, 1984. The Tigers beat McNeese State, 8-6, in front of 645 fans.

It was a small opening of a big and beautiful relationship between LSU fans and Bertman that continues today, more than 20 years after he coached his last game at the Box, on May 27, 2001. He won that one, too – a 14-9 NCAA Regional victory over Virginia Commonwealth in front of 5,224.

My scoreboard gig was short-lived once Bertman noticed the balls and strikes were not being updated quickly enough. He was patient, though, as he was while I worked on this book.

I owe a special debt of gratitude to fellow author Leo Honeycutt, who wrote a Bertman manuscript that went unpublished. Excerpts from a number of Honeycutt's interviews appear here, as does some of his in-depth reporting and anecdotes from his exhaustive and impressive work.

This book covers Bertman's time as LSU baseball coach and his tenure as Athletic Director, as well as his five National Championships and a lot more. So, it isn't intended to be read in one sitting. Just the one chapter on his secrets to success, Chapter 19, is a lot to take in and think about.

Hopefully, while reading this book you will feel – as I did while researching and writing it – like you're back in the old Alex Box or Rosenblatt Stadium with Skip and the Boys.

– Glenn Guilbeau

Acknowledgements

I owe a debt of gratitude to all who contributed to the content of this book, starting with Skip Bertman, who sat for more interviews than I can count.

I want to thank the 38 former LSU baseball players who Skip coached and who I interviewed in person and on the phone. Their names and a little about them can be found in the Sources under Personal Interviews toward the back of this book.

Special thanks to LSU baseball Sports Information Director Bill Franques for his interview and for providing nearly all of the pictures that appear on these pages.

Thanks to former *USA Today* Louisiana/Lafayette editor Brett Blackledge, a truly great editor, who allowed me to write this book while covering LSU and the Saints.

I'd like to acknowledge the many sportswriters whose articles were used for reference as I wrote through these chapters. So, thanks to former Baton Rouge *Advocate* sportswriters Lee Feinswog, Sam King, Jim Mashek and Dave Moormann; current *Advocate* sportswriters Jeff Duncan, Joe Macaluso and Scott Rabalais; former *Times-Picayune* sportswriters Teddy Allen, Charlie Bennett, Peter Finney and Brian Allee-Walsh; former Shreveport *Times* sportswriter Scott Ferrell; current Lake Charles *American Press* sportswriter Kenneth "Scooter" Hobbs; and former Alexandria *Daily Town Talk* sportswriters Michael Lough and Jeff Nixon.

And thanks to Derrick Goold, Cardinals beat writer for the St. Louis *Post-Dispatch*, who covered Bertman's last championship season in 2000 for the *Times-Picayune*.

Thanks also to Marc Kinderman, producer of "Hold The Rope," the Skip Bertman documentary on ESPN/SEC Network, for his contribution.

Special thanks to Skip Bertman's wife, Sandy and their daughters, Jan, Jodi Lisa and Lori; Skip's sister, Marlene; childhood friends Richard Berger and Louie Hayes; Skip's Miami Beach High players Joel Misler, Gary Kelson, Nelson Ferreira, and Danny Marrero; and University of Miami coach Ron Fraser. Those interviews were for my special section, "Skip Bertman – Architect of a Baseball Dynasty," published by the Baton Rouge *Advocate* in 2001 and used in this book.

Thanks to Trent Angers of Acadian House Publishing and Baton Rouge businessman Eric Lane for their patience amid the pressure to finish this book.

And a heartfelt thanks to my understanding wife, Michelle Guilbeau, who was *Advocate* news reporter Michelle Millhollon when we had our first date, in Omaha's Old Market after Bertman's last national title, in June of 2000.

– G.G.

What I learned from a great teacher

By Warren Morris

I don't think I would have become the athlete that I became or the person I am now without the influence of Coach Skip Bertman. God puts certain people in our lives at just the precise times when we need them the most to mold us into the person that He intends for us to be.

I was one of the lucky ones to have been able to learn from one of the greatest leaders of our time. I tell people today, as a player at LSU under Coach Bertman you received more than just an education in baseball. You got an education in life.

Many of the same lessons that were so vital to help us win games, I use today to succeed as a husband, father, employee, and friend. Sports is a great metaphor for life. It teaches valuable lessons to all who play. I feel like I was able to get a "PhD" from what Coach taught us.

I was not recruited to play baseball by any college. Not one college assistant coach or recruiting coordinator ever came to one of my games. But a friend of my family, Don Boniol, who had coached with my father, William Morris, years before, knew Coach Bertman well from working LSU summer camps for many years. He told Coach Bertman I was a good player, and that opened a door.

I soon got the chance to meet Coach Bertman, not in Baton Rouge, but in my own ballpark: Bringhurst Field in Alexandria, where I played my high school home games. I saw Coach's Tigers play Louisiana College there on March 14, 1992, when I was a junior at Bolton High School. I went to the game with my father. Toward the latter innings of LSU's 23-2 win, I was shocked to hear the stadium announcer say over the speakers:

"Warren Morris, please report to the LSU dugout."

So right there, as the game was going on, beside the dugout, my father and I met Coach, and he offered me the opportunity to be an "invited walk-on." Wow! I didn't see that coming when I decided to go to the game that day.

I will never forget my very first team activity as a new player on the LSU baseball team. We had an introductory meeting in the locker room. We were all in chairs circled around Coach Bertman as he laid out the goal and expectations for the coming season. It was clear from the beginning that the only baseball prize we were focusing on was a national championship. Omaha, Nebraska, was the Promised Land that we planned on reaching.

I red-shirted that first year, in 1993, and learned a lot from Coach. Everything we did had a purpose and a reason behind it. It wasn't enough just to know what to do, we were quizzed on why we do it that way. There was an attention to detail to everything we did. Even on something as simple as making a call to catch a pop-up. When is the right time to say, "I got it?" Who has priority within the infield and outfield? How many times should we call for the ball? What does the person not catching the ball do?

We spent a lot of time discussing the mental and psychological side of the game. Coach talked at length about how great teams separate themselves from the others by mental toughness. The game of baseball is not easy. It truly is more mental than physical.

I can remember him saying, "We want pressure. We invite it." I had never had a coach put it in those terms or talk so much about the mental side of the game. Coach also talked a lot with us about the importance of imaging: being able to see yourself succeeding in your own mind. He would often tell us, "Be the star of your own movie." He had a great quote he created and repeated:

"Anything you vividly imagine, ardently desire, sincerely believe, and enthusiastically act upon, must, absolutely must come to pass."

See it in your mind. Feel it with your senses. Even smell the smells of the concessions, so it's like you are truly there. I needed someone like Coach to provide a tool so I could convince myself that I could make it on this level.

* * * * *

Coach won his second National Championship in 1993 with me watching the 8-0 win over Wichita State on TV in Alexandria. It wasn't a big surprise that we won. There was just a feeling around the program that this is what we do. We win. It wasn't cockiness, it was a mindset. You can't fake it. And it all started at the top with the man in charge.

Coach Bertman had a history of winning before he ever came to LSU. He would tell us he had won over 80% of the games he coached. He shared that with us, not to brag, but to say, "You can trust me. When I tell you to do something a certain way, it's because I know it has worked before." He had a system in place. We just had to execute the plan and buy into the system.

"If it doesn't work," he'd say, "I'll take the blame. Over time, it is successful more times than not."

I always felt like we had an advantage over the other team because Skip Bertman was in our dugout. Quite simply, he was smarter than the other team's coach. It was uncanny how many times he would call a pitchout on the exact pitch on which the opposing team tried to steal. He would tell us much of the game is putting the odds in your favor. If you can get your best hitter to the plate with more runners on base, odds are you will score more runs because he has the best chance of getting a hit.

When my parents met with Coach Bertman soon after I arrived, he told them your son will grow up a lot here. In fact, he said, "After the first semester when you see him, you won't recognize him." It wasn't just physical growth and getting on a strength training program, it was growing from a boy to a man.

In 1994, when I began playing, I was ready.

I quickly found out that like most great coaches, Coach Bertman demanded much from his players. He could be harsh at times, but there was always a purpose. I may not have understood this at the time, but, looking back, it was just another way to prepare us. He understood people and that different things make different people tick. Some he would come down harder on because that is what they responded to best. He pointed out others' mistakes in more subtle terms.

But, make no mistake, he would let you know when you did not meet expectations. It was a tough love in front of the team. One on one, I found that he was much more approachable and understanding. Even the pressure that he put on us was for a purpose. He knew if we could perform under pressure at practice or in early-season games, it would translate into being able to come through in bigger games later.

Coach was a great communicator. He stressed two acronyms: H.W.A. (How-to-Win Awareness) and T.O.B. (Transfer of Blame). H.W.A. was the ability to understand a situation quickly and react without having to be told what to do. The more players with heightened H.W.A., the better the team would be. H.W.A. is a base runner rounding second and seeing the outfielder make a slight bobble of the ball, taking off to third base and sliding safely without the aid of the third base coach. If you have to wait for the coach to tell you to take the next base, it's too late. You have to be instinctive and understand the game. Not all players have this. We were to be active in every step of the game, not just reactionary.

The same is true of great citizens. They seek out ways to improve their community. They take the initiative and lead the charge, rather than wait for someone to seek them out. It works for winning at baseball and everywhere else.

T.O.B. is not something you want. We've become a culture that seeks excuses rather than own up to our mistakes and learn from them. Coach said this bad habit stops here. T.O.B. would not be allowed. He would often point out examples of T.O.B., and we would seek to avoid them. No one was allowed to make an excuse for his error or missed assignment. Instead, we admitted our mistake and moved forward from there.

That is one of the most powerful lessons a young adult can learn as he or she grows in responsibility and leadership. Champions don't pass the buck. They improve and own up to their actions.

Before a big game, Coach would remind us that in baseball when you try to do too much or press yourself into playing above your normal level, it rarely goes well. Instead he urged us to just play our game. When you do this and play aggressive and confident, the same way you have all season, it frees you up to do extraordinary things in these big games. Attention to detail was a common theme.

We all had to pitch in to do our part to make sure the field and facilities were clean and looked professional. I had the job as a freshman with others to clean and dust the baseball offices and coaches' locker room. Some painted the batting cages. Others picked up trash. There was a reason behind this. Even something as menial as this contributed to our success. Coach wanted to make sure all the nets in the batting cages were in good shape with no holes. All the balls and equipment were picked up. Everything was freshly painted.

The reason was when the opposing team came in to practice on Thursday night before the Friday series opener, we wanted to make sure their first impression was that this was a first-class program with everything in order. This conveyed a sense of success and even a slight level of intimidation for the visitors before they ever took the field. If things were in disarray, it gave the sense that this program wasn't in very good order. That would build confidence in the opponent. We always wanted whatever edge we could get.

Everything mattered.

* * * * *

I felt Coach was a sincere person. He didn't always put his caring side in the open for all to see, but he always wanted us to give back to others. We were asked to read to elementary school students. He encouraged us to sign autographs and had us do caring things for people around Baton Rouge.

In 1996, while I was injured and no doctor anywhere seemed to be able to determine what the problem was, Coach called upon his contacts all throughout Major League Baseball to speak to trainers, hand experts, and anyone who would listen. I know he wanted me back in the lineup, but more than that I think he wanted to help make me better again. He went above and beyond the call of duty of a coach, and it was extra special for me and the team to be able to help bring him the championship that season.

We have always had a fraternity of former players who support one another. Coach's first few teams laid the groundwork for the success that came in the 1990s. Over the years, we all had heard the "Hold the rope" story many times. We lived it. None of the success I enjoyed would have been possible without those before me paying the dues they did. That's the beauty of playing on a team. It's the closest thing to a blood family I know. You live with these brothers day in and day out. You go through the fire with them, suffer with them, and celebrate with them. Everyone grows up together.

Even beyond the teammates I shared, others who played under Coach share a special bond. We are all part of *the system* that changed everything in college baseball.

Coach was very open to bringing spiritual guidance into the program. For me, growing up in a strong Baptist home, weekly church attendance was a no-brainer. I really didn't know what sort of religious outreach he allowed in the clubhouse. I found out early that each Sunday a Christian chaplain, Charlie Clary, was allowed in to share a message with the team. Each Sunday, he would speak for 15 to 20 minutes. There would have been a great void in my college experience had Coach not allowed Charlie that access. Sure, there were plenty of avenues for me to meet my spiritual needs outside of the team. But it wouldn't have been the same. This made it more like home to me.

Coach would tell us before certain games:

"Someone may hit three home runs today or pitch a no-hitter. Why not you? Why not today? See yourself succeeding and believe you can. Today could be your day."

One of the acronyms Coach liked to use is W.I.N. (What's Important Now). It's a simple concept, but still very powerful. It focuses on living in the moment. It's a concept that works for any task: Focus on the job at hand and be the best you can be.

I was in the moment with two outs and Brad Wilson on third in the bottom of the ninth against Miami in the National Championship game on June 8, 1996. My single focus was just to stay aggressive. Coach always taught us that most mistakes are made when you become passive. It's better to take a calculated (not careless) risk by being aggressive. I can remember thinking, "Even if I strike out, I'm going down swinging."

Before I knew it, I was back at home plate on the bottom of a pile of all my teammates. What a moment – a dream come true! I had been the only player in our lineup without a home run, and I just hit a championship-clinching walk-off home run on the grandest stage.

In conclusion, I'd like to repeat what I shared with my fellow Red River Bank employees about teamwork in June of 2016. It goes like this:

When everyone is on the same page and doing their all to help the team, great things can happen. Details matter, too. My LSU coach, Skip Bertman, always said, "If you take care of the little things, the wins will take care of themselves." That's what personal excellence is all about – giving your best in big and small ways so that you can achieve greater things. Everything matters.

Introduction

Hot coffee and clean restrooms

In the 1984 movie, "The Natural," the angry manager of the New York Knights was cussing his team and his life in a battered dugout with a bad water fountain.

"Wouldn't you think I could get a fresh drink after all the years I spent in this game?" Pop Fisher asks his assistant, Red Blow.

"I should've been a farmer," he says. "Since the day I was born, Red, I should've been a farmer."

Stanley "Skip" Bertman was already 45 before his first season as LSU's baseball coach in 1984. He would have preferred to be the baseball coach at the University of Miami, which went to the College World Series five straight times from 1978 to 1982 with Skip as the associate head coach/pitching coach and won the national championship in '82.

Instead, he inherited LSU and its humble 2,500-seat Alex Box Stadium with its bad drinking fountains and horrible showers without soap dishes.

Basically, Bertman was like a farmer given a drought-ravaged, decaying piece of land on Nicholson Drive on the LSU campus.

For now, he would have to make do with what he had. So, he made a list. Among the first entries were new tile, shower heads and soap dishes.

A member of the newly formed Coaches Committee to help finance baseball, which was Bertman's idea, asked Bertman what he needed first.

"A diaper-changing station in the women's bathroom," Bertman said.

The answer floored the businessman who asked the question.

As the home opener approached on Feb. 22, 1984, Bertman reminded everyone who would listen of the simplest and one of the more important marketing tools for sporting events.

"Keep the coffee hot and the bathrooms clean," he said.

"Skip always wanted the restrooms clean," said Stanley Jacobs, a former LSU Board of Supervisors member and original member of the Tiger Athletic Foundation (TAF), a fundraising arm for LSU athletics that started in 1987.

"He always understood the fan experience," Jacobs said. "Skip's more than just a great baseball mind. He understands the promotional part of it. I started going to games that first year and said, 'Hey, this is kind of neat.'"

And on this farm, Bertman had "hired hands" who were on scholarship.

"He had his players in there with buckets of paint painting the locker room, cleaning the toilet. We used the players, probably illegally, as the workers," said Baton Rouge businessman Richard Lipsey, who started TAF.

"The first thing I picked up at LSU wasn't a baseball," said pitcher Mark Guthrie, who was in Bertman's first recruiting class and played and worked from 1984 to 1987. "It was a paint brush and a shovel."

And this was after lifting weights and running.

"We had these practice schedules that said, 'batting practice' and 'infield,' and then these two: 'paint crew' and 'landscaping crew,'" recalled pitcher Stan Loewer, another original Bertman employee who played and worked from 1984 to 1987.

"In the early years, you did grounds work," Loewer said. "You painted. You pressure-washed the stadium. You did everything it took from a grassroots level to build a program. Nobody was above any task that was needed by the team."

And Loewer, who grew up on a farm near Eunice, was one of Bertman's top recruits. He could have gone to more established baseball schools that didn't include the work-release programs.

"I remember my father saying, 'You can go wherever you want to go, but it takes something special to build something,'" Loewer said.

That exactly was Bertman and assistant coach Ray "Smoke" Laval's pitch.

"The ability that Skip had to articulate a vision was something that inspired me to build something that was special," Loewer said. "I'd come from a manufacturing and fabrication family on a farm. We built everything we needed. So, to go and be a part of building a program, that was very appealing. And that's what we did. We started small. Skip was big on the little things, you could say. Skip and Smoke sold it, and the rest is history."

One might think that the author of the biggest, brightest moment in the history of college baseball would not believe in such little things.

Warren Morris, a native of Alexandria and a Bolton High graduate, didn't have to paint and power-wash by the time he arrived at LSU in 1993, but he knew about small things.

Before he hit his two-out, two-run, bottom-of-the-ninth, walk-off home run to beat Miami, 9-8, for the National Championship in 1996, Morris threw a runner out at the plate and had three other hits. These included a double and a bunt single in a 4-for-4 afternoon.

"I think people that don't know baseball as well sometimes think it all comes down to who gets the big hit in the ninth inning," said Morris, who should know. "A lot of times, the game is won or lost in the second, third or fourth inning. Skip taught us that everything counts and about winning the game early. It's the little things. He taught us a lot about baseball, but we also got an education about life. Take care of the little things, and the wins will take care of themselves in baseball and in life."

* * * * *

To Skip, everything mattered, including the type of film in a camera, as LSU baseball publicity director Bill Franques of Lafayette found out one day at Ole Miss in 1989. Bertman wanted to take pictures of various improvements at stadiums around the SEC. He was on a mission to enhance Alex Box, which would gradually grow to a capacity of 7,760 and would lead the nation in attendance for nearly a quarter of a century, starting in 1996.

But Franques, in a rare mistake, gave him the wrong kind of film.

"Let me explain something to you," Bertman told Franques. "You see, I'm trying to build a program here. I'm trying to be excellent. Everything counts with me. There is nothing too small.

"If we go to someone else's field, and I see there are holes in their batting cage nets, I know I can beat that team. If the coffee's cold and the bathrooms aren't clean, I know that coach doesn't care enough about his program. That won't happen at LSU, because I won't allow it to happen."

Two years later, in 1991, Bertman and LSU won their first national championship. Another one followed in 1993, and in 1996 and in 1997, but Bertman never stopped paying attention to the details.

One Saturday morning in April of 2000, LSU was at Florida and the Tigers were having breakfast before the start of a doubleheader. Bertman noticed the eggs, ham, grits and assorted pastries on the buffet. But something was missing. He went up to Franques, who by now was easily one of the best college baseball publicity directors in the game.

"Bill, where's the toast? How can you order a breakfast for us without toast? Let me explain something to you," Bertman said. "You see, we're trying to be excellent here. Everything matters."

Two months later, Bertman won his fifth national championship in 10 years at LSU. It was a 6-5 victory over Stanford on a walk-off, line drive single to left field by Brad Cresse on June 17, 2000, at Rosenblatt Stadium in Omaha, Nebraska – a place LSU fans turned into "Alex Box-North" with seven trips in the 1990s and three in the 1980s.

Only one other coach, USC's Rod Dedeaux, won more national championships in the history of college baseball with 10 from 1958 to 1978. Augie Garrido also won five national titles, but over a 26-year period, from 1979 to 2005.

"I've been going one year at a time for several years now, and I'm still going one year at a time," Bertman, then 62, said after the game. "I'm going to be back in 2001."

That same night, Bertman, wife Sandy, and daughters Jodi and Lori were watching the replay of the championship game at the Crowne Plaza hotel restaurant and bar in Omaha.

Less than a month later, on July 5, 2000, Bertman announced that 2001 would be his last season as LSU's coach, and he came within one win of reaching a 12th College World Series that season. His last game was a 7-1 loss to Tulane in the Super Regional championship game on June 3, 2001, at Zephyr Field in Metairie.

* * * * *

But Bertman was far from done. There were extra innings in his future as he was named LSU's Athletic Director even before coaching his final game. He took over officially right after the 2001 baseball season.

Four more national championships would follow by coaches whom Bertman would hire – Les Miles, in football in the 2007 season; Dennis Shaver, in women's outdoor track in 2008; Paul Mainieri, in baseball in 2009; and Chuck Winstead, in golf in 2015.

The Bertman touch also helped produce two Final Fours in basketball.

Bertman refused to yield to pressure to fire men's basketball coach John Brady following LSU's second straight first-round loss in the NCAA Tournament in 2005. He then helped Brady with his scheduling and media persona. A year later, LSU won its first SEC title and first NCAA Tournament game since 2000 before advancing to its first Final Four in 20 years.

In 2007, Bertman hired four-time WNBA champion coach Van Chancellor to guide the women's basketball program, and Chancellor took the Lady Tigers to the SEC title and a Final Four appearance in the 2007-08 season.

In all, Bertman is directly responsible for nine national championships at LSU in five sports – five in baseball as coach, and one apiece in football, women's track, baseball, and golf as the Athletic Director who hired the coach who won it all.

Along the way, he ushered in a state-of-the-art, costly, and unpopular but profitable football season ticket licensing plan. LSU was still reaping the financial benefits of the plan more than a decade after Bertman retired as Athletic Director in 2008.

"He was so popular that he was the only guy who could've gotten that ticket licensing fee passed without getting crucified," said LSU Baseball Coaches Committee founder Wally McMakin. (A former Tiger third baseman from Monroe, McMakin is the one who conducted the search to hire Bertman from his job as Miami's pitching coach in 1983.)

Bertman also raised money and helped design a new, 10,326-seat Alex Box Stadium that opened in 2009.

"Oh, he was a fabulous Athletic Director," said Richard Lipsey. "Skip put together a great team in the Athletic Department. As an Athletic Director, Skip did more than any other Athletic Director we had. Skip brought the whole package. He was ahead of his time. As a coach, you have to compare Skip to the only person you could compare him to: John Wooden."

Wooden won 10 National Championships from 1964 to 1975 as UCLA's men's basketball coach.

* * * * *

Bertman farmed LSU baseball, then farmed LSU athletics overall like no other.

Like a good farmer correctly forecasting the weather by only looking up, Bertman had a knack for saying what was about to happen in a baseball game.

"I was always fascinated by Skip's ability to predict things," said Todd Walker, one of LSU's greatest hitters, the guy who led the Tigers to the 1993 National Championship.

"Inevitably, he was pitching out when a guy was about to steal second base," Walker said. "It was incredible what he knew on the field, and I was just in awe of watching it as I was playing the game. I always locked into everything he said, because it seemed like every word out of his mouth was gold."

Walker, a Bossier City native, played for 12 years in Major League Baseball before going to work in 2016 as a college baseball analyst on the SEC Network.

"I can't even begin to tell you how blessed I feel to have played for him because of what he's meant not only to the players he's coached, but also college baseball," Walker observed. "If you look at the college stadiums now around the country, you can't help but think that Skip had a lot to do with that. What you see today with games being on TV all the time, Skip had a piece of every bit of that."

And it all started with a paint brush and a shovel.

"We were picking up rakes," Walker said. "We were fixing our own batter's boxes. And we were pulling tarps and fixing nets with zip ties. We were doing all of that, and that was Skip making us. We took pride in that work as well as the games."

Then it was time to play.

"Before games, he'd always come up with something he had read – some story for every game we had," Walker said. "It was amazing."

Bertman would say a version of the following before every game – a mid-week affair against an in-state school or the national championship:

"Stick together. We're one as a unit. We're dynamite. Now, you represent LSU. You represent your family. You represent your Maker. I want you to enjoy the moment. Have a ball and play like champions. Let's go!"

* * * * *

Over the following pages, we will take you around the bases of LSU's five national championships under Bertman along with the other trips to the College World Series and some of the games that got LSU to Omaha.

We will take you inside the LSU Athletic Department that Bertman led with much the same style as he directed his baseball teams. We will go behind the scenes as Bertman tries to keep football coach Nick Saban.

We will also go back to the beginning with Bertman in Miami and the twist of fate that brought him to LSU with its barren barn of a stadium and unplowed field that would become the greatest diamond in college baseball.

Because everything mattered.

Table of Contents

Preface .... *v*

Acknowledgements .... *vi*

Foreword .... *viii*

Introduction .... *xiii*

  1. It almost didn't happen 23

  2. Bon Jovi rocks LSU baseball 29

  3. The 'other' national title: Assault on A&M 35

  4. College Station hangover 47

  5. The weekend Alex Box became another Tiger Stadium 53

  6. 5th time's a charm 61

  7. The 1991 National Championship 67

  8. Mr. Skip doesn't go to Washington 75

  9. 'That's baseball' is no excuse (Sometimes you just lose) 79

  10. LSU's 'façade' National Championship of 1993 83

  11. Walk-on Warren Morris' walk-off to immortality 93

      Photo Section 97

  12. 'Gorilla Ball' and the 1997 National Championship 117

  13. A fist full of titles (The 2000 National Championship) 129

  14. 2001: A Skip odyssey - The final season 147

  15. Shifting gears: From baseball coach to Athletic Director 159

  16. Athletic Director, but still hawking tickets 167

  17. More than 'just a coach' 175

      Photo Section 177

  18. Nick Saban should have listened to Skip 195

  19. Skip's secrets to success 199

Afterword: 'Holding the Rope' in LSU baseball 215

Appendix 1: Living proof of the Bertman touch 221

Appendix 2: Timeline: The life and times of Skip Bertman 222

Appendix 3: Skip's original check list 230

Sources 231

Index 238

About the Author 246

EVERYTHING MATTERS IN BASEBALL

The **SKIP BERTMAN** Story

Chapter 1

It almost didn't happen

"You'll be making a mistake if you don't take the LSU job."
— Miami football coach Howard Schnellenberger to Miami associate head coach/
pitching coach Skip Bertman in the spring of 1983

LSU Athletic Department employees in the early 1980s used to refer to the sudden influx of people from South Beach, Florida, to their department as the "Miami Mafia."

There was Athletic Director Bob Brodhead, who came to LSU in June of 1982 from a business manager post with the Miami Dolphins. It was Brodhead who fired LSU football coach Jerry Stovall during the 1983 season and hired Miami Dolphins defensive coordinator Bill Arnsparger to replace him. Then Arnsparger hired University of Miami defensive backs coach Mike Archer to be his defensive backs coach, and Archer became LSU's head coach in 1987.

And on April 25, 1983, University of Miami's associate head coach/pitching coach Stanley "Skip" Bertman was introduced as LSU's baseball coach.

But it took nearly a year of wooing.

"What I don't think people realize is Skip wasn't initially excited about coming here," Brodhead's daughter, Mindy, said during a 2001 interview. "My dad had to sell the job."

Bertman was hesitant to come to LSU in part because it was always his dream to become Miami's head baseball coach. Bertman, a Miami graduate and former Hurricane's catcher and outfielder from 1958 to 1960, had lived most of his life in Miami. He had been Miami Beach High's baseball coach from 1965 to 1974. While there, he developed trick plays while also teaching driver's education, physical education, and sex education classes.

Bertman preached practice, practice, practice – on the baseball field, primarily. He wanted his players to see it first, so he had his players practice putting him on their shoulders before the 1970 state championship game against Leto High of Tampa. His Hi-Tides won, 4-0, and Skip rode high.

As Miami's pitching coach from 1975 to 1983, Bertman was considered the "defensive coordinator" under head coach Ron Fraser. At the 1982 College World Series, the day before Miami was to play the Wichita State Shockers in a second-round game, Bertman and a fellow assistant coach had the Hurricanes practice a fake pick-off throw to first base.

The opportunity to use the trick play presented itself during the actual game. The first baseman, the relief pitchers in the bullpen, the right fielder, the second baseman, and Hurricane players in the first base dugout all acted as if pitcher Mike Kasprzak's throw to first got by the first baseman and bounced into foul territory. But Kasprzak still had the ball on the mound.

Bertman would call the play if he noticed a runner on first base diving back to the bag head first on the first pick-off attempt. If the fake was on, Bertman would put his finger in his ear, and then the pitcher would casually put his finger in his ear on the mound to signal the rest of the team. He'd make one or two real tosses to first before the trick.

In the game against the Shockers in the sixth inning with Miami up 4-3, it was the right time. Aggressive Wichita State base runner Phil Stephenson – who happened to be the nation's leader in stolen bases with 86 – got on first with a walk. Stephenson dove in head first when Kasprzak threw over to first to keep him close. Bertman's finger went to his ear. Kasprzak's finger went to his ear. It was on.

Kasprzak faked his next throw to first. The second baseman and right fielder ran toward foul territory for the imaginary ball. The relievers in the bullpen jumped or ran out of the way of the invisible ball. Players in the dugout shouted directions to their teammates on the ball's whereabouts.

Even Miami's bat girls – the Sugarcanes – began jumping up and down and running away as if a ball was coming their way. They didn't know about the play. They didn't practice it. In a bit of *lagniappe*, they just fell for it, as did the base runner, who took off for second.

Kasprzak calmly threw the ball to shortstop Bill Wrona, who had covered second while pretending to be looking for the ball in the right field foul area. Wrona easily tagged the shocked Shocker out on his way to second on a play that become famously known as the "Grand Illusion."

Miami held on for the 4-3 win. Then the Hurricanes beat Texas, 2-1, in 12 innings two days later as Bertman's pitchers tossed another gem. Then they beat Maine, 10-4, and defeated Wichita State with no tricks, 9-3, in the championship game for their first national title. And Bertman became the most well-known assistant coach in college baseball.

Bertman was up for the Florida head coaching job after the 1982 season, but Jack Rhine, who was named interim coach the previous January, retained the job.

Brodhead called Bertman not long after Miami won the national title. The two met in Brodhead's home in Fort Lauderdale, Florida, with some other LSU people, including super-fan and booster Augie Cross. But Bertman turned down the offer to take over the LSU program because Jack Lamabe, whom Bertman knew, was still the LSU baseball coach. This was what coaches did at the time.

"I'm certainly not leaving when there's a coach at LSU. Jack Lamabe is a hell of a guy," Bertman told Brodhead. "Well, I know, but we're waiting to see if you can come up. And if you take the job, we're going to fire Jack," Brodhead said.

"Well, sorry, I can't do that," Bertman said.

Brodhead was miffed, but he didn't give up.

"He seemed to think I was acting with some kind of nobility," Bertman said. "He didn't realize that was protocol. He didn't know. They didn't run the Athletic Department at LSU right at the time."

Midway through the 1983 baseball season, Brodhead – without informing Lamabe – advertised the position with a Help Wanted ad in the Baton Rouge *Advocate*.

Now realizing the LSU job would be open, Bertman went to see Coach Ron Fraser.

Bertman: "Ron, how long are you going to coach?"

Fraser: "Hey, I'm going to be the athletic director, and naturally you're going to be the coach."

The athletic director at the time, Harry Mallios, was leaving, and Fraser thought for sure he was going to get the job. *Great*, Bertman thought. He and his wife Sandy could send all four of their daughters – Jan, Jodi, Lisa, and Lori – to Miami, a private college, for free and stay with the program he helped to build.

Bertman thought he would inherit a much better team at Miami than at LSU, which was 77-76 over Lamabe's last three seasons, while Miami had reached five straight World Series, from 1978 to 1982.

Meanwhile, though, South Alabama, which at the time had a much better program than LSU, was also interested in Bertman in 1983 to be its new coach. South Alabama was replacing Eddie Stanky, a former Brooklyn Dodger second baseman, who was retiring.

LSU had been below .500 in the SEC 10 times from 1972 through 1983 with one NCAA appearance and one SEC title under Coach Jim Smith. Interestingly enough, Smith's main job was equipment manager for the football team.

"You'd go in to interview him in his office, and there were football helmets all over the place," recalled Lake Charles *American Press* sports editor Scooter Hobbs, who worked as a Sports Information student-assistant while attending LSU in the 1970s. Hobbs traveled with the baseball team in 1977 when the Tigers produced their worst SEC record ever at 4-15. This was just two years after LSU went 40-16 under Smith, winning the SEC title and reaching the NCAA postseason for the first time.

Once, upon returning home after getting swept on the road in 1977, the gate where the bus parked was closed. As the driver got out to retrieve a key from LSU police, a player in the back of the bus yelled, "We're so bad, they've locked us out."

* * * * *

Bertman came to LSU with Miami in 1977 for a two-game regular season series that it split with the Tigers.

"Coach Smith drove us around," Bertman recalled. "We stayed in the football dorms. And I thought it was cool. See, I'd never seen a real campus. Miami wasn't like that. It was an urban, commuter campus. LSU has such a beautiful campus."

But Alex Box Stadium – named after a former LSU outfielder and World War II hero who was killed in action in North Africa in 1943 – wasn't much to look at then. Bertman would visit Alex Box again for a game with some LSU power brokers in the 1983 season.

"I looked up in the wooden stands and saw about 300 people watching. And they sat like this," Bertman said as he sat on his hands. "Still. There was no standing or clapping. You could hear the guys' spikes as they ran, it was so quiet."

But Bertman still preferred LSU to South Alabama because it was the state's flagship institution and located in the Capital City.

"Eddie Stanky's program at South Alabama had some oomph," Bertman said. "Whereas, LSU – nothing. I liked the signs they had up at Stanky Field, too. I liked the fact that someone had worked hard at that, and the field was really nice for those days."

Bertman would later visit Stanky Field again and model some of his improvements to Alex Box after it, particularly the signage.

"I called people who said that LSU had a chance to be good. And I thought to myself, *I'd rather go to the one school that's the best in the state*," Bertman said. "I just figured if I'm at LSU, there's no LSU State. It's the only major school. South Alabama couldn't say that with Alabama and Auburn.'"

But in the spring of 1983, with Coach Fraser supposedly soon moving up to athletic director, LSU and South Alabama did not matter as much to Bertman as Miami did. He intended to coach where he always wanted to coach.

That all changed one day that spring when Bertman was walking through the first floor of Miami's Athletic Department building, and Ron Steiner, the sports information director for football, tapped him on the shoulder.

"Coach Bertman, Coach Schnellenberger wants to see you," Steiner said.

And Bertman froze in fright. Howard Schnellenberger, the football coach at Miami, was on the second floor.

Nobody ever goes up there, Bertman thought.

Schnellenberger, then 49, was in the process of turning a Miami football program virtually left for dead into a national champion. After a 5-6 campaign in his first year in 1979, Schnellenberger produced three straight winning seasons, from 1980 to 1982, for the first time at Miami since the mid-1960s and would win the 1983 national title.

Bertman had a scary thought. He had been teaching several football players in his physical education classes over the years, including quarterbacks Jim Kelly and Mark Richt. Bertman had just given another top player an F, since he was not coming to class.

"Now, Schnellenberger wants to see me," Bertman said. "And I went pale."

Bertman makes his way to the second floor and into Schnellenberger's office. He smells the pipe Schnellenberger always smoked as he walks across the shag carpet.

"C'mon in, coach," Schnellenberger says in his characteristic gruff baritone.

"Yes, sir," Bertman recalls saying in a non-characteristic high squeal. "I sit down, and lucky for me he doesn't say anything about my class."

"Coach, I read in the newspaper, where you might be going to LSU," Schnellenberger says. "What's stopping you is, you want to know whether Ron's going to be the athletic director or not, right?"

"That's true," Bertman said with his normal voice back. "And if Ron [Fraser] becomes athletic director, I'm not going anywhere."

Schnellenberger exhales a large billow of smoke.

"Ron's not going to be athletic director," he tells Bertman matter-of-factly.

"Well, how do you know this?" Bertman says as the high, frightened voice returns.

"I won't allow it," Schnellenberger says. "You'll be making a mistake if you don't take the LSU job."

Bertman pauses and says "Thank you."

"Football coaches, of course, ran everything in those days," Bertman says reflectively. "It was 1983."

After Bertman left Schnellenberger's office that day, he immediately called his wife, Sandy.

"I want you to come with me on a trip," he said. "To Baton Rouge."

Chapter 2

Bon Jovi rocks
LSU baseball

"My wife Sandy and I are big Bon Jovi fans.
You know, 'Wanted Dead or Alive!'"

– LSU baseball coach Skip Bertman telling his team practice was being cancelled
on Feb. 2, 1989, because of a Bon Jovi concert at the Pete Maravich Assembly Center

Nothing came easy for LSU baseball in 1988.

Skip Bertman had his second of only two sub-40 win teams ever at LSU. That was the only Bertman team, other than his first one in 1984, that failed to reach the NCAA postseason. And it followed back-to-back CWS teams in 1986 and '87, dropping from 55-14 and 49-19 seasons to 39-21.

One of the most maddening, most frustrating things was that the Tigers lost 10 of 17 one-run games, including its last seven.

"We just couldn't win a one-run game down the stretch," recalls first baseman Pete Bush.

LSU lost nine of its last 11, but it wasn't because of the pitching.

"But that team, man, we could pitch," says catcher Mike Bianco, the only LSU player to play for Bertman, coach under him, and coach against him.

LSU pitching led the SEC in strikeouts in 1988 with 519 behind two Louisiana sophomores who gave hope for 1989. Russell Springer of Pollock fanned 156 in going 7-7 with a 2.95 ERA in '88. The 6-foot-7 star was Ben McDonald of Denham Springs, who went 13-7 with a 2.65 ERA and 144 strikeouts after playing basketball his freshman year, in 1986-87.

"We just didn't score," Bianco says.

So Bertman decided to mix things up for 1989 in a concerted effort to try to return to Omaha.

"We're going to do something a little different," Bertman said at the first team meeting of the new year. "We're going to have two-a-days."

Bertman, who often commented on the "football mentality" at LSU, was reverting to football culture? A drastic step indeed.

"We're going to practice in the afternoons, and then certain nights we'll have intra-squad scrimmages," he said.

The scrimmages were on Tuesdays and Thursdays, and Feb. 2, 1989, was creeping up and Bianco was getting worried.

Why was that Thursday night so important?

Well, the previous November, Bianco had gotten clearance from assistant coach Ray "Smoke" Laval to tell the rest of the players they could go ahead and buy concert tickets for Bon Jovi, a soaring rock band from New Jersey. Bon Jovi and lead singer Jon Bon Jovi would be at the Pete Maravich Assembly Center on Thursday, Feb. 2 as part of the "New Jersey Tour" that was showcasing chart-topping hits from their recent smash albums "Slippery When Wet" and "New Jersey."

"Slippery When Wet" spent eight weeks at No. 1 and was the best-selling album in 1987 with such singles as "You Give Love a Bad Name," "Wanted Dead or Alive" and "Livin' on a Prayer," which is still constantly played at college football games.

"We had to buy the tickets in advance that November or December, and nobody wanted to pay the money if we were going to have practice or lift weights the night of the concert," Bianco points out.

"You go get the tickets," Laval had told Bianco. "I'll handle the Skip-meister. Don't worry about all that. I got it."

So virtually the entire team bought Bon Jovi tickets at roughly $25 a pop, which would be $50 if players purchased tickets for girlfriends.

"And then it's like a week before the concert," Bianco recalls. "And Smoke's now into baseball mode. We're like, 'Wow, we got this concert, and Skip doesn't know about it. We're going to miss it because of these scrimmages.'"

So, Bianco and Bush dispatched new graduate assistant Jeff "Rooster" Southall, a pitcher at LSU in 1982 and '83 and a liaison with the players, to broach Bon Jovi with Bertman.

"I stuck my head in his office and said, 'Hey coach, we're about to have a mutiny,'" Southall said before explaining the situation. Then he reported back to the team.

"Hey guys, bad deal. I don't think it's going to work. The boss man went berserk," he says.

"I'm trying to win a (expletive deleted) national championship, and now these guys want to go to a concert after the way we played last year," Bertman told Southall.

Players began considering selling their tickets and some did. Pitcher Russell Springer kept his, and trying to instill a little team ownership, he said, "Why can't we do both?"

Bertman covertly was thinking the same thing.

The week of the concert arrived, and the Tigers were in Bon Jovi limbo. But after the scrimmage on the Tuesday before the concert, Bertman called the team together after a workout.

"And then Skip, in perfect fashion, did one of the things that makes him so great," Bianco recalls.

"Guys, listen, this two-a-day thing that we've been doing on Tuesdays and Thursdays, I can really see it making a difference," Bertman began. "It's doing what we need it to do. But listen, I've got some bad news. We're not going to be able to scrimmage Thursday. I don't know if you realize it or not, but Bon Jovi's coming to town. And my wife Sandy and I are big Bon Jovi fans. You know, 'Wanted Dead Or Alive.'"

Bertman gives the thumbs up sign as he correctly names the song. "And, 'You Give Love a Bad Name.'"

Thumbs up again. Southall had given Bertman the Bon Jovi batting order, so to speak.

"Sandy and I can't miss the concert, guys," he said.

"Now, the players are ecstatic. They're fired up," Southall says.

"We're all cheering and going crazy," Bianco recalls. "It was the greatest."

And on Feb. 2, Bon Jovi blasted the Assembly Center in front of 11,772 – not 11,774, as Skip and Sandy did not attend. But LSU senior outfielder Scott Schneidewind bought Bertman a concert T-shirt.

Before practice the next day while Bertman is talking to the team, Schneidewind asks Bertman if he can get up and say a few words, and he's holding something.

"Sure, Schneids. Come on up here. C'mon," Bertman says, forever wanting his players to *take ownership*. (This was a decade before Nick Saban supposedly coined the phrase as LSU's new football coach.)

"Coach, listen, we know how much of a Bon Jovi fan you are, and we realize that you and Sandy weren't able to make the concert," Schneidewind opens. "But Jon Bon Jovi had a little gift for you."

Schneidewind unfurls the black T-shirt so everyone can see, "Bon Jovi, 1989," on the front with "*Skip* Back Kickin' Ass" on the back. Schneids had someone steam "*Skip*" above the regular writing on the T-shirt.

Skip burst out laughing when he saw it, and the team laughed along with him.

"He kept going around saying, 'Ooh, Jon Bon Jovi kicks ass,'" says then-LSU pitcher Chad Ogea of Lake Charles. "It was so funny. We laughed about that all year."

Mutiny foiled. Team ownership taken. Togetherness tightened. All because of a T-shirt.

"Skip's a fun guy," Bush points out. "He was a taskmaster. But he always made sure we had fun."

The hits kept on coming for Bon Jovi as the "New Jersey" world tour moved on through the United States, Europe, and South America for another year.

Nine days after Bon Jovi's Baton Rouge stop, LSU opened the 1989 season

– and the hits started coming. The Tigers beat TCU, 8-2 and 10-5, and Southern Mississippi, 10-1, on their way to a 22-2 start, including 7-1 in the SEC and 3-0 in one-run games.

And Bertman kept invoking the name of Bon Jovi.

"He'd pull out a *USA Today* or *Billboard* in the dugout and say, 'Hey, who the hell is Milli Vanilli and Debbie Gibson? Bon Jovi blows them away,'" Southall recalls.

* * * * *

On Saturday, April 15, LSU was 35-3, second in the SEC at 12-3, and ranked No. 3 in the nation. Mississippi State was 28-6, atop the SEC at 12-1, and ranked No. 2 as it entered Alex Box Stadium for a doubleheader of seven-inning games. (That was the SEC series format at the time with nine-inning games on Sundays.)

At the time, the Alex Box Stadium attendance record was 5,189. The available tickets would go on sale a few hours before the opening pitch.

"We pull up into the parking lot across the street from the old Box three or four hours before the game to get dressed, and the line is all the way down almost to the Mississippi River," Bianco remembers.

"It was past the Vet School (the last building before the river levee)," Southall points out.

"People are standing in line to get tickets. Then it's over 6,000 for BP [batting practice]. Our big crowds at the time were like 3,000 or 4,000. Now, we know it's going to be crazy," Bianco says.

Bertman was ready. He had been preparing for weeks for this weekend against Mississippi State and its coach, Ron Polk, his rival and old friend who would visit him at his home when the Bulldogs played at LSU.

A month before the Mississippi State series, Bertman had Southall ditch his coaching uniform for street clothes and sit in Alex Box for the Tigers' series against Florida to sample the concessions and check the bathrooms. Bertman, as usual, wanted to make sure the coffee was hot and the bathrooms were clean. Southall also sampled the acoustics around the Box, and they were not clean.

Just in time for the Mississippi State series, Bertman had a brand new, powerful Bose sound system installed.

"The new speakers would've been sufficient for Bon Jovi," Southall says. "It blasted. So that place was in a frenzy."

As game time approached, a record crowd of 6,977 was on the way in. The Alex Box capacity at the time was listed conservatively at 6,000.

Bertman gathered his team up just before the game.

"Hey guys, listen, tonight is one of those nights. This is why you came to LSU," he said. "To play in front of the largest crowd in Alex Box history. To play for an SEC championship. To play the best team in the country. And so guys, tonight, don't hold anything back. Dive for every ball. Swing as hard as you can. Pull out all the stops tonight. Don't hold anything back. You represent LSU, your family, your country, and your Maker."

But as he was wrapping up, Bertman threw a curve. He began to slowly unbutton his jersey, and there was the Bon Jovi T-shirt proclaiming "*Skip –* Back Kickin' Ass!"

"And everybody was like, 'Yeah!'" Bianco recalled.

"Of course, we ended up losing two one-run games just like in 1988, but it was one of the greatest pre-game talks ever."

LSU did manage to win game three on Sunday, 19-9, but finished second in the SEC to Mississippi State at 18-9 to 20-5.

In the end, though, the Tigers and Bon Jovi made it to Omaha for the World Series, and State did not.

Chapter 3

The 'other' national title: Assault on A&M

"You just can't underestimate the power of the mind."

– Skip Bertman, touting the power of positive thinking after the Tigers
battled Texas A&M for a trip to the College World Series in 1989

Some may think the LSU-Texas A&M rivalry began in November of 2018, when the Aggies beat the Tigers, 74-72, in a seven-overtime football game at Kyle Field in College Station, Texas.

That's when Texas A&M assistant coach Dameyune Craig (who had been fired by LSU coach Ed Orgeron two years previously) and Aggies' head coach Jimbo Fisher's nephew, Cole Fisher, started a fight near midfield after the game. Craig ran up and jawed with LSU personnel. Fisher, at first trying to hold Craig back, pushed LSU offensive analyst Steve Kragthorpe in the chest where he has a pacemaker for Parkinson's Disease. Fists flew from LSU staff member Kevin Faulk and safety John Battle. And all hell broke loose.

But that's not where the rivalry began.

Around the corner from Kyle Field is Texas A&M's baseball stadium, Olsen Field, where 30 years earlier the Tigers and the Aggies nearly came to blows on May 28, 1989. As he was being thrown out at first base, an A&M batter allegedly tried to spike LSU first baseman Pete Bush early in the first of two games.

"Everybody saw it," LSU reserve third baseman Pat Garrity said. "We started coming out the dugout, but they stopped us. It didn't progress from there. But from then on, it was pretty salty."

Yes, for the next eight hours, and more than three decades, it was salty and hot. Temperatures frequently reached between 95 and 98 over the four-day weekend as Aggie fans prepared to roast the Tigers mercilessly.

From the upper deck of Olsen Stadium, batteries, ice, soft drinks and coins heated by cigarette lighters rained down hard from the Aggie fans, including the Corps of Cadets, onto the Tigers, their fans, girlfriends, and families. And particularly on LSU ace Ben McDonald, who came in at 13-2 with 179 strikeouts in 133 innings.

"I'd never seen fans like that – not even at Yankee Stadium," said McDonald, a 6-foot-7 right-hander from Denham Springs with a 90-plus m.p.h. fastball who would be the first pick in the Major League Baseball draft a week later. (By September, he would be pitching for the Baltimore Orioles and off to a 9-year pro career.)

* * * * *

The big game pitted No. 11-ranked, No. 2-seed LSU – 51-15 and coming off two College World Series appearances in three years – against No. 1-seed Texas A&M – 58-5 and No. 1 in the Collegiate Baseball and Baseball America polls. A&M hadn't been to the College World Series in Omaha since 1964.

The first pitch was scheduled for 2 p.m. that Sunday in the double-elimination NCAA Central Regional, with a trip to Omaha on the line.

LSU had come through the loser's bracket with wins over Nevada-Las Vegas and South Alabama on Saturday. But if LSU were to beat A&M in the first game, then the two teams would play again at 7 p.m. Sunday. The Aggies needed only one win.

A&M had blown through three Regional games by 65-13 – over Jackson State, Brigham Young, and South Alabama – and rode a 10-game win streak. They were also 41-2 at Olsen Field on the season, including a 4-1 mark against Omaha institution Texas. The Longhorns had dominated the Aggies with 23 wins in their last 25 games.

This was clearly the Aggies' year. They had their best team ever: shortstop Chuck Knoblauch, a future Yankee second baseman who would go in the MLB draft's first round a week later; third baseman John Byington, a third-round pick by Milwaukee; first baseman Mike Easley; second baseman Terry Taylor; and catcher Eric Albright. The Aggies started the season 26-0 and were No. 1 for 11 weeks in Collegiate Baseball's poll.

LSU, on the other hand, was a pedestrian 11-11 from April 9 through the Southeastern Conference Tournament. But the Aggies knew LSU's brand was better, and they were lying in wait.

"We pulled up there Wednesday for practice, and their students are waiting for us," LSU student manager Russ Rome said. "They're yelling at McDonald and throwing Big Mac bags at him. They're flippin' us off when we leave on the bus."

But this was only a taste of what was to come on Sunday.

"A&M fans threw rocks at our bus during the game," Pat Garrity said. "They were throwing stuff at us in the dugout – rocks, batteries, cokes."

Garrity remembers a public address announcement asking for LSU's driver to move the bus to a safer location.

"It was as crazy an environment and as intimidating an environment as I've ever seen, still today," said Mike Bianco, LSU's catcher in 1988 and '89 and an LSU assistant from 1993 to 1997.

"They had their cadets on the second tier, and they threw rocks," Coach

Bertman recalled.

"My mom and other parents got hit with ice chips. Our girlfriends and fans were right in the striking zone of their student section in the upper deck," Pete Bush said.

"I couldn't believe it. They're throwing things at Ben in the bullpen. The fans were getting rocks off the railroad tracks near the stadium. The cops had to stop them," Bianco reported.

Texas A&M also played walk-up songs for its hitters, which is not allowed in NCAA postseason play.

This was before the days of LSU fans traveling by the thousands to away games. There were maybe 200 in LSU's contingent in College Station, and most of those were family and friends. They were outnumbered, out-volumed, and showered with debris.

'Pillage the Village'

But Bertman was ready for everything, and he had been since the previous Monday when the NCAA Selection Committee sent his 48-14 Tigers to College Station.

"He went to medieval terms," Garrity recalled. And this was five years before Quentin Tarantino's "Pulp Fiction."

"I was really mad," Bertman said. "They sent us there to make it a great crowd. We should've been sent somewhere else for more balanced regionals."

Instead, the six teams in College Station had the most combined wins of any of the other seven regionals, with 264 wins going in – 55 by Texas A&M, 48 by LSU, 47 by Brigham Young, 43 by South Alabama, 39 by Nevada-Las Vegas, and 32 by Jackson State.

"That really got to me. So, I had to do something," Bertman said.

"So, he tells us early in the week, 'We're not just going to win. We're going to Pillage the Village.' That was the calling card the whole weekend," Bianco recalled.

"And steal all their goods," Bertman says now, laughing. "And take all their land. Well, they just went crazy with that."

Players taped a "Pillage the Village" sign in whichever dugout LSU had for a game in College Station.

"He kept saying it, 'We want to Pillage the Village,'" Garrity recalled.

"And drink their beer," Bush added. "It was hilarious. When you're 18 to 21 years old, and your coach says, 'Pillage the Village,' your toes are tapping."

Bertman also did some homework. While the Aggies had a gaudy record and huge scores, they hadn't won a lot of tough games. They had 16 double-digit wins, but they didn't play a lot of great teams.

Under pressure, it's different, Bertman thought. *They'll soften just as they did the two previous seasons in regional finals.*

The pressure was mounting on fifth-year A&M coach Mark Johnson to get the Aggies back to the CWS for the first time since his predecessor Tom Chandler went 25 years earlier, in 1964. Meanwhile, A&M's dominant rival, Texas, had reached Omaha 16 times since '64 and won its fourth National Championship in 1983.

"Skip did a marvelous job of preparing the team," said Jim Wells, who was an LSU assistant from 1987 to 1989 before becoming Northwestern State's coach and later Alabama's.

"As the days went by, he kept saying, 'There's a lot of pressure on them,'" Wells recalled. "He kept saying that. He kept telling the guys, 'You know, they're *supposed* to win. They haven't been to Omaha in *forever*.'"

Then Wells just smiled.

"I look back 30 years ago," Wells said. "And I'm like, 'Yeah, that was pretty good by Skip.' We felt no pressure, and we were in the loser's bracket almost the whole time."

Bertman also skillfully surmised that what his team didn't see wouldn't hurt them. Texas A&M beat Jackson State, 23-3, Brigham Young, 25-4, and South Alabama, 17-6, but there were no Tigers watching. Usually, what players do at tournaments when they're not playing is watch the other games.

"One of my jobs was to find entertainment for the guys in between games," Wells said. "Take them to a movie or find something to eat. The easy thing was to load 'em up and go to the other games. Sometimes, it was mandatory. But this time Skip said, 'Don't take 'em, because A&M's beating the hell out of everybody.'"

The don't-watch rule extended to A&M's batting practice on Sunday, too. The Tigers would see the Aggies enough during eight hours of ball.

Texas A&M woke up Sunday without two straight losses at Olsen since Texas visited two years earlier. The Aggies' starter would be veteran right-hander Keith Langston, who was 12-0 on the season and would be a 12th-round pick in the upcoming MLB draft.

The Aggies' pitching staff was well rested and stress-free behind a robust offense, winning lopsided scrimmages at night on Thursday and Friday with a matinee blowout on Saturday against South Alabama.

Tickets for a second game were not even printed.

"That just showed that the idea of them losing never came into play," Pat Garrity said.

"They were so overconfident and cocky," Bush said. "And I don't ever remember us thinking, 'We're walking into insurmountable odds.'"

The Ogea factor

LSU, meanwhile, played Thursday, Friday, and Saturday in the sweltering sun before a night game on Saturday. In all, the Tigers had used only eight pitchers. But Bertman had thrown No. 2 starter Curtis Leskanic as a reliever in three of four games, logging eight innings in all and winning twice to go to 13-2. No. 4 starter Paul Byrd (6-2 on the season) also relieved in three of four games for seven innings.

McDonald had been rocked for 10 hits and five runs in the opener on Thursday against UNLV in just three innings before LSU came back to win 12-10 with Byrd, Leskanic, and closer Mark LaRosa. So, McDonald (13-2) was well rested for Sunday, and he would need it.

No. 3 starter Russell Springer, who was 8-3 on the season, was not. He had started Friday and threw five and two-thirds innings, allowing just two runs to South Alabama before LaRosa took the 6-4 loss. None of LSU's front line pitchers threw in the first game Saturday against UNLV other than LaRosa, for two-thirds of an inning. This would end up being very valuable in the second game Saturday and both games on Sunday.

That was because Bertman pulled a bulldog out of his cap on Saturday morning – freshman right-hander Chad Ogea of Lake Charles.

Entering College Station, Ogea (1-0, 3.10 ERA) had started exactly one game, and that was on March 23 against Northwestern State. He had thrown only 20 and a third innings all season, with his longest outing at three and a third innings against Southeastern Louisiana.

Before the games at College Station, Ogea was basically off on weekends. And for this reason, Leskanic was worried Ogea might not be ready for such a big game.

"Instead, he rose to the occasion and just pitched lights out," Leskanic said.

But first, Ogea had to get up off the ground. Early in the game, he took a line drive off his shin.

"I thought I broke my leg," he recalled.

Pete Bush ran to the mound from first before trainer Phillip Page could get there. When Page pulled Ogea's sock back, there was an open wound on his shin.

"It hit right on the bone and sliced him," Bush observed.

The ball bounced foul, almost into UNLV's dugout.

"I went down, and then I got back up because Bush told me to," Ogea said. "I told the trainer, 'Uh, I'm not coming out of this game.'"

And a bulldog was born. Ogea lasted eight innings with nothing but a fastball that hit its spots and an odd-looking slider. He scattered eight hits, but allowed only two earned runs with seven strikeouts and left with a 13-3 lead. LSU won 13-8.

Bertman was asked why he threw Ogea instead of a well-rested McDonald in a critical elimination game.

"I expect to win the tournament. I didn't come here to make a good showing," Bertman said, delivering his own fastball.

"We'll throw McDonald in the first game Sunday and then Springer, Leskanic, Byrd for game two," he said matter-of-factly.

One more speech, and a cool nap

With the "Pillage the Village" mantra resonating through day three, Bertman still had one more motivational speech in him for Sunday morning at the hotel.

"Hey guys, listen, I figured it out last night," he began. "I figured out how to beat A&M. See, they're not better than us. It's not what you think. They haven't played anybody. And we're better than them. And I'm going to show you right now."

Bertman went around the room and compared each A&M starting position player to each one from LSU.

"Pete Bush is better defensively than Mike Easley at first base," he said and continued on to each starter. "And by the way, what you guys don't understand is we have *Ben McDonald*. We have the single most deadly, lethal weapon."

Bertman continued with his bold, confident predictions.

"Guys, they're under so much pressure," he said. "If we win the first game, they'll be under that much more pressure. Look at their faces when we switch dugouts after we win the first game. They're not going to win the second game. It's over if we win the first game."

And co-captains Bianco and Bush had a plan for the rest advantage A&M had. Instead of taking batting practice early Sunday after two games on Saturday, Bianco told top assistant coach Ray "Smoke" Laval, the team will be napping in the A&M locker room. LSU had the home dugout for the first game.

"Some guys did hit in the cage, but we had played two games the day before," said Bianco, who caught 35 of 36 innings Thursday through Saturday. "And we were going to play two more. So, most of us went in the air conditioning and turned out the lights."

Bertman arrived later, expecting to see his team taking batting practice. When he went in the locker room, he saw the sleepy calm before the storm instead.

"Great. They've taken over the team," Bertman told assistant Randy Davis.

"He loved that stuff," Bush said. "He had a lot of respect for guys who would take charge. But it wasn't really taking things into our own hands. Even at 11 a.m. out there, it was scorching. And it was such a tough game the night before."

LSU and starting pitcher Jason Wall had trailed South Alabama 4-0 in the second and 5-3 in the fifth Saturday night before Tigers' second baseman

Tookie Johnson broke up a 5-5 game in the bottom of the eighth with an RBI single for the game-winning hit in a 6-5 win. Johnson also hit a three-run homer in the second.

"We didn't get home and unwind until 1 a.m.," Bush said. "So, the nap was more out of exhaustion. It was like, 'We've got to save our energy. We've got to beat these guys twice.'"

LSU at Texas A&M – Game 1

It turned out that the Tigers didn't need batting practice after all. In the first game, they clobbered the Aggies with 15 hits for a 13-5 win in front of nearly 6,000 fans. LSU took a 5-3 lead in the fourth as they roughed up A&M's star pitcher Keith Langston for five runs on five hits. Langston lasted just three and a third for his only loss of the year to finish 12-1.

Bianco homered in the second as LSU took a 2-1 lead. Matt Gruver added a two-run homer, and Tookie Johnson went 4-for-5 with three RBIs and a triple. Wes Grisham went 2-for-4 with three RBIs as did Craig Cala. No. 9 hitter Ron Lim went 3-for-4.

McDonald allowed 10 hits and five runs through seven innings, including a lead-off home run to All-American John Byington in the second inning for a 1-0 deficit. But he was ahead most of the game and struck out seven with only two walks.

After he struck out Byington to end the top of the fifth up 6-3, McDonald threw a taunt right back at the A&M crowd with a "Gig 'em Aggies" thumbs up. It was clearly out of character for McDonald, but he had been dodging rocks and batteries all day.

He left the mound up 8-5 in the seventh inning. Bertman was not comfortable with the lead, though, and put McDonald in left field – just in case he needed him to return to the mound. But LaRosa threw a no-hit shutout over the final two innings.

The game ended just before 5:30 p.m., and the teams prepared to cross paths on their way to the other's dugout.

"Look in their eyes, and you'll see they weren't expecting that. They're scared now," Bertman said.

"He was right again," Pete Bush said.

"You could tell from looking at them, A&M was defeated," Garrity chimed in.

The stage was set for the championship game at 7 p.m., though the Tigers and their staff and followers were starting to feel the fatigue.

LSU at Texas A&M – Game 2

With some makeshift tickets, another 4,177 filed through for Game 2.

Junior Russell Springer was LSU's other 90 m.p.h. preseason All-American in 1989. He had set the LSU record and led the SEC in strikeouts in 1988 with 156 in 119 innings. He would be a seventh-round pick by the Yankees the next week and would pitch for nearly 20 years in the Majors.

So, Bertman felt good about giving the ball to an established starter in LSU's sixth game of the regional – the fourth in 36 hours. But Springer struggled with home plate umpire Bob Jones, walking five and allowing three earned runs in two and a third innings as A&M took a 4-1 lead.

Through four innings against A&M starter Pat Sweet, LSU was still down 4-1. Despite all his motivational tactics, confidence, and clearly the better pitching staff, Bertman worried out loud.

"I always sat by him and watched what pitch he'd call because I had to position the outfield," Wells recalled. "And in that game, he was saying to himself, 'We got a chance. We can make this last longer.'"

But Byrd, who had thrown four innings of one-run relief in the 6-5 win over South Alabama Saturday night, came on to throw a one-hit shutout over four and a third into the seventh. It was his fourth appearance in four days. In all, he allowed three earned runs on eight hits and three walks through 11 and a third with seven strikeouts and a 2.38 ERA.

Meanwhile, the Tigers cut A&M's lead to 4-3 in the fifth on a two-run home run to left-center – Wes Grisham's 19th on the year.

LSU tied it 4-4 in the eighth on Bush's RBI single, scoring pinch-runner Scott Schneidewind. Schneidewind had stolen second to give Bush the opportunity for a "timely hit," as Bertman called it.

As Schneidewind rounded third, he wasn't thinking about a possible trip to Omaha.

"I was trying to think of what I could do to agitate their fans because they were so awful," Schneidewind said in a 2019 interview. "So, I did the 'Hook 'em Horns' sign as I crossed the plate because A&M hates Texas. At that point, it was nothing about the game. It was about those fans because it was such a brutal atmosphere."

The best pitcher in the tournament – LSU's Curtis Leskanic – had come on in the seventh for his fourth appearance in four days. On Saturday night against South Alabama, he was superb through three and a third, one-hit scoreless innings as he threw 42 pitches, 39 of which were strikes. Leskanic struck out three and earned his second win of the regional to go to 13-2.

And he was on again Sunday as he shut out the Aggies on three hits over four innings with one very questionable walk and four strikeouts into the 11th.

LSU took a 5-4 lead in the top of the 11th. Craig Cala smashed a one-out double to right-center off right-handed reliever Scott Centala. Bianco's ground out got Cala to third. Freshman third baseman Luis Garcia, a right-handed hitter, was due up with two outs, but most of LSU's righties were missing

Centala's curve. He had eight strikeouts after relieving Sweet in the sixth. So Bertman tapped the last lefty in the dugout.

Sophomore backup third baseman Pat Garrity of New Orleans was 4-for-19 on the season for a .210 average. His last hit was an RBI single on March 15 in a win over St. John's. Since that night, LSU had played 46 games, and Garrity batted three times without a hit.

"I had no idea I might be going in," Garrity said. "I was shocked."

But Bertman had a hunch Garrity could see Centala's curve well.

"I knew Pat could hit that guy because he waits on the ball so well," Bertman said.

Bertman was now more confident than earlier in the game. Garrity battled to a 2-and-2 count, and then a Bertman prediction again came true.

"He threw a breaking ball and left it up a little bit on the inner half," Garrity said. "I knew I hit it good, and I saw the right fielder turn around and take off. I thought it had a chance, but it hit the wall. Probably a foot from going out."

Cala scored easily for the 5-4 LSU lead, and Garrity reached second with a double as LSU's dugout went wild. Olsen Field suddenly went quiet – rocks and all.

Joe Macaluso of the Baton Rouge *State-Times* wrote that he heard a dejected Aggies fan yelling to the A&M dugout: "Don't you guys want to go to Omaha?"

The Aggies were about to miss Omaha by one win for the third straight year. Texas A&M first baseman Mike Easley walked up to Garrity defiantly, though.

"It ain't over," he said.

"Yes, it is," Garrity responded.

Phil Espinosa was retired to end the inning. And Garrity went to third base for the bottom of the 11th. Leskanic went to the mound for his fourth inning, seventh in two nights, and 12th of the regional.

"My uniform was soaking wet," Leskanic said.

"I really started to feel it," said Bianco, who crouched down behind home plate for his 55th inning in four days. "The legs were really heavy."

Leskanic retired two batters in the 11th, bringing up the No. 9 batter, freshman designated hitter Trey Witte, who was 0-for-3.

On a full count, Leskanic fired a fastball right over the middle of the plate. Witte stepped away as if he was out, and Bianco exploded out of his crouch. But home plate umpire Bob Jones called ball four.

Suddenly, the Aggies had life as Leskanic vehemently argued the call, and Bertman decided to replace the tiring pitcher.

Speedy leadoff hitter Kirk Thompson was on deck, and Bertman summoned McDonald from the bullpen.

"As soon as their fans saw Ben coming out, it took the air out of the stadium immediately," Garrity said.

As McDonald warmed up with Bertman and Bianco on the mound, Garrity – a frequent defensive substitution at third — walked up.

"Coach, do you want me to guard the line?" Garrity asked.

Bertman did not believe in the conventional baseball wisdom of guarding the line late in games to avoid extra-base hits as he said more balls go through toward the middle of the field.

"Sure, Pat," Bertman said, without a lot of concern before returning to the dugout.

"He didn't really care because he thought Ben was going to strike this guy out," Bianco said.

But Thompson hit it hard down the third base line.

"If Pat's playing where he normally plays, that's a double, and they could've tied it 5-5," Bianco said.

Instead, Garrity fielded it deep behind third. He couldn't throw to second for a force out, because Tookie Johnson at second base was playing too deep to get over. So, Garrity made a great, long throw to just get Thompson out at first.

And it was over.

"We win. We go to Omaha. It could've been a double. But that's Skip – the magic man," Bianco said.

"It was a two-hopper," Garrity recalled. "When Skip said to play on the line, I was straddling it. I took like one step over and waited for it. There was a big hole between me and shortstop. If I'm playing regular, that's a double."

"You could've heard a pin drop," Ogea said. "Those people were in shock."

The Tigers dogpiled on Olsen Field, but they were not thinking about Omaha yet. They still wanted to get back at the Aggie fans. Third baseman Phil Espinosa thought of the perfect way to remind A&M that it used to be No. 1.

Video has survived of Espinosa exiting the dogpile and slowly, gradually flipping his middle finger high and hard toward all the Aggie fans – lower and upper decks, foul line to foul line, on the railroad tracks, and everywhere in between.

Espinosa may have committed errors in the Regional, but his hand delivered an instructional video for the ages on how to flip off an entire stadium.

"You can go look at it frame by frame," Bush said. "We're all throwing stuff and jumping on one another. And then you see Espy peel off from the pile, and he starts shooting the bird at everyone. It's hilarious."

* * * * *

And the party continued back at the hotel.

"That was the No. 1 team in the country we beat back-to-back there," Leskanic said. "It was euphoric. You just don't forget those feelings."

Leskanic's performance was memorable, too, and he should have won the NCAA Central Regional MVP – three wins in four days, only six hits allowed, four walks, 12 strikeouts, zero runs in 12 innings for an ERA of 0.00.

"I remember back at the hotel with all the parents being around," said Leskanic, who would later pitch for the Boston Red Sox. "Really, to be honest with you, it was like a World Series reception. When we were in the World Series with the Red Sox, we'd go back to the hotel, and it was all family, and like a big party everywhere you went."

And LSU did drink A&M's beer.

"When you're a 21-year-old and you're having a couple of beers with the parents and team, it was like, 'Wow, this is really happening. We're going to the World Series.' It's amazing," Leskanic said.

McDonald, who got the save for Leskanic after winning the first game Sunday, was named regional MVP.

"Truly, this was a team victory," Bertman said after the game. "These last 36 hours were incredible. I mean, you just can't underestimate the power of the mind. These guys really believed they could win. It's the greatest accomplishment of a team in my 28 years of coaching. It's one of the greatest victories in LSU sports history."

Pat Garrity finished 5-for-20 on the season with one game-winning hit.

"I really believe in situations like that; good things happen to good people," Bertman said. "Pat has been one of those players who comes out every day, never complains, always is there working as hard as a starter. I just somehow knew he would do it. Don't ask me how. I just knew."

LSU left the Village on Monday morning. The Tigers had a game on Saturday in Omaha against Miami. On the bus back to Baton Rouge, they sang with joy: "*Hit the road, Pat, and don't you come back no more, no more, no more, no more...*"

* * * * *

Texas A&M never quite got over it.

"People were absolutely shattered, as we were, to lose that game," Texas A&M's Coach Mark Johnson said 25 years later to a Bryan-College Station newspaper reporter.

In 1993, Johnson had finally gotten the Aggies to Omaha – and they promptly lost to LSU in the second round, 13-8. They went again in 1999. In 2004, Johnson got A&M to the Super Regional round, where his team lost back-to-back games at LSU. He was let go by A&M after the 2005 season, and he was replaced by Rob Childress, who reached Omaha in 2011 and 2017. A&M has never won a national title in baseball as of this writing.

Johnson finished his coaching career in 2011 at Sam Houston State before becoming an announcer for Aggie baseball broadcasts.

"That game was such a shocker and such a heartbreaker that it affected people," Johnson said. "People were crushed. It's incredible. Regardless of age, the conversation goes to the '89 team."

"You talk to people over there, and it's still a fresh wound," Bush said. "It was one of the worst losses in any sport they've ever had."

Ben McDonald, who is on the SEC Network television crew for baseball, found that out when he did the LSU series at Texas A&M in 2014.

"I just happened to be there when they were celebrating the 25-year anniversary of their '89 team," he said. "When I stepped off the plane in College Station, a flight guy recognized me. He said, 'We still can't believe you guys beat us. That's the best team we've ever had here.'"

Bertman calls the 1989 defeat of A&M his "sixth national championship."

"I can tell you this, as far as my college days go, I don't think there was anything better," said McDonald, who was the first pick in the MLB draft, won the Golden Spikes award, and played on LSU's Elite Eight basketball team in the 1986-87 season.

"Knocking off a No. 1 team twice in front of a rowdy crowd like that – that's about as exciting as it gets."

Chapter 4

College Station hangover

"OK, here's where I made the greatest mistake I've ever made."

– Coach Skip Bertman, on the 1989 College World Series

Texas A&M, in a way, never recovered from its doubleheader loss to LSU at home in the NCAA Regional championship round on Sunday, May 28, 1989, with Omaha on the line. The Aggies were No. 1 that day and for most of that season.

Well, LSU also struggled in its own way to recover from its "Pillage the Village" weekend, with four wins in 36 hours after falling to the loser's bracket in the double-elimination format. When the Tigers arrived in Omaha the next Thursday, they were still lingering in a College Station state of mind.

"We all still talk about how when we got to Omaha, it was anticlimactic," LSU senior first baseman/captain Pete Bush said. "Not that we weren't trying to win, but we spent so much emotional energy beating A&M, which was probably the best team in the country. I wouldn't say we were physically exhausted. We had time to recover. But mentally, man, what it took to overcome the odds over there."

The No. 6-seeded Tigers did get a Saturday night opener at the College World Series against No. 3-seed Miami on June 3 and a full five days rest for ace Ben McDonald, who had just picked up Baseball America's College Player of the Year award. He would also win the Golden Spikes Award for the nation's best amateur baseball player.

But the Tigers found themselves right back in the loser's bracket after falling, 5-2, to the Miami Hurricanes.

McDonald struggled, allowing four runs on nine hits in eight innings, including a pair of two-run homers in the first three innings. More critical, though, than anyone imagined at the time was a nagging blister on the tip of his right, throwing middle finger that had first surfaced as LSU left for A&M a week earlier.

Miami ace Joe Grahe, who would pitch for seven seasons in the Majors, held LSU to five hits and one earned run in nine innings.

Bertman had asked McDonald if he wanted to wait and start the second game in Omaha because of the blister.

"It was bothering him," Bertman said. "But to his credit, and his guts, and his belief in the team, he said, 'No, I'm good.' And he did a good job. He gave us a chance to win, but we only got five hits off Grahe."

The following Monday, McDonald became the only LSU player in history to be the first selection in the Major League Baseball draft as he went to the Baltimore Orioles. That afternoon, McDonald watched LSU No. 2 pitcher Curtis Leskanic beat Long Beach State, 8-5, for his fourth win in 12 days to keep the Tigers alive as he set the school win record for a season, improving to 15-2.

The next night, McDonald relieved LSU starter Russell Springer in the ninth with a 6-3 lead over Miami and one out with a man on. He struck out the next two looking with a minimum of pitches and not much of a blister issue, earning his fourth save of the season.

Springer, whom the Yankees took in the seventh round, struck out nine around six hits in eight and a third killer innings for the win to go to 9-3.

"Man, did Springer pitch great!" Bertman said. "He was pitching so well, but I wanted to get Ben some confidence."

It was Bertman's first CWS win over Miami, where he was pitching coach and associate head coach before coming to LSU in 1983. Bertman had entered the game 1-5 against Miami overall as LSU's coach.

Two nights later, LSU (55-16) met No. 2-seed Texas (53-17), which had blown through its two CWS games with 7-1 and 12-2 wins over Long Beach State and Miami. The Tigers would have to beat the Longhorns that Thursday night and again on Friday to reach the National Championship game on Saturday.

It seemed like A&M all over again.

Bertman decided to go with his first-round draft choice, though McDonald was tailing off with some arm fatigue and the blister. The starter for Texas was ace Kirk Dressendorfer (17-2, 2.38 ERA), who was also ailing with some arm fatigue and upper back spasms.

While McDonald was a shiny 14-3 with a 2.91 ERA and 194 strikeouts in 148 and a third innings, he was slipping. Over his five NCAA postseason appearances starting at A&M, he had allowed 14 earned runs on 29 hits in 19 innings for a 6.63 ERA. Though tiring and tender on the blistered middle finger, McDonald was still an effective power pitcher in that 5-game span; his record was 1-1 with two saves and 21 strikeouts against five walks.

"He said he was good to go again. That's how Ben is," Bertman said. "But I shouldn't have pitched him in the first game against Texas. I should've started Leskanic, but not expecting him to go nine."

An eighth-round pick by Cleveland, Leskanic had just thrown seven and two-thirds innings on Monday. But he was on fire with a live, fresh, and "aerodynamic" arm. (He had a teammate shave his arm before every start.) In his four NCAA postseason appearances, Leskanic was 4-0 with a 2.29 ERA in 19 and two-thirds innings, allowing 16 hits with 15 strikeouts against five walks.

"He was hot," Bertman said. "He was a unique player who was pitching extraordinarily well – a great pitcher. He just blew the ball by people and had a hard breaking ball."

And lately, Leskanic did not require much rest.

"Here's where I made the mistake. Here's why," Bertman said. "We had never won a National Championship. And I couldn't imagine at the time going into a National Championship game without having Ben McDonald to pitch. If he pitched Thursday against Texas some, there was enough time for him to rest for the National Championship."

Bertman said he should have started McDonald on Friday, assuming Leskanic and a reliever or two would have beaten Texas on Thursday. No. 4 starter and reliever Paul Byrd could have relieved on Thursday and Friday. He was a sophomore who finished 6-2 with a 3.38 ERA in 1989. He had pitched only once in Omaha so far, earning a save against Long Beach State with an inning and a third of one-hit, shut-out relief.

"I could've used Ogea, too," Bertman said.

Chad Ogea was a seldom-used freshman, but he had just beaten UNLV at A&M with eight innings of two-run pitching and seven strikeouts to keep LSU alive.

"Then I would've had to pitch Springer in the National Championship, which would have been fine," said Bertman, who later mixed and matched pitchers more in Omaha regardless of the "ace" tag.

"Now that I look at it, that was my mistake," Bertman said. "I could've used Springer in relief on Thursday, too, and bring him back Saturday if Leskanic got tired in the fifth or sixth. But Curtis was on fire.

"That was the biggest coaching error I've had. I've had a lot, of course. But that was the biggest one because we had a great team. I should've started Curtis that Thursday."

McDonald walked leadoff hitter Lance Jones in the top of the first. Then David Tollison singled. A pickoff try to second by McDonald sailed to center field, putting runners on second and third. Scott Bryant tripled for a 2-0 lead. Arthur Butcher's RBI single made it 3-0 before McDonald threw wildly to third for another error after fielding a bunt to put the Longhorns up 4-0.

"I thought I could pitch through it like I had been," McDonald said. "But in the second inning, the blister ripped all the way through. It wasn't completely healed."

A bandage was applied, but it didn't matter.

"I couldn't feel the ball. It affected my fastball and my curve," McDonald recalled.

"His velocity was down into the mid-80s," his catcher Mike Bianco said.

"He's throwing and wiping blood on his pants. He just couldn't do it."

Texas went up 6-0 in the second and 7-0 in the third on a solo homer by Steve Bethea.

"I remember the umpire throwing balls out of the game because they had too much blood on them," McDonald said. "I'm sitting there bleeding on balls. They were too red, and I'm trying to pitch through it."

The Longhorns made it 11-3 in the fourth as McDonald exited after three and a third, allowing 11 earned runs on nine hits with three walks and six strikeouts.

"Skip still kicks himself for not throwing Leskanic," Bianco said. "But he didn't know at the time the blister was going to be an issue. Neither did Ben."

In the end, LSU had nine hits and scored enough to win had it been a well-pitched game, but the Tigers fell 12-7 and were eliminated. Ogea threw three and a third of one-hit, shut-out relief with four strikeouts, and Byrd allowed a run and a hit in two innings.

"We were on top of the world. Then you go to Omaha, and it was a different feel," Ogea said.

"You guys are really good," Texas coach Cliff Gustafson told Bertman before losing the national title, 5-3, to Wichita State two days later.

"And I said to myself, 'I blew this one,'" Bertman said remorsefully. "You see, Ben did have a blister, but I'm not blaming the blister. That's not his fault. That was my fault. We had six Big Leaguers on that pitching staff. I should've used more of them."

Indeed, six pitchers from the 1989 team would reach the Majors and pitch a combined 60 seasons from September of 1989 with McDonald's debut through Springer's final pitch in 2010: Springer (18 seasons), Byrd (14), Leskanic (12), McDonald (9), Ogea (6) and John O'Donoghue (1).

McDonald finished in the 1989 NCAA postseason with a 10.07 ERA, having allowed 25 earned runs in 22 and a third innings with 38 hits, 27 strikeouts and eight walks. This was not the same Ben McDonald who started the season by breaking the 26-year-old SEC record of 37 consecutive scoreless innings by hurling 44 and two-thirds of those and opening the season at 11-1.

"He wasn't himself in Omaha, that's for sure," team captain Pete Bush observed.

McDonald finished 14-4 with a 3.49 ERA through 152 and a third innings in 1989 after throwing 79 and a third on the 1988 Summer Olympic team that won the gold in Seoul, Korea, with Bertman as pitching coach.

"Ben McDonald did everything he could for us," Bertman said. "He had pitched in the Olympics. He rested all fall, but that's still a lot of innings. But he was such a unique athlete."

McDonald had punted and kicked on the Denham Springs High football team. He was more heavily recruited as a basketball player than for baseball out of high school. He was a 6-foot-7 backup forward on an LSU basketball team that reached the Elite Eight in the 1986-87 season before focusing solely on baseball.

"Sometimes pitchers aren't real athletes," Bertman said. "Ben was. Ben was one of the greatest athletes ever to play at LSU. He was the greatest baseball player for sure. I screwed up '89 with Ben, as I've told him and Leskanic."

McDonald's 202 strikeouts in 1989 is still the SEC season record, and he is second in consecutive scoreless innings at 44 and two thirds. (Tennessee's Todd Helton had a stretch of 47 and a third in 1994.)

Bertman would make very few mistakes over the next 12 years as he won five National Championships in 10 years (1991, '93, '96, '97 and 2000) and reached Omaha in three other seasons (1990, '94 and '98).

But 30 years after the 1989 season, Bertman was still wondering what might have been.

"Because of Ben's blister, I should have used another pitcher," he said.

* * * * *

LSU finished the 1989 season at 55-17, tying the school record for wins. And suddenly the Tigers were among the elites of college baseball, with three Omaha trips in four seasons in Bertman's sixth year.

He was on his way, and the *Times Picayune's* Teddy Allen already had immortalized Bertman – in press boxes at least – with a poem to the tune of "Take Me Out to the Ballgame." It remarkably captured Bertman's diction, marketing skill, and baseball philosophy … all in nine lines.

It should be noted that Allen wrote this before Bertman took the blame for not pitching Leskanic against Texas:

Take me out to the ball-yerd
Take me out to see Skip
Where the bathrooms are clean
And the coffee's hot
Football mentality, he hasn't got.
Oh, it's root, root, root for Skip Bertman
If they don't win, he's not to blame
A heater he'll light, he'll smile, and say … 'That's baseball'
At the old ball game.

Chapter 5

The weekend Alex Box became another Tiger Stadium

"I don't recall tailgating being a big thing at all before 1990."
– Bill Franques, LSU Baseball Sports Information Director, recalling
Alex Box Stadium's rise to national prominence

Alex Box Stadium public address announcer Bill Franques cued up the perfect crowd-pleaser – Bruce Springsteen's "Born to Run" – as Rich Cordani swung on deck with the tying run on first in the bottom of the seventh. LSU was trailing USC, 6-5, in the NCAA South I Regional championship game on May 28, 1990.

USC coach Mike Gillespie headed for the mound to try to settle down Jackie Nickell, his closer. Nickell had just hit Keith Osik to start LSU's inning and rev up a raucous, record-breaking Alex Box crowd of 5,809 in the then-6,000-seat stadium. Cordani batted third in the order and had eight home runs.

"Oh, hell yeah, I remember that," Cordani said three decades later in his thick Boston accent. "We had some Springsteen fans with Northern roots on that team. This gets me all excited just talking about it. This is history. This will never die."

Cue up "Glory Days."

Coach Skip Bertman did bring LSU to the College World Series in Omaha in just his third season, in 1986, in nothing short of a miracle, considering where the program was just two years earlier and for much of its history. Two more trips were to follow, in 1987 and '89, though not out of Alex Box.

But the glory days didn't come overnight.

It took seven years for Bertman to make Alex Box what it became on that Memorial Day weekend in 1990: an NCAA Regional destination dynasty.

In LSU's first home Regional, in 1986, the Tigers drew just 3,000 fans to watch them beat Tulane, 7-6, and reach Omaha for the first time. Only 3,957 had filed into the stadium to watch LSU beat Jackson State, 14-11, in the '86 Regional opener. The next Saturday morning, just 3,048 watched LSU beat Louisiana Tech, 7-4, in the winners' bracket final.

Coming off that first College World Series appearance and Bertman's first SEC Championship in 1986, LSU went 43-17 in 1987 but lost the NCAA Regional host site to the University of New Orleans, which was 42-17.

At the time, UNO was still *the* baseball power in the state and the first Louisiana school to reach Omaha, in 1984.

"UNO bid more money than we did," Bertman said. "It was hard to convince Joe Dean (LSU Athletic Director from 1987 to 2000) in 1987 how important it was to host a Regional and how we could make money. I was upset about it."

The Tigers still defeated UNO at Privateer Park twice and No. 1-seed Cal State Fullerton in '87 to reach Omaha. In 1988, LSU failed to reach the postseason, and it was sent to Texas A&M in 1989.

On May 14, 1990, LSU finally got its home Regional site with a bid of $140,000 – significantly higher than what it had been bidding. Its overall record was 47-16, 20-7 in the SEC, and SEC regular season and tournament titles.

"Ultimately, Joe started to understand by 1990 after we kept getting sent away," Bertman said. "We had to make larger bids, because we were also competing with Mississippi State, UNO, and other schools in the area."

Dean reluctantly had to guarantee that 75 percent of the $140,000 would be retained by the NCAA. But Bertman had been trying to tell him for years that LSU could make that much and more through ticket sales and concessions.

"I knew we would make much more than the $140,000 because we got to keep the groceries," Bertman said, referring to revenue from concessions and ticket sales. "But we had to pack the place with 5,000 or 6,000."

But that was not seen as easy at the time since LSU had drawn as few as 2,000 fans for a few SEC home games that season.

Were the misses in Omaha in 1986, '87, and '89 taking their toll on fan interest?

* * * * *

"In 1990, people in Baton Rouge didn't really believe in Skip's vision yet," said Bill Franques, LSU baseball's publicity director. "The fans hadn't accepted LSU as a real powerhouse."

Bertman repeatedly told reporters that the fans had to show up in large numbers at the Box for the Regional.

"That's how you get Regionals year after year," he said. "We really need the fans. That's how you go to Omaha every year or almost every year."

After LSU and Mississippi State shared a rain-shortened SEC Tournament title in Birmingham, Alabama, on May 20, the Tiger Nation answered Bertman's plea with gusto.

A single-game Alex Box record crowd of 5,642 watched LSU beat Louisiana-Lafayette, 8-0, in a 7 p.m. game as the NCAA South I Regional opened on May 24. Another 3,660 saw LSU beat Georgia Tech, 11-5, the next afternoon. For a winners' bracket final on Saturday, 4,724 watched No. 2-seed USC edge No. 1-seed LSU, 5-4.

LSU fans were crestfallen, but at least some of them had interrupted their usual Memorial Day weekend plans. They were there. And something else happened that weekend before and after games at the Box like never before. LSU fans were tailgating before and after *baseball* games.

What would become a tradition in Omaha – Louisiana cuisine outside Rosenblatt Stadium for friend and foe alike – began cooking on this weekend in Baton Rouge.

"I don't recall tailgating being a big thing at all before 1990," Franques said.

After the loss to USC, just over 3,500 showed up to watch LSU on a Saturday night for a game against Georgia Tech, which the Tigers won, 6-4.

* * * * *

Just two teams remained now, LSU and USC, a pair of football schools – one trying to build a dynasty in baseball, the other trying to re-build one. (In 1987, USC coach Mike Gillespie had replaced the legend Rod Dedeaux, a New Orleans native who won 10 National Championships between 1958 and 1978.)

LSU would have to beat the Trojans twice, too – first at 2 p.m. Sunday, and then in a nightcap.

But the weather was a problem. After LSU held on to beat USC, 5-4, on Sunday afternoon, a storm packing 80 m.p.h. winds shredded stage scaffolding and injured 31 in downtown Baton Rouge at "Fest For All" and mangled the right field fence at Alex Box Stadium.

The NCAA South I Regional title game was rescheduled for high noon on Memorial Day. The Tigers' starting pitcher would be Paul Byrd, who had beaten Georgia Tech on Friday in seven innings to go to 16-5 on the season and set the school record for wins in a season.

Considering how the first two LSU-USC games delivered, this championship tilt figured to be a classic. Both previous meetings were intense, one-run games with each ending in the bottom of the ninth with the tying run in scoring position.

"Two photo finishes, nail-biters. Both were almost mirror images of the other," Gillespie said diplomatically. "The real shame here is that two teams have battled each other to the wire in two games, and somebody who deserves to go to the College World Series will not go."

And there was something else. LSU's fans were more rabid than usual when the Tigers played USC.

"Those were football crowds at the USC games," said superfan Marvin "Big Ragoo" Dugas. "That 1990 Regional was the first really great Regional at LSU, and it might have been the loudest ever."

And it featured a villain.

The star of the Regional's first four days was unquestionably USC junior shortstop Bret Boone, who would go on to a 13-year Major League career from 1992 to 2005. He found his home run stroke in Alex Box as he entered with six home runs on the season and departed with 12. He had hit .578 (11-for-19) with five home runs and 10 RBIs in USC's first four games heading into the final.

USC, which normally plays with a high of 72 degrees and minimal humidity, clearly was not used to the semi-tropical climate of south Louisiana.

There was something in the air. In just three LSU-USC games in history – two so far in 1990 and an early season game in 1988 – the Trojans and Tigers resembled sweaty SEC rivals.

"It's so emotional, these games," Bertman said wearily after the Sunday win.

"I don't think either team has an advantage," said Boone, who then on Memorial Day Monday gave his team a 3-0 lead with a three-run homer off Paul Byrd in the first inning of the title game.

It was Boone's sixth homer in five games and third against LSU.

The Tigers cut that lead to 3-1 in the second on a Johnny Tellechea RBI groundout. LSU took a 4-3 lead with a three-run fifth inning off starter Rick Cirillo and went up 5-3 in the sixth on a solo home run by Lyle Mouton.

USC scored three in the top of the seventh to take a 6-5 lead. John O'Donoghue allowed two runs (with the third charged to Byrd) on four hits, a walk and a wild pitch. But he did manage to strike out Boone with the bases loaded amid all that to help limit the bleeding.

Mark LaRosa relieved O'Donoghue with the bases loaded and one out. He struck out one batter and got another to fly out to end the inning and keep LSU within 6-5.

The Tigers' first batter of the seventh inning, catcher Keith Osik, got on first base as a hit batsman, though that call proved to be controversial. The crowd was nervous and rowdy, as might be expected. "Born to Run" was playing loudly, and the fans and players seemed to be stoked by its lively tune and simple lyrics.

The left-handed Rich Cordani stepped up to face the right-handed Jackie Nickell. Cordani had just singled up the middle off Nickell in the fifth to tie it 3-3.

"Our fans were so loud," Cordani said as though he could still hear them. "There were so many people there. They had people standing everywhere. And my back was up against the wall."

Cordani was hitting just .105 in the Regional entering the game, so he went to a slightly smaller bat on his father's advice.

"I was struggling, and I'm like, 'This is it. I've got to do something for us,'" he said.

And down went Cordani on the first pitch.

"That got me even more jacked up because he went right at my kneecaps, and I fell completely on my face," Cordani said. "I got up, and I was staring into the dugout at my boys and I said, 'There's no way this guy's getting me out. No way.' We had been howling at this guy because he kept having a coach bring a towel to the mound. Of course, it was hot, but we're like, 'What's this about?' We were all hamming it up the whole game. That's the type of team we had."

Cordani stood in again.

"The type of team we were, you want to get in a little bit of a street fight. And that's what that Regional was for three days," Cordani said. "It was like a game seven of a World Series. They had great players. We had great players. So, I said, 'All right, you come inside again, you'll see what happens.' He tried again...."

Cordani slammed the pitch over the light tower beyond the right field wall for a 7-6 lead.

"He came back inside, and he learned," Cordani said.

"I had a great view because I was on first base," Osik said. "I mean, that ball was launched. He pulled it right over my head, so I was able to turn around, and then it was just like we were flying around the bases. We were as light as a feather."

But USC had six more outs, and the feared Boone would bat again.

LaRosa, who had been on crutches Thursday after getting hit in the foot on an errant bullpen pitch by Greene, allowed only a harmless single in the eighth.

Boone led off the top of the ninth. If he were to hit his seventh home run of the Regional, it would tie the game 7-7. He and LaRosa went to a full count.

"I think it was beyond nervousness," Boone said.

"He was fightin' and fightin' in the ninth," LaRosa said. "On three-and-two, I just said I've got to give it my best shot. And I did."

Boone took strike three.

"And I loved it," LaRosa said.

"LaRosa worked me away every pitch," Boone said. "It got to a full count, and he busted a fastball by me for a strike. It was a great pitch. I was looking away, and he knew that."

Actually, Bertman knew that.

"We were trying not to pitch to him," Bertman said. "We were very careful. We were throwing way out of the strike zone to keep him from pulling the ball over the fence. And then it goes 3-2, and I'm thinking, *We're going inside*, which is different. And LaRosa strikes him out. I mean LaRosa delivered a wonderful pitch."

With two outs, Mark Smith grounded to shortstop. LSU's Scott Bethea bobbled it as the fans gasped, but he recovered and threw him out to end the game.

LaRosa, who had lost four postseason games in the 1989 and '90 seasons, collected his second win of the Regional to go to 7-2 and felt like a new man.

"This is the greatest feeling of all to go back to the World Series," he said as he threw his arms up. "Unbelievable. I can't explain it. Our crowd gets into such a frame of mind and so much into the game that nothing can beat you."

And it was time to start a new tradition that continues today. After eliminating USC, LSU did the first Omaha victory lap around Alex Box, where fans can literally reach out and touch the players.

"I remember fans actually bent the fence around the stadium as we took the victory lap," Osik said. "The atmosphere was amazing. What a night!"

So, make that two fences up for repair or reconstruction before the 1991 season.

The construction of the fan base, though, was done.

"That Regional was the big starting point," said "Big Ragoo" Dugas. "Everybody jumped on the bandwagon and stayed on after that."

Not only did LSU draw 34,467 over the weekend, but the fans were knowledgeable. They cussed and taunted the Trojans, but they also cheered their great plays, and applauded Boone when it was all over.

Bertman's idea to dispatch players and assistant coaches into the stands at the Box in his early years was paying off. They'd go up to explain to fans why certain coaching moves were made in certain situations and to answer questions.

"I really have to thank the people of Baton Rouge and the surrounding areas for their support," Bertman said after the game. "That means a lot to me personally and to the players. The fan support really made a difference. It was tremendous. You could feel it in the dugout."

* * * * *

Three decades later, Bertman remembered when Alex Box took a giant leap to national prominence.

"The fans really rocked out in 1990," he said. "Yes, 1990 turned it around. The thing about it is we probably shouldn't have won that Regional. We weren't a great team yet, and USC was very good. But we were better because we were at home."

And in the end, LSU made USC feel at home. Some of the hard feelings dissipated after the final out, and Boone and some of his teammates even joined LSU's players, Athletic Department staff, and fans at Tiger Bar in Tigerland.

"Just a massive celebration," Franques said. "The Tiger was the players' hangout, and there were a lot of them out after that game. Everyone was in the place. Then it spilled out into the parking lot."

The Box left its mark on USC coach Mike Gillespie, who would not get to Omaha until 1995 – 17 years after the Trojans' last appearance.

"Their crowd was a factor, and that's to their credit," he said. "LSU has something to be cherished here. Their fans were great, and they played great baseball. So, did we. We had three of the greatest games I've ever been involved with."

"You can barely hear yourself in that stadium," Gillespie told Bertman.

Bertman would hear a similar comment from several coaches, including South Alabama coach Steve Kittrell, who would be sent to the Box for Regionals in 1991, '92, '93, and '97.

"The word spread that we were the place to play. And now Joe Dean understood that we can have the thing every year because we would always have about 6,000 and make money," Bertman observed.

It was now clear nationwide that LSU Baseball was no longer a minor sport on the field or in the stands.

* * * * *

LSU went on to host these six-team NCAA Regionals every year from 1990 through 1998. The Tigers advanced to Omaha every time except in 1992 and 1995, and won National Championships in 1991, '93, '96, and '97. USC and Gillespie finally reached Omaha in 1998, eliminated LSU, and won it all.

Bertman reached four NCAA Regionals from 1986 to '90 and won all four – two away and two at home. The last two were won in stunning fashion out of the losers' bracket over teams that were ranked No. 1 at some point that season.

Unfortunately, things didn't go well for the Tigers in Omaha in 1990. They were done in four games for the second straight year after having to win a combined seven elimination games to get there. The A&M and USC Regionals may have been too draining. Either way, LSU was 0-for-Omaha through four trips, with a pedestrian 7-8 record.

Nevertheless, LSU was making gradual, incremental improvement the *Kaizen* way – the Japanese business philosophy preached by Bertman that stresses continuous, methodical progress.

In 1989, LSU showed it could win its way into Omaha amid the most difficult of circumstances – two wins in one day at No. 1 Texas A&M. In 1990, LSU launched the greatest home field advantage in college baseball. That's progress.

"LSU first showed it was a consistent, national brand by reaching Omaha for the third time in four years by winning twice at A&M," Franques said. "In 1990, we showed how strong we could be at home. We swept first place Georgia to win the SEC outright in front of some big crowds – a huge statement. Then that Regional against USC – unbelievable! Those two weekends solidified the connection between our fans and the program that has thrived since then."

Landing on and traversing Omaha for a few days was no longer enough, though. Next on *Kaizen's* list for Bertman was to plant LSU's flag between home plate and the mound at Rosenblatt Stadium.

"After this year, I can honestly say LSU will always be a contender for the National Championship no matter who plays for them," pitcher Paul Byrd predicted boldly and prophetically as the 1990 season ended. "The team that comes back next year will realize you want to peak during the World Series."

And that team would be basically the same as the 1990 team with so many players returning: pitchers Paul Byrd, Chad Ogea, Rick Greene, Mike Sirotka, and Mark LaRosa; third baseman/outfielder Rich Cordani; outfielder Lyle Mouton; second baseman Tookie Johnson; first baseman Johnny Tellechea; catcher Gary Hymel; designated hitter Pat Garrity; and third baseman Luis Garcia. It would be the largest group of returnees from an Omaha team that Bertman ever had.

"We probably overachieved a little bit throughout 1990," Ogea said. "We were terrible that previous fall. We lost to everybody. We got better as the season went on, but we peaked against USC. When we lost at Omaha again, we were like, 'We'll be back here.' We knew what kind of team we had coming back. We knew we could do much more."

Or, as "Born to Run" says:

We're gonna get to that place, where we really want to go,
And we'll walk in the sun.

Five times in 10 years, to be exact.

Chapter 6

5th time's a charm

"Personally, I'm glad the tournament from hell is over, to be very honest."

– Skip Bertman, after losing the SEC Tournament title amid the mud
and the muck of Alex Box Stadium in 1991

In 1991, LSU had it all. The Tigers were full of veterans who had already been to Omaha in back-to-back seasons – unprecedented at LSU.

Could this be the year when LSU would finally, finally win the national title?

Talented veterans included junior starting pitchers Chad Ogea and Paul Byrd, senior reliever Mark LaRosa, senior left fielder Rich Cordani, senior second baseman Tookie Johnson, senior designated hitter Pat Garrity, and junior infielder Luis Garcia.

And there were five others who had been to Omaha in 1990: sophomore closer Rick Greene; sophomore starting pitcher Mike Sirotka; senior first baseman Johnny Tellechea, who was a junior college transfer the previous season; junior right fielder Lyle Mouton, a true power hitter; and senior catcher Gary Hymel, who was tutored by Mike Bianco in 1988 and '89 and now had more power at the plate.

In addition, Bertman got junior third baseman Chris Moock back full time after he missed most of 1989 and all of 1990 playing quarterback at LSU during spring practice. And LSU signed two sophomore transfers who became starters – center fielder Armando Rios from North Carolina-Charlotte and shortstop Andy Sheets from Tulane.

"I actually thought our '90 team was better than '91 for a while, at least numbers-wise," Mouton said. "Sometimes, it's the hot team. And in '91, we got hot and just had a very good, cohesive team. You couldn't concentrate on one or two or three hitters. We had a whole lineup of guys who could hurt you."

When Dan Canevari, the coach at Coral Gables High and a Miami pitcher under Bertman, arrived for his first of 11 seasons as an assistant coach under Bertman, LSU's lineup was virtually locked.

"I walked into Skip's office in December of '90, and he said, 'Just let 'em go. They know what to do,'" Canevari recalled. "They were a team that knew they could win if they did the right things. They'd tasted it."

And they were tired of leaving the Omaha table still hungry.

"We were sick of getting there and not winning it," said Tookie Johnson, who had been starting at second base since 1988 and was full time since 1989. "Yeah, it's wonderful to go to Omaha. But going there and losing? It's the same as losing in a Regional."

Of course, LSU had not lost a Regional since 1985.

"We were determined to win it all in Omaha," Johnson recalled. "Experience was the key to the '91 team – Omaha experience. And of all my years there, it had the best team chemistry."

* * * * *

LSU, a preseason No. 5, immediately showed what was to come with a 6-4 win over SEC rival Mississippi State in the season-opening American Baseball Coaches Association Hall of Fame Tournament at Alex Box.

Armando Rios, a native of Carolina, Puerto Rico, dashed in from center field and performed a complete flip into the infield that shocked nearly everyone. A picture in the Baton Rouge *Advocate* the next day captured Rios parallel to the ground at the 6-foot-5 Greene's chest. Bertman saw the picture.

"Armando," he said the next day before LSU beat No. 2 Oklahoma State, 6-0, behind Ogea's two-hitter. "See, this is LSU. We expect to win here. I don't ever want to see you do that again – unless, we win the national championship."

The Tigers were soon ranked No. 1 and boasted a record of 12-1. By mid-April, the Tigers were still No. 1 and 33-8 overall, 11-0 in the SEC, with a four-game lead going to Tennessee (29-9, 7-5 SEC). But the Tigers lost a Saturday doubleheader to the Volunteers, 5-3 and 6-5.

"We ran 56 sprints after that," remembered Ronnie Rantz, a 6-foot-5, 250-pound left-hander from Alexandria whom Bertman nicknamed "Jumbo."

"One sprint for every win we would need to win the national championship that year," said Rantz, who later founded a company to televise LSU baseball games that he called the Jumbo Sports Network.

The extra leg work did not benefit the team in the short run as the Tigers were swept at Kentucky a week later amid frigid temperatures, 17-7 and 11-7 on Saturday, and 7-3 on Sunday.

A 15-2 drubbing to Southeastern Louisiana followed – which was the Tigers' fifth loss to an in-state team in a mid-week game that season. Suddenly, many fans thought the team was not Omaha-worthy.

"But that was a veteran team," said baseball Sports Information Director Bill Franques. "They had heard all Skip's stuff before. To their credit, they definitely performed when it mattered."

Bertman had had such an impact on his players for so long that he didn't realize they had it under control because of him and no longer always needed to hear it from him.

The Tigers went on to prove once again that mid-week game results do not matter much as they took seven of the last nine SEC games to end the regular season at 44-16, 19-7 in the league, for Bertman's third SEC Championship.

The only thing that could curtail LSU for long in '91 was the weather.

* * * * *

The weather was terrible in the SEC Tournament in May at Alex Box as weeks of torrential rains continued, turning the outfield into what you could call a Woodstock Revival on the Mississippi River – which was located just a few blocks from the stadium.

Hard rain postponed the LSU-Mississippi State game on Friday night, May 17, with the Tigers trailing 1-0 in the top of the third. After more rain, all remaining games of the double-elimination tourney were cut to seven innings.

Auburn was eliminated in its third game of the tournament, 1-0, by Mississippi State on Saturday, and it did not reach NCAA play.

LSU's veteran players, meanwhile, had no worries.

"We're loose. We're more focused on the Regional next week and Omaha than this," Garcia said.

LSU beat Mississippi State, 8-2, on Saturday to finish that game, but lost to Florida, 7-1, in the late game that went past midnight. The Tigers eliminated Mississippi State, 9-4, on Sunday, setting up a Florida-LSU championship round. The Tigers would have to beat the Gators twice, and thus play three games in one day to win the title. But the SEC Tournament was thought of basically as a nuisance string of mid-week games for LSU and others that would reach NCAA Tournament play either way – Florida, Mississippi State, and Alabama.

"I didn't want to play," Bertman said. "I wanted to get to Omaha, and I didn't care who won the SEC Tournament."

Bertman opened with mid-week starter David Herry and did lose to Florida, 8-4. The loss gave Bertman the chance to rest his pitchers and his deteriorating field.

"Personally, I'm glad the tournament from hell is over, to be very honest," Bertman said as laughter broke in a muddy, smelly press tent.

Bill Franques smiled in agreement. Needing a shave, shower, and sleep, Franques resembled a B-movie Indiana Jones with his Panama Jack hat, shades to match, and mud caked all over both legs.

An LSU facilities worker told reporters how he drilled a 30-inch hole in the outfield the morning after the SEC Tournament, and by 3 p.m. this hole to hell was filled with Mississippi River water.

LSU was granted special permission from the NCAA to start its South Regional the next Friday at the Box instead of the usual Thursday, so the field could dry and be patched up by LSU's overworked maintenance crew. And by whatever other means necessary.

Bertman got Acadian Ambulance to send a helicopter over for free to basically blow-dry the field. "The 'copter went just over the outfield, and the water was flying," Bertman reported.

Assistant athletic director for facilities John Symank then mixed a cocktail of sand, sawdust, hay, clay, and woodchips to top it off.

"We used straw, too, and all kinds of clay, but the river was too high," Bertman said.

In the end, the field was still a gooey mess.

"I'm going to wear my galoshes, put studs in them, and hope the water doesn't run up to my calves," left fielder Rich Cordani told the *Times Picayune*. He knew those outfield waters. He had performed a 10-yard belly flop and slide and actually went underwater while trying to snag a low liner in a loss to Florida.

* * * * *

Come hell or high water, Bertman wanted his team ready despite conditions so as not to repeat what happened in the Kentucky cold a month previously.

"I'll never forget it," Johnson said. "After batting practice the week of the Regional, he read us the riot act. We weren't playing badly, but I think he wanted to give us that little edge and put us in our place."

Johnson, Cordani, Hymel, Mouton, Ogea, and others looked at one another.

"And a couple guys start talking, 'Who in the hell is he kidding? He can say whatever he wants. We're going to win the whole damn thing,'" Johnson said.

"Skip, you loved him and hated him," said Ogea, who would later pitch in the Major Leagues for six years. "When he got on your ass, you hated him. But you wanted to prove him wrong, and that probably drove us more than anything. You also loved him for doing that and making you a better player."

Players called it the "WrestleMania" speech.

"He'd go right down the roster and get in everybody's face," Johnson said. "Everybody got a scathing review. You never knew when he'd do it. Part of the magic of him was he'd time it just right. His timing with everything was impeccable. He knew what to say to get you going. He thought we were overconfident."

With buttons pushed, LSU would not lose another game in 1991.

The Tigers ripped Northwestern State, 13-2, on Friday night to open the Regional before all three Saturday games were pushed to Sunday after more rain. The Tigers sloshed their way to a 4-0 mark and a Regional title for the first time since 1987, beating Oklahoma, 4-3, on Sunday; Texas A&M, 7-1, on Monday; and Louisiana-Lafayette, 8-5, on Tuesday.

Finally, the Tigers did not have to survive the losers' bracket to win a Regional – as at Texas A&M in 1989 and versus USC in 1990 – which drained them emotionally and physically pre-Omaha. But they now had to open the

CWS in just three days on Friday night against a team it had just lost to twice – No. 5-seed Florida.

Omaha, though, would be a cool, dry heaven compared to the Alex Hot Box of Mud. LSU arrived at Rosenblatt Stadium rested, refreshed, and clean as the No. 4 seed at 51-18.

Bertman and his team had high hopes. This could be their year to win it all.

"I had a spot picked for the national championship trophy…, " Bertman said. "In our old trailer office next to Alex Box, I had a shelf with SEC Championship trophies and other trophies. And right in the middle, it was empty. I'm a big believer in all kinds of visualization. A star in your own mind. That was one of my big phrases. And people saw my vision. It was easy after a while because people believed we were going to win."

Chapter 7

The 1991 National Championship

"I had decided on the Dean Smith method. I stayed calm.
Business as usual. I walked across, shook hands, hugged our coaches.
Remember now, I've always seen this. So, when I walked across,
I felt like I'd done this a thousand times."

– Skip Bertman on winning his first National Championship as LSU's coach

J ust as LSU surged into Omaha with its most experienced World Series team and one of its better squads overall, the Tigers were immediately reminded of past failures.

"When we walked into practice at Rosenblatt, the workers getting the field ready laughed at us," said junior pitcher Paul Byrd, who would start LSU's opener on Friday night.

"I'm like, 'Why are they laughing at us?' I couldn't believe it," said Byrd, now an Atlanta Braves announcer after 15 seasons in the Major Leagues. "And one of them goes, 'Hey, welcome back guys. Five times a charm.' And we were ticked off. Is that what we're known for? We keep coming back, and we can't close the deal? I remember being really angry."

Bertman was, too, because of the draw. He was paired with the only other SEC team in the eight-team field, Florida, and LSU had just played them. The Gators were throwing ace John Burke, who soon would be the sixth pick of the first round in the MLB draft. Burke had just tossed the first no-hitter in the NCAA postseason since 1974 – the year before the aluminum bat – to beat Furman, 2-0, in the Regional.

A win could pair LSU with No. 1-seed Florida State on Sunday as the Seminoles would play No. 8-seed Fresno State Friday afternoon.

"I remember saying to myself, 'Boy, that's a bad draw,'" Bertman said.

But Bertman convinced his team otherwise – as he had done after a bad draw before LSU won twice in one day at No. 1 Texas A&M in the 1989 NCAA Regional. LSU had dominated Florida in the regular season, beating Burke, 6-5, in the Busch Challenge in New Orleans in March, and 6-5, 5-3, and 12-6 in Alex Box in April.

"Guys, we've already beaten these guys four times. We're the best team here," he told the team.

"He knew when to get on us and when to give us a pat on the back," second baseman Tookie Johnson said.

"We were better than everybody else," Bertman remembers saying. "And the belief system by then was such that the players thought we could do anything if we put our minds to it – if we *believed* that we can."

Bertman repeated what he had been preaching since he arrived in Baton Rouge in 1983:

"Anything you vividly imagine, ardently desire, sincerely believe, and enthusiastically act upon, must, absolutely must come to pass."

It was on.

"I don't care if you brought in the 1927 Yankees, we were going to win," Johnson said. "That was the mindset. It wasn't a cockiness as much as it was an overwhelming confidence."

Bertman did not vividly imagine a gargantuan, estimated 500-foot home run over the 420 mark in center field and the 25-foot double deck by Lyle Mouton off Burke. But he got that for a 1-0 lead in the first inning. The tone was set.

"Lyle took two steps, and it was gone," Bertman said.

"It was the first 'pimp' after a home run I ever saw in college baseball. Mouton hit it, dropped the bat, and just watched it. Nobody did that back then," assistant coach Dan Canevari said.

Even Florida third baseman Herbert Perry enjoyed the view. He turned to the LSU dugout at his right with a look of amazement as Mouton rounded the bases.

"It's 420 feet out there!" Perry exclaimed.

Mouton added a 390-foot grand slam off the scoreboard in left center for the 8-1 final in the seventh inning and finished 3-for-4 with five RBIs. The junior from St. Thomas More High School in Lafayette became just the 13th player in CWS history to homer twice in a game. It was Mouton's 12th homer of the season.

"They ought to give that guy a steroid test," a grounds crew worker said after the game while raking the batter's box. "I've been working here 10 years, and I ain't never seen a ball hit that far."

Mouton was not on anything, but something was on him. He told Joe Macaluso of the Baton Rouge *Advocate* that his father, Lyle, gave him a small bottle of holy oil before the World Series.

"I put it on my body and my bat," Mouton revealed.

Pat Garrity, the hero of the 1989 NCAA Regional title at College Station, added a home run in the fourth for a 3-1 lead.

Byrd allowed one run on four hits in four and two-thirds innings and would have gotten the win had he been allowed to finish the fifth. But Chad Ogea came on to pitch two and a third innings of relief with four strikeouts for the win.

* * * * *

LSU's updated "Murderer's Row" rolled on Sunday in a 15-3 win over Fresno State as Gary Hymel homered to left field for a 1-0 lead in the second inning. It was his 22nd homer and broke the school record for a season. He added a two-run homer in the sixth for an 11-2 lead and became the 14th player to homer twice in a CWS.

Sophomore left-hander Mike Sirotka allowed two earned runs in six innings for the win to go to 11-0 on the season. LSU was now 2-0 in a College World Series for the first time. The team had two days off before its next game, which would again be against Florida on Wednesday.

Hymel continued his precursor to Gorilla Ball with bookend three-run home runs in the first and ninth innings to give him four for the week. Mouton added a home run to give him three for the CWS as the Tigers eliminated the Gators, 19-8. LSU scored 42 runs on 40 hits with eight home runs in three games.

Paul Byrd allowed four runs in five innings for the win, and Chad Ogea and Rick Greene each worked an inning to stay sharp for the national championship game at noon Saturday on CBS after another two days off.

"We really beat the crap out of everybody," Bertman said. "Hymel and Mouton were destroying the ball. The combination of Byrd and Ogea with Sirotka was terrific."

And LSU hardly needed Greene, whose killer, sinking fastball had him atop the nation with an LSU season record 13 saves as well as the LSU career saves mark of 20.

Bertman basically relaxed for three games – something he had rarely done in Omaha.

"I didn't have to make many decisions," he said.

But he would make a very important decision before the championship game against Wichita State and 11-1 right-hander Tyler Green (no relation to Rick Greene of LSU).

For the third straight year, the Tigers were staying at the Embassy Suites on 72nd Street in Omaha, and by 1991 this was LSU's office. Bertman had a large suite to himself with video equipment while his wife, Sandy, and a daughter or two or friends would stay in the suite next door.

Ogea, a third-round pick of the Indians that week, would start the championship game at 13-5 with a 3.11 ERA. He was summoned to the Skip Suite.

"We looked at video and watched the Wichita State hitters for hours," Ogea said. "It was like, 'This guy does this. This guy does that.' And I remember him saying, 'We're going to win the game.' And he said, 'You've been working towards this your whole college career.'"

Rick Greene (7-2, 3.30 ERA) also visited the suite.

"The guy was full of wisdom, and he had been around the game for so long that you would just sit there and listen," Greene said of Bertman. "His knowledge based on percentages and tendencies made you so confident that you couldn't be beat."

Bertman and various hitters studied film of Wichita State's Tyler Green, who had a devastating split-finger breaking ball and a 90 m.p.h. fastball. Bertman noticed he would throw the knuckle curve only when he was ahead in the count.

"After strike one, boom, he'll throw it," Bertman told his hitters. "One ball and two strikes, boom. It looked like a fastball strike coming at you, and then the bottom would drop out of it. He rarely threw it for a strike."

And Bertman made his decision to take pitches. The team that had staged a home run derby for three wins by a combined 42-12 score on 40 hits was *not* going to be aggressive?

Yes, because the team was prepared.

"I wanted every advantage, see," Bertman said. "I always told the players the person with the most information wins in life. And the team that has the most information usually wins."

LSU would be passive-aggressive at the plate, according to Bertman's film-educated guesses of Tyler Green's pitches.

There was information and always motivation. At a team dinner with families at Anthony's steak house under the big steer at 72nd and F streets, Bertman delivered an emotional speech to go with the film study.

"Raise one of your hands," he told the players. "Can you raise it a little bit higher? Can you go a little bit higher? That's what we need to do Saturday."

They had heard it before.

"And we're like, 'Really, again?' But he always put that mental and emotional part of the game plan into place," senior left-fielder Rich Cordani said. "It was the makeup of us, and he made us. Believing in a system, believing in one another, and believing in the team concept."

Everything mattered.

"You couldn't get anything past him," Cordani said. "Not that you would try to. But he would always be ahead mentally, situationally, anything. He's got elephant-brain, that guy."

Green, the opposing pitcher, would learn that quickly.

"I gave a lot of take signals when I was sure he was going to throw that breaking pitch," Bertman said. "It didn't matter what the count was."

And Green was suddenly off his game from the first inning. He walked Tookie Johnson and Armando Rios on full counts, then moved both runners over on a wild pick-off throw to second. Cordani's sacrifice fly to deep center field gave LSU a 1-0 lead. Pat Garrity's two-out RBI single made it 2-0.

"We were always so prepared," said Garrity, now a lawyer in New Orleans. "There really wasn't a situation that was going to come up in a game that we were not ready to deal with."

Wichita State cut it to 2-1 in the bottom of the first on an RBI ground out. LSU took a 4-1 lead in the second after two outs on a single by Johnson and a two-run home run by Rios to left-center field. As Rios rounded third and passed Green, the two had words.

Green walked Andy Sheets on four pitches to start the fourth and then he was gone. Replacing Green was freshman Darren Dreifort, who would become a two-time All-American and the second pick of the 1993 draft. After a double play cleared the bases, Dreifort hit Rios with his first pitch, and it appeared not to be an accident.

Rios didn't give a flip.

"I thought it'd be stupid if they hit me, because I figured we'd score," Rios said.

He was right and would soon perform his first flip since the opener. Dreifort walked Mouton and gave up a two-run triple to right to Cordani for a 6-1 LSU lead.

"Again, they tried to come inside like USC the year before," said Cordani, whose two-run homer in the seventh at the 1990 Regional gave LSU a 7-6 win and a trip to Omaha. "And I love when they come inside. I turned on it pretty good."

Wichita State cut the lead to 6-2 in the fourth with another manufactured run and drew within 6-3 in the eighth on a lead-off home run by Tommy Tilma. Ogea walked the next batter on five pitches, and Bertman replaced him with Rick Greene.

Ogea had allowed two earned runs on four hits and four walks, but he may have saved his most competitive outing for his last at LSU.

"Chad was magnificent," Bertman said. "He memorized what we watched on film. One of the most competitive games I've ever seen pitched at LSU was Ogea in that final game. He was so strong. He worked so hard every pitch."

* * * * *

Ogea quietly told Greene as he walked off the mound, ***"Hold the rope."*** That referred to an oft-told baseball fable by Bertman that led to his first SEC West title, in 1985, with a 4-3 win at Auburn in 14 innings in the regular season finale.

The story goes, if everyone is confident that everyone else is holding the rope, then when your team is about to make the last defensive out to win it, everyone acts as if the out will be made and doesn't just watch and hope.

"Skip had told that story early in the year, and it just wasn't in the forefront of our minds," Greene said. "But when Chad whispered, 'Hold the rope,' it just kind of clicked and took me back to when we first heard the story. And I thought, *OK, now it's my turn to be the guy on top of the cliff holding onto the rope for the next guy. This is my time.* It was amazing because it broke my anxiety that I had in what was a really big moment."

* * * * *

LSU was one out away from victory when ninth batter Jason White stepped up.

"I specifically remember looking at the very last hitter and thinking to myself, *This guy does not want to strike out to end the season*," Greene said. "So, I threw a slider, and he pulled it to Chris Moock at third on the first pitch."

If anyone could handle the last play in front of 16,612 at Rosenblatt for LSU's first national championship in a major sport since the football team won it in 1958, it was Moock.

"It was routine, but you still have to finish it. And sometimes those are harder," Moock said. "You have to assume it's coming to you, and this is what I'm going to do. That's something that Skip was always big on – visualization. You visualize yourself making the play, getting the hit, or whatever."

Moock was also used to playing in front of big crowds as Baker High's quarterback and as an LSU quarterback. After suffering a broken ankle just before the 1990 football season, Moock returned to complete 4 of 8 passes for 73 yards with a touchdown to help beat Tulane, 16-13, in the season finale in front of 67,435 at Tiger Stadium.

"The national championship game at Rosenblatt was the first time I experienced a baseball atmosphere that felt like, 'Wow, this is a really big event.' And for me, it was relaxing. And, sure enough, the last batter hits me the ball."

"I had to decide to charge or sit back," he said. "They tell you not to, but I sat back, and it was fine. I had enough time to throw it across for the out."

And before he even threw it to first base, LSU's players in the dugout were already running on the field to celebrate – as in the "Hold the Rope" story.

"I turned around and watched Moock catch it and throw," Greene said. "The ball seemed like it took forever to get across the diamond. It was in slow motion to me, but when I watched the replay, it was a missile, probably 90 m.p.h. By that time, Luis Garcia, and Chad, and the rest of the guys were already literally across the foul line because they knew it was going to be an out."

Moock turned to Andy Sheets at shortstop.

"We had these amazed looks on our faces," he said.

Rios did his first complete flip since the season opener in the infield.

"Then I just jumped right in the dog pile," Moock said.

So did Byrd, whose elbow accidentally nailed Moock right in the forehead. He suffered a cut that would need immediate stitches, causing him to miss the team picture. Meanwhile, Ronnie Rantz was at the bottom.

"My face was getting pressed in the dirt," he said. "It took everything I had just to get up enough to not suffocate. I was yelling, 'Get off! Get off!' It was terrible. I remember finally getting up and crying."

And it was wonderful. There *is* crying in baseball.

"A lot of us were. It was amazing," Rantz said.

"I was actually a little sad," said Byrd, who had been picked in the fourth round by Cleveland. "We're all jumping on top of people, and I'm like, 'It's over. It's done. I'm not going back to LSU. No more practices. We're not going to the weight room.' It was just a little weird for me, and a very surreal moment."

On the very top of the pile was Luis Garcia in a picture that went across the country.

Bertman did not join the dogpile. Instead, he simply walked across the diamond and shook hands with Wichita State coach Gene Stephenson.

"I had decided on the Dean Smith method," he said, referring to the North Carolina basketball coach who won the 1982 National Championship in his seventh trip to the Final Four. "I stayed calm. Business as usual. I walked across, shook hands, hugged our coaches. Remember now, I've always seen this. So, when I walked across, I felt like I'd done this a thousand times."

Garcia then grabbed and hugged Bertman.

"Coach, we did it," he said.

"We were supposed to do it. We're supposed to win," Bertman said.

"Who says that? Someone who believes it 100 percent," Garcia commented.

After the celebration on the field, Bertman spoke to the players and reminded them of the chain of players before them who built the road from Alex Box to Omaha – Ben McDonald, Stan Loewer, Mark Guthrie, Clay Parker, Barry Manuel, Wes Grisham, Keith Osik, Eric Hetzel, Mike Bianco, Pete Bush, Rob Leary, Jeff Reboulet, Robbie Smith, Andy Galy, and others.

"It was a perfect way for the older guys to end our college careers," Johnson said. "It really was. It was the way it should be. We had paid our dues, gotten our taste, and then we won it. And we won it for the guys before us."

And they did it with style. LSU set College World Series records for most runs per game with 12, highest slugging percentage at .603, best fielding percentage at .993 with one error in 148 chances, and highest slugging percentage by a player as CWS MVP Gary Hymel finished at 1.357 with 19 total bases in 14 at-bats. The Tigers also tied the record for most home runs in a CWS with nine.

"We set a lot of records that didn't last long, because future LSU teams would break them. But we really peaked at the right time," Mouton said. "Gary Hymel said it best. 'This was a business trip,' because we had been there. We didn't go to the zoo. We didn't get caught up in the baseball Christmas that is Omaha. It wasn't new to us. With our massive amounts of fans there, it was almost like Alex Box of the North."

As the team walked into the Embassy Suites, a.k.a. "Hotel LSU," fans unfurled a banner of tied bed sheets from a top floor toward the atrium with No. 1 painted in purple.

"People were on the balconies cheering and chanting," Rantz reported.

The Coaches Committee set up a victory party on the top floor with Dom Perignon and cigars for everyone.

"Luis Garcia was walking around interviewing people in Spanish," Rantz recalled. "Skip had a cigar. He was happy and proud."

On their fifth try, the Tigers fittingly won their first national championship under Bertman – figuratively flipping off those stadium workers who laughed at them upon arrival at CWS No. 5. The fifth time *was* a charm, and it opened the title tidal gates.

Chapter 8

Mr. Skip doesn't go to Washington

"The fans were waiting for us at the airport. It was just awesome. When we bussed over to the Box, it felt like a playoff atmosphere. It was packed."

– Pitcher Paul Byrd describing the reception the Tigers got in Baton Rouge after winning the 1991 National Championship

The first National Championship took nearly 100 years of LSU baseball and 22 coaches. It even took Coach No. 22, Skip Bertman, eight years and five trips to Omaha.

And within two days of the last out on June 8, 1991, all 31 players had scattered from Baton Rouge to Alaska, to Puerto Rico, to both coasts, and all points in between for pro ball, summer ball or just home.

But what a party it was on that roof of the Embassy Suites in Omaha as the Tigers were the ultimate "fat cats" until the wee hours of Sunday morning, June 9. There was no game to prepare for on Sunday.

No, only a cool plane ride for the bleary and weary, and the sweet swag of success like no other.

"Just the feeling of accomplishment. Finally, to take the next step," said senior Pat Garrity, who had lost in Omaha the two previous years.

"We were great in '91," third baseman Chris Moock recalled. "We were the best. Finally, we could stop and realize what we had accomplished."

There was, however, one last date at Alex Box Stadium for the 1991 Tigers: a "Welcome Back" pep rally set for 11:15 a.m. that Sunday at the Box with the team expected to land at Baton Rouge Metropolitan Airport mid-morning.

No rest for the champions.

University officials asked that folks not go to the airport for security reasons.

"But the fans were waiting for us at the airport," said junior pitcher Paul Byrd, who would be leaving soon for the minor leagues. "It was just awesome. When we bussed over to the Box, it felt like a playoff atmosphere. It was packed."

The players were not expecting such a reception that would go unequaled anywhere in Louisiana for a sports team until the Saints flew back to New Orleans the day after winning the Super Bowl in February of 2010.

"We were shocked that the old Alex Box was *packed,*" Moock said. "People were *everywhere.* We were like, 'Wow!'"

75

It felt like an NCAA Regional title game day because several thousand had crowded the Box. The grandstand was full, and fans overflowed into the bleachers.

"People were screaming when Skip introduced each of us," Byrd recalled.

When Armando Rios was introduced, naturally, he repeated the full body flip he had just performed the day before at Rosenblatt Stadium after the last out.

"Man, how do I follow that?" Byrd asked himself. "So, when Skip said my name, I did a cartwheel. Everybody started laughing, and I said, 'Oh, my gosh, did I just do that? What an idiot!' But it was just a really cool moment."

After the big pep rally, there would be another poignant gathering for the team in Baton Rouge.

Because it was LSU's first National Championship in a major sport since football in 1958 with Billy Cannon, Governor Buddy Roemer had the team over to the Mansion for apple pie, courtesy of Kansas Governor and bet-loser Joan Finney. There was also a visit to the State Legislature for a proclamation in the Louisiana State Capitol.

But the *piece de resistance* would take place exactly one month after the national title party at Alex Box when Skip's boys reconvened at the White House.

* * * * *

Now, the White House was occupied at the time by President George H.W. Bush, a former Yale first baseman/team captain who played in the first two College World Series, in 1947 and 1948. It just so happened that President Bush was having Joe DiMaggio and Ted Williams over to commemorate the magical Major League Baseball season of 1941. DiMaggio hit in 56 straight games that season for the world champion New York Yankees, and Williams hit .406 for the Boston Red Sox. Neither mark has been touched since.

Both baseball superstars received Presidential Citations and met the LSU team before flying with President Bush on Air Force One to Toronto, Ontario, for the MLB All-Star game that night.

The national champion Tigers shared the Rose Garden with the two greatest living baseball players and the leader of the free world, fresh off the Operation Desert Storm victory in Iraq and 43 years removed from two CWS appearances himself.

In a super serendipitous slice of Americana, Bertman, who had two CWS titles himself (one with LSU, one with Miami in 1982) and was not long from being labeled the greatest living college baseball coach, could go elbow to elbow with two of his boyhood idols, and meet the President – all in the same mid-summer afternoon.

However, Bertman, who had lived with intense pain in his hips all season long, would have to sit this one out. He was still recovering from left hip-replacement surgery.

"Skip, I bet those hips aren't hurting you right now," a friend said during the national title celebration atop the Embassy Suites.

"I'll bet you're wrong," Bertman retorted. "The hips don't know we won."

A little Crown Royal didn't help much either.

Bertman's hips had been painful since 1990. He wouldn't charge umpires in recent years because of excruciating pain from degenerative arthritis, perhaps stemming from his youth as a catcher at Miami from 1958 to 1960 and lineman on the Miami Beach High football team.

Bertman hated missing out on the White House visit, but he was more than glad that he had had the surgery.

"My hip was killing me," he said. "The team went to the White House. I went to my bed. Joe DiMaggio and Ted Williams – they were my two idols coming up."

But the surgery worked like a charm.

"Right after they replace the hip, there's no pain immediately," he said. "There was recovery time, but I mean the pain is gone the day they do it."

Acadian Ambulance offered to get him to D.C. by chopper, but he decided he needed to recover more.

"I can tell you this," Bertman assistant Dan Canevari said nearly 30 years later. "I just had my own hip replaced, and I don't know how Skip coached before that. But he was probably happier to get the hip replaced than to meet Joe DiMaggio."

Sandy Bertman, Skip's wife, made the trip as did virtually all the players and every assistant coach.

"Sandy loved it," Bertman said. "She was very excited, and President Bush called her up to the podium. DiMaggio and Williams both spoke to the team. I saw it on television."

Bertman was struck by how happy the players looked.

"Certainly, they were glad to meet the President and two of the all-time greats in baseball," he said. "But it seemed like they were almost happier about seeing each other."

As the players milled around trying to talk to President Bush, Williams, DiMaggio, and one another, Armando Rios seemed anxious to get a word in with President Bush.

"Man, I've got to go talk to the President," Rios said, but got tongue-tied as he neared the President.

So, his teammate Ronnie Rantz stepped up to help:

"Mr. President, can I ask you something? Armando Rios here wants to know when Puerto Rico will become the 51st state."

Bush started talking to Rios, a hero of the 1991 National Championship game, but suddenly Rios was unable to speak.

"There he is in his Rico Suave (1990 song by Gerardo Mejía) suit, but he was so nervous he couldn't say anything," Rantz recalled.

"I would've loved to have been there," Bertman said.

Upon landing in Baton Rouge, Mrs. Bertman was asked by a reporter about Skip missing the trip.

"He'll just have to win next year to get to go," she laughed.

Chapter 9

'That's baseball' is no excuse
(Sometimes you just lose)

*"My first reaction is to the game of baseball, I guess.
It's such a strange game."*

– The late coach Augie Garrido, after his Cal State-Fullerton team became the first to
eliminate Skip Bertman from an NCAA Regional in Alex Box Stadium, on May 23, 1992

A funny thing happens after winning a National Championship, particularly one that was built incrementally over years. Such was the case with the LSU baseball program's first national title in 1991, under Coach Skip Bertman after moderate success at the College World Series in Omaha in 1986, '87, '89 and '90.

People start to believe they can't lose. Even when they lose, they think they didn't really lose. Their winning was just delayed. Yes, by 1992 LSU baseball was becoming like Alabama football: great winning seasons were expected all the time. And Omaha was a scheduled summer sojourn for south Louisianians like so many trips to Gulf Shores, Ala., or Destin, Fla.

Something else happens after a National Championship, or a world championship in professional sports: the "Medicine Year," as Lafayette, La., sportswriter Kevin Foote calls it.

You take your medicine after you win it all. This even happened to Tom Brady and Bill Belichick after their first Super Bowl title in the 2001 season. They went 9-7 in 2002 and did not make the playoffs.

This also happened to Coach Sean Payton and the New Orleans Saints after they won Super Bowl XLIV in the 2009 season at 16-3. The next season they fell to 11-6, with a Wild Card playoff loss to 7-9 Seattle.

But it didn't look like this was going to happen to LSU in 1992. The Tigers rolled to a 21-3 start and a 48-14 mark pre-NCAA postseason behind super freshmen Todd Walker of Bossier City at second base and Russ Johnson of Denham Springs at third. On the same team was pitcher Lloyd Peever (14-0, 1.98 ERA), a consensus first team All-American and Collegiate Baseball magazine's National Player of the Year.

LSU became the first team to win three straight SEC regular season championships since Alabama did it in the 1940s. Then the Tigers took the SEC Tournament in New Orleans with five wins in six games.

LSU was No. 3 in the nation, and Walker – the Collegiate Baseball and Baseball America National Freshman of the Year – was hitting .409 with 11 home runs and 74 RBIs when the team opened the NCAA South I Regional at Alex Box. They eased past Providence, 8-1, and Omaha looked like a sure thing.

The Tigers were 14-1 in NCAA Regional games in the Box since 1986 when they took the field against No. 4-seed Ohio State on Friday, May 22. The Buckeyes had lost, 3-2, in the opening round to No. 3-seed Cal State-Fullerton.

And LSU lost, 5-0, to a No. 2 starter who froze the Tigers with killer changeups and held them to five harmless singles. Even Walker went 0-for-3.

Meanwhile, Ohio State catcher Tony Khoury, hitting just .257 with two home runs all season, had what Bertman liked to call a "career day." He belted a two-run home run in the fourth inning for the 5-0 lead.

"That's what tournaments are all about," Bertman said. "Guys getting hits who usually don't. That's baseball."

It was the first shutout of LSU ever in NCAA and SEC postseason – a stretch of 89 games dating back to the SEC playoffs in 1961.

"There was no way we could've won today," Walker said.

"They had the two components that win 97 percent of all baseball games," Bertman said. "Pitching and timely hitting. We had neither. That's baseball."

They shrugged it off.

"It just wasn't our day," a young mother told her two little girls as they exited the stadium.

"And I bet one of the kids said, 'That's baseball, Mom. We just didn't get the timely hits today,'" LSU Sports Information Director Herb Vincent said as he laughed in the press tent.

It seemed that Bertman clones were everywhere, and they were getting younger, these Children of the Box.

LSU recovered to eliminate Tulane, 7-3, in the early game Saturday as Chris Moock hit a grand slam, and left-hander Ronnie Rantz struck out seven in six and a third innings for his sixth straight win to go to 7-2 on the season.

LSU seemed reborn and appeared Omaha-bound again late that night before playing Cal State-Fullerton in front of an Alex Box record crowd of 5,972 rejuvenated fans. They and the players rocked to "Shout" from "Animal House" just before the first pitch with closer Rick Greene (5-3, 2.48 ERA, 8 saves).

The place was electric.

How could LSU lose?

Bertman was 15-2 in the Box in NCAA postseasons since 1986 with zero eliminations through three previous home Regionals.

"Win the SEC, host a Regional, win a Regional, then go to Omaha," Greene said. "That just became part of our yearly routine."

Then Cal State-Fullerton won, 11-0.

LSU guzzled its medicine straight to the tune of a season-high six errors and just four hits, while four of its pitchers allowed 11 hits. The defending national champs were shut out for the second time in 27 hours after scoring in their previous 89 postseason games.

Walker finished 0-for-10 for the Regional, but still batted .400 for the season. He also made two errors after entering the Cal State game with only eight and a .972 fielding percentage.

Greene, who led the nation with 14 saves in 14 opportunities in 1991 and just one run allowed through four CWS appearances, was not himself either. He allowed four runs on five hits in three innings in this, his last collegiate appearance. And LSU finished 3-for-30 with runners in scoring position.

In baseball, there's just no telling how things will turn out in any given game.

"My first reaction is to the game of baseball, I guess. It's such a strange game," said Cal State coach Augie Garrido, after his team's resounding victory over LSU.

But that night at Ivar's sports bar on Perkins Road, Greene – who would be taken a week later with the 16th pick of the first round of the MLB Draft by Detroit – took it in stride.

"That's baseball," he said.

Or was it medicine?

Nearly 30 years later, Greene would observe, "In 1992, we had a good group of guys. I don't think we had as good a meshing of a team as we did in 1991."

Bertman still says it was simply baseball.

"The 1992 team was a perfect example of it," he said. "That was absolutely one of our better teams that couldn't get out of the Regional. But Fullerton was better than us. Sometimes teams not as good did get to Omaha."

Fullerton eliminated Ohio State, 13-1, the next day in front of just 891 and reached the National Championship before losing to Pepperdine, 3-2.

Just baseball, maybe, but losing leaves a bad taste in one's mouth.

"Oh, that was devastating," Rantz said. "In '92, we were really good. Won the SEC, won the tournament. I was on fire. I just thought we were going to be in Omaha."

Most thought the same thing.

"It was definitely disappointing," Walker said. "But I would argue that that's what won it for us the next year. We had the same basic team coming back, and it had that experience of what getting beat in a Regional felt like."

In 1993, LSU would also be loaded with talent and great team chemistry – and that's baseball, too.

Chapter 10

LSU's 'façade' National Championship of 1993

"Having Skip in there in the dugout,
it's like having your own little angel on your shoulder."
– Former LSU and San Francisco Giants center fielder Armando Rios

Skip Bertman rarely sweated over recruiting. He delegated much of that to assistants and just kind of gathered players at the end like someone Christmas shopping on Dec. 24.

After he was established with five trips to the College World Series as LSU's coach from 1986 to 1991 and the national title in '91, he had a standard line for new prospects:

"If you want to come, great. If not, we'll get somebody else. We're going to Omaha with or without you."

So, in April of 1992, when the Tigers were to play at Northwestern State, Bertman gave a call to Todd Walker, a stud, left handed-hitting second base prospect from Bossier City, La. Future Hall of Fame coaches from Oklahoma State and Arkansas – both of whom had taken their teams to the CWS multiple times in recent years – were already all over Walker. So was the Texas A&M coach.

Walker had visited all three. Each was offering 85 percent of a scholarship, which is about as good as it gets. Walker was the 1991 Class AAAA Louisiana Player of the Year and likely would have been recruited even more nationally had he not hurt his throwing arm his junior season and had rotator cuff surgery, which prompted a move from shortstop to second base.

Bertman was offering only 25 percent. And he didn't go to the prospective players. They came to him. So Bertman called Walker and asked him to drive the hour and 10 minutes from Bossier City to his motel in Natchitoches, where LSU would be staying for the Northwestern State game on April 9.

"The funniest thing is I didn't really recruit Todd hard," Bertman said. "It's not like today where everybody plays in those tournaments, and you get a chance to see them as juniors in high school. You had to wait to see who could play. And I was waiting because I heard Walker could hit, but he had a bad arm, and he couldn't play shortstop."

Most college second basemen played shortstop in high school. One doesn't usually recruit a high school second baseman to play second base in college.

"But if he can hit, he'll play second base, or I'll find a spot," Bertman said. "So, the only time I ever spoke to him is when we went to Natchitoches."

Walker showed up at the motel.

"I barely talked to Skip before that," Walker recalled. "It was all Beetle Bailey (LSU's hitting coach from 1988 to 1995). Oklahoma State was always in Omaha; their offer was intriguing, for sure. Arkansas was awesome, too. Texas A&M was an up and comer. Plus, the 85 percent ride. I was considering going out of state."

Then Walker knocked on Bertman's motel door.

"We talked for a while," Bertman said.

"He said, 'You can sign here, or you can sign somewhere else.' That was the philosophy. You were left to figure out whether you wanted to be part of the ride," Walker said.

"And then I said, 'I've got a 25 percent scholarship, and I want you to take it,'" Bertman recalled saying.

"Yes, sir," Walker replied in a matter-of-fact manner.

So ended the recruitment of one of the greatest baseball players in LSU history.

"Hey, I'd grown up in Louisiana, and ultimately, that's where I wanted to go to school," Walker says now.

"Todd Walker's the best three-year player I've ever had," Bertman says upon reflection.

After Walker hit .400 in 1992 and was the National Freshman of the Year, he was ready for the next step in 1993: Bertman's Embassy Suites room in Omaha for opponent video sessions.

Two seniors, whom Bertman also wrapped up late without much shopping, would also have huge parts in 1993 on LSU's sixth trip in eight years to Omaha for the College World Series.

Those were center fielder Armando Rios, a hero of the 1991 World Series title, and pitcher Mike Sirotka, who was 11-0 with a 2.80 ERA in '91 but played a supporting role in Omaha behind ace Chad Ogea and Paul Byrd. After struggling to a 6-3 mark and a 4.48 earned run average in 22 appearances in 1992 following shoulder surgery, a healthier Sirotka was ready to take a leading role in 1993.

Rios is from Carolina, Puerto Rico, the home of the first Latin American baseball player to make the Hall of Fame – Roberto Clemente, in 1973. Carolina (pronounced Caro-lee-na) is called *Tierra de Gigantes*," meaning the Land of Giants, because a local man, Felipe Birriel (1916-1994), was nearly eight feet tall.

Rios transferred to LSU from North Carolina-Charlotte after the 1990 season.

Bertman did not see Rios until he showed up at LSU at all of 5-foot-9 – more than two feet shorter than Birriel.

"This is him? Really. Whoa, he's not a big guy," Bertman told his staff.

"I guess he was expecting somebody taller from the Land of the Giants," Rios said, laughing. "But he got the real deal. He couldn't win it all until I got there, right?"

Sirotka had already committed to Texas A&M out of high school in Houston when LSU assistant coach Randy Davis jumped on him.

"LSU came into the recruiting process on the late side," Sirotka said. "I took a visit in the middle of my senior season (1989), but it wasn't even an official one."

But Sirotka noticed that eight of Bertman's pitchers had been drafted from LSU since 1985.

"I said, 'OK, this sounds like the place to go pitch,'" Sirotka said.

But Bertman was not impressed with Sirotka, who was 6-foot-1 and weighed in at only 160 pounds.

"Skip never saw me throw," Sirotka said. "I show up on campus, and he tells Randy Davis, 'Who in the hell did you bring over here? Is this guy a manager?'"

Davis didn't mean to recruit Sirotka. He had gone to Houston to watch another prospect, who did not pitch well.

"Some coaches told him to go watch me because I was pitching against a really good-hitting team. And I had a nice game," Sirotka said.

Bertman had few questions for Davis after watching Sirotka throw on the side.

"I threw a few curveballs, and we were okay from there," he said.

"Sirotka was the best four-year pitcher I've ever had," Bertman says now.

Rios was a classic Bertman overachiever who improved as his career went on.

Walker was joined by two other freshman All-Americans entering the 1993 season: third baseman/shortstop Russ Johnson of Denham Springs, La., and right-handed pitcher Scott Shultz of Sterling, Va. Johnson hit .338 in 1992 with seven homers and 49 RBIs. Shultz was 8-3 with a 2.90 ERA.

With all that talent plus prized recruit Brett Laxton, a 6-foot-2 right-hander from Audubon, N.J., the 1993 season opened with a preseason No. 1 ranking for the Tigers in three polls. But that quickly turned artificial with a 3-3 start – LSU's worst since 2-4 in 1981.

LSU regrouped to win 12 in a row, but then started 3-2-1 in the SEC after losing two of three at Tennessee with little offense.

"People said that team was sort of a façade – top heavy, and it made a lot of errors," LSU baseball Sports Information Director Bill Franques said.

This façade, though, was still strong enough to win LSU's fourth consecutive regular season SEC title.

They also led the SEC with 103 errors and would set a school record at 125. The bullpen finished with all of seven saves. (By comparison, former Tiger Rick Greene had eight by himself in 1992 and a school record 14 in 1991.)

"It was weird," Sirotka would say years later. "I went through our roster not too long ago, and I'm like, 'How did we make it through that year?' We didn't have relief pitching. We didn't have a true closer. We made a lot of errors."

* * * * *

The Tigers charged into the NCAA South Regional at Alex Box on May 27 at 45-15-1 and ranked No. 3 in the nation. They did have Walker, who was hitting .409 with 16 home runs and 78 RBIs and had set the SEC record with a 33-game hitting streak from March 23 through May 8. (That would stand until 2007.)

After a 7-2 win over Western Carolina in the Regional opener, LSU fell to No. 3-seed Kent State, 15-12. The Tigers led 11-6 in the top of the eighth, but three relievers allowed nine runs and six straight two-out hits to fall behind 15-11, imploding the façade. LSU pitching allowed a season-high 19 hits, including 13 by the bullpen. Kent State had never defeated a higher-ranked team.

In a 13-6 elimination win over Baylor on Saturday morning, Walker hit a three-run homer and drove in four to set the record of 86 RBIs on the season. LSU won big again, 11-4, that night over South Alabama to reach the championship game against No. 5-seed South Alabama, which eliminated Kent State, 7-6, early Sunday.

But the Tigers faced elimination that night against the Jaguars, who led 4-3 – courtesy of five LSU errors – when the Tigers came to bat in the bottom of the seventh. South Alabama starter Jamie Ybarra had retired 15 of the previous 17 Tigers, and the Jags were counting the outs for their first trip to Omaha.

But most of LSU's record Regional crowd of 6,223 also came to bat in the seventh.

"I tell you, I've been to College Station, Tallahassee, Austin, and I don't think I've ever heard college baseball fans this vocal," South Alabama coach Steve Kittrell said. "I have to rate LSU the best."

Senior Jim Greely walked to open the LSU seventh. Ryan Huffman, also an LSU quarterback, pinch-ran. Kenny Jackson doubled to right center to tie it 4-4, and the Box was exploding.

"The fans really helped us," Bertman said. "It was incredible. It was as vocal as it was in 1990 when USC was here."

Freshman third baseman Jason Williams singled in the go-ahead run for a 5-4 lead.

"I've never heard anything like that," Bertman beamed. "It's amazing. It's intimidating. It's inspiring – and I'm not an emotional guy."

After Rios bunted Williams to third, Johnson doubled down the left field line for a 6-4 advantage and later scored on Harry Berrios' single for a 7-4 lead. LSU added two more in the eighth for a 9-4 final. And it was off to Omaha.

"They were standing for the whole seventh," Bertman said. "I've never seen that."

Alex Box was clearly not a façade, though the team still resembled a house of cards. The Tigers committed 11 errors and allowed nine unearned runs in five games in the Regional with a team ERA of 4.39.

"So, I'm sittin' there going, 'How did we even make it to Omaha?'" Sirotka said.

Sirotka, who was named MVP, was one reason. He won two complete games in four days with a 1.49 ERA and more than 200 pitches. He held South Alabama to one run on nine hits to get to 10-5 on the season. Not counting Sirotka and Laxton – who beat Baylor on four hits and a run in seven innings to go 11-1 – LSU's overall ERA was 8.10.

Another reason was Todd Walker, who hit three homers with a grand slam, drove in 12 runs, and scored six times. Russ Johnson hit .500 (10-for-20) with 11 runs scored and four RBIs. Armando Rios hit .350 (7-for-20) with eight runs scored and a homer, and Jim Greely hit .333 (4-for-12) with two home runs.

"Some teams that got out of the Regional at the Box weren't really the best team," Bertman said. "The '93 team was one of those. The Box helped the '93 team like it helped the '90 team that beat USC."

LSU and Bertman – the angel on the Tigers' collective shoulder – also just knew how to win as the Box enveloped and intimidated the team's opponents.

The Tigers' late heroics against South Alabama would be like muscle memory for the team in the coming World Series at "Alex Box North."

* * * * *

LSU, the No. 5 seed in Omaha, started slowly again against No. 4-seed Long Beach State, and trailed 1-0 after six innings on Friday, June 4. But the Tigers erupted for seven runs over the final three innings to win 7-1. Jim Greely hit a three-run homer and a two-run blast to give him four in five NCAA games after just one in an injury-marred regular season.

No. 1-seed Texas A&M, a robust 52-9 and in its first CWS since 1964, also took an early lead against LSU. The Aggies went up 7-2 in the fifth on Sunday night off Laxton and LSU's typical two errors. The Tigers came back and cut their deficit to 8-7 after seven.

It was Tiger time in the eighth. Mike Neal and Jim Greely singled to start the inning, and a Kenny Jackson ground out tied it, 8-8. "Omaha" Rios followed with an RBI single to give LSU its first lead. Russ Johnson walked to load the bases and bring up Todd Walker, who was 0-for-7 for the CWS.

On a full count with two outs, Walker homered to the opposite field in left for a 13-8 lead that would be the final. It was his 20th homer of the season and third grand slam.

"I was here in '91, and we had great talent," Rios said. "But this team deserves to win it all, too, because we have great heart. Coach keeps saying we need to score earlier, but that's us. Don't count us out if we're down in the eighth or ninth."

But don't count on LSU's pitching late in the game, either. After taking an 8-5 lead over Long Beach State into the seventh on Wednesday, Long Beach State cut it to 8-6 in the seventh.

With a man on first to start the eighth, Bertman went to Sirotka, whom he wanted to start in the championship game on Saturday. But he had no closer. Sirotka got two batters to ground out into fielder's choices, and it looked like LSU's ace would get out of it.

* * * * *

Enter Eddie Davis, a junior outfielder from New Orleans via Southern University in Baton Rouge who just happened to go to the Skip Bertman Baseball Camp in 1988 and '89 when he was in high school in New Orleans. Davis had won the best all-around player at one of the camps.

Davis was hitting .227 with four home runs when he was announced as a pinch-hitter. LSU catcher Adrian Antonini recognized Davis from the Cape Cod League from the previous summer and told Sirotka to stay away from fastballs, but Sirotka was already thinking that.

"He was a big guy," Sirotka said. "I knew he could hit a home run with the wind."

Davis, who had struck out 23 times in 109 at-bats, worked the count to two balls and one strike.

"If I'm a hitter, I'm thinking fastball, so I threw him a slider," Sirotka said. "It was a decent pitch, but he got it up."

Davis had already been figuring breaking ball, too.

"I'm thinking Antonini probably told him no fastballs," Davis would say more than 25 years later. "So, I said, 'I'm going to stay back on the pitch and not be too aggressive.' And I got it."

So, Davis camped on the pitch and hit Sirotka's slider 408 feet over the center field wall to tie it at 8-8.

"I guess I taught him how to hit," Bertman joked.

Long Beach State got another home run for a 9-8 lead then manufactured a run for a 10-8 lead that was the final.

"It was a dream come true because LSU never recruited me," Davis said.

"Everybody who grew up in Louisiana wanted to play for Skip."

The LSU loss set up a semifinal between LSU and Long Beach State two days later, and Davis – a pinch-hitter in each of his previous games against LSU – was suddenly starting in center and batting third with Sirotka on the mound again.

And Davis delivered another two-run homer for a 2-0 lead in the first inning for the Tigers' fourth straight opening deficit in the series.

"When he took me deep again, I was like, 'Who is this guy?'" Sirotka said.

Sirotka and Davis settled down after that, but LSU's defense didn't, committing five errors and helping Long Beach State to a 5-3 lead going into the bottom of the ninth.

Adrian Antonini, hitting .227 on the season, led off with a single but pinch-hitter Mark Stocco struck out. Long Beach State was two outs away, but Jason Williams drew a walk to bring up Rios, who doubled in both runners to tie the game, 5-5. Johnson was walked intentionally before Todd Walker came to the plate. Walker was 3-for-4 with two RBIs in the game. And he delivered a walk-off single to win the game, 6-5.

"We were against the wall: We lose, we go home. But we just had that feeling. Nobody was desperate. We had Skip," Rios said.

"This has been one of the most miraculous World Series I've ever seen in my 12 years here," Bertman said.

Sirotka threw his eighth complete game in his last nine starts as he held Long Beach State to two earned runs on nine hits with eight strikeouts.

"And Eddie Davis went to the beach," Sirotka cracked after the game.

"That was one of the most courageous games I've ever seen pitched," Bertman said. "He battled on every pitch. He wasn't a 95 m.p.h. thrower, but his curve ball on both sides of the plate was just excellent."

* * * * *

The Tigers (52-17-1) advanced to play No. 7-seed Wichita State (58-16) at noon the next day, Saturday, on CBS.

"We had to rush back Friday night to the hotel and throw the film on for Wichita State," Bertman said. "The whole team watched film. Everybody came running. They felt it. They could tell. You've got to be able to smell how close you are. We pretty much knew what was going to happen, you see, before the game."

From a pitching perspective, that is. Bertman didn't see an easy game coming. But Walker hit a two-run homer in the first inning. It was the Tigers' first lead to open a game in the series.

Walker added an RBI single in LSU's three-run second for a 5-0 lead, and Rios' bases-loaded, two-out, two-run single off reliever Darren Dreifort put LSU up 7-0 in the third. The screaming liner right at Dreifort was sweet revenge for Rios, whom Dreifort intentionally hit in the 1991 championship game after Rios' two-run homer off first round pick Tyler Green. Green and Rios had had words as Rios rounded third that day.

"Well, I hope he enjoyed his last game of baseball," said Dreifort, who was the second pick of the 1993 MLB Draft.

Rios would get revenge for that remark, too, as he became Bertman's first LSU player to reach the Big Leagues without being drafted. He would record his first Major League hit, which was a home run, as a San Francisco Giant in 1998 off Darren Dreifort in Dodger Stadium.

* * * * *

LSU won the National Championship by an 8-0 final, and Brett Laxton became the first pitcher since 1961 to throw a complete game shutout in the title game. He set a title game record with 16 strikeouts on mainly fastballs in the mid-90s with some sliders.

"That was the perfect storm," said Laxton, the national Freshman of the Year, who finished 12-1 with an SEC-best 1.98 ERA. "Wichita State had a bunch of big swingers. That fit my game. I was effectively wild at times. We got a big lead pretty quick, and I just kept pouring it in there."

The Shockers got no one to third base and managed only three singles off Laxton, who struck out every Wichita State hitter at least once with eight going down looking.

"Brett was so competitive," Bertman said. "That kind of stuff means a lot to me. Those guys, Sirotka and Laxton, every pitch meant something to them. That's why they won."

Laxton just felt like a kid.

"That championship game was where you actually saw yourself when you were 7 or 8 years old," he said. "I saw myself being that guy, and the next thing you know, you're there."

Walker won the MVP after a 1-for-11 start at the plate as he finished 7-for-20 for a .350 average with three home runs, a grand slam, 12 RBIs and that game-winning hit to beat Long Beach State and get LSU to the title game. He was 6-of-9 with two homers and six RBIs in the Tigers' last two games. Walker finished with a .395 average, 22 home runs, and an SEC record 102 RBIs that stood until LSU's Eddy Furniss topped it three years later.

Sirotka and Rios, who were both runts on arrival, finished as giants.

Sirotka's career record ended at 30-11 with a 2.87 ERA, and he left with the LSU record for innings pitched at 372 and tied for the LSU season complete games mark with 10. In three trips to Omaha, Sirotka was 3-1 with a 2.30 ERA allowing only seven earned runs in six appearances through 27 and a third innings. He would pitch for six seasons in the Majors with the Chicago White Sox from 1995 to 2000.

Rios was the classic overachieving Bertman player who got better. He batted .319 as a senior, which was 80 points better than the previous year, with 61 RBIs, which was one more than he had his first two seasons. In two national championship games, he was 3-for-6 with six RBIs, a two-run homer in 1991, a two-run single in 1993, and two sacrifice flies.

Russ Johnson led the team in hitting in 10 NCAA postseason games, going 17-for-38 for a .447 average with six RBIs and 16 runs scored. Scott Schultz battled an ankle injury most of the season but finished 7-3 with a 4.91 ERA and three saves.

The 1993 team was LSU's first to be No. 1 at the beginning and at the end of the season. Bertman skillfully built a foundation from what only appeared to be a façade.

"I wouldn't say the '93 team got lucky or overachieved, because Todd Walker and Russ Johnson were two of the best players in the United States," Bertman said. "But we didn't have that Barry Manuel or Rick Greene closer. We worked around it, and Todd was terrific. Russ Johnson was the greatest, Jim Greely surprised us in the postseason, and you couldn't beat Sirotka and Laxton."

And it was a blast.

"The most fun I ever had in baseball was that World Series in 1993," Rios said. "Coming back against Long Beach was awesome. What made it special was that we knew. Having Skip in there in the dugout, it's like having your own little angel on your shoulder. If there was a devil on the other side, with Skip as your angel saying, 'It's going to be OK,' then we're going to do it. It's just a matter of following him."

Chapter 11

Walk-on Warren Morris'
walk-off to immortality

"Pick me up."

– LSU catcher Tim Lanier to next batter, Warren Morris,
after Lanier struck out for the second out in the bottom of the ninth
of the national title game against Miami

At exactly 3:29 p.m. on June 8, 1996, it happened.

"The world changed," Skip Bertman proclaimed some 25 years later, extending the pronunciation of the last two words as if atop Mount Rosenblatt in Omaha.

Second baseman Warren Morris' two-run home run to right field on the first pitch from Miami closer Robbie Morrison with two outs in the bottom of the ninth gave LSU a walk-off, 9-8 victory for its third National Championship.

It was the 50th anniversary of the College World Series, and such a scenario had never happened before in the history of college baseball or Major League Baseball – a two-out, walk-off home run in a do-or-die world championship game.

• Bill Mazeroski's solo homer for Pittsburgh that beat the New York Yankees, 10-9, in 1960 is the only walk-off in a World Series Game Seven in history, but Mazeroski led off the bottom of the ninth.

• Joe Carter's walk-off, three-run homer for Toronto that beat Philadelphia, 8-6, in the 1993 World Series came with one out in the ninth, and it was a Game Six.

• Bobby Thomson's walk-off three-run homer for the New York Giants to beat the Brooklyn Dodgers, 5-4, in 1951 came with one out in the ninth of the finale of a best-of-three series – not the World Series. It was for the National League pennant. The Giants lost the World Series to the New York Yankees.

Morris' renowned homer came during the championship game, televised at high noon on CBS under a brilliant sun amid crisp 69-degree temperatures in front of 23,905 at Rosenblatt Stadium.

Skip Bertman's inspirational video of LSU highlights for National Championship Saturday had been played to the tune of CBS' "One Shining Moment" and his *piece de resistance*, Bonnie Tyler's "Holding Out for a Hero."

LSU players wore their bright, new, sunflower-gold jerseys – undefeated since their unveiling just two weeks prior for the NCAA Regional opener against Austin Peay at Alex Box Stadium.

"You guys are a special team," Bertman told them. "Never has an LSU team worn this."

They were bright like the sun.

"The room erupted like Christmas morning when kids see what Santa has left them," Morris said.

These jerseys would become Warren Morris Gold.

"I felt we were meant to win it all that season," Morris said, looking back. "I know that sounds crazy, but I honestly felt that way. Even late in the game against Miami, when we fell behind, I had no panic. I knew somehow it would work out. It's hard to describe that mindset I had. It was just an assurance I had. Plus, we don't lose in those gold jerseys!"

Designated hitter Brad Wilson, batting sixth in the order, was 1-for-16 in Omaha when he stepped up in his gold jersey to lead off the ninth vs. Robbie Morrison. He scorched one down the left field line. But Eddie Rivero's pinpoint throw beat him to second.

"Only Brad did a backdoor slide, threw his hand in the air and got it on the base," Bertman said. "I still thought the ump would call him out because the throw beat him, but he called him safe. It's just crazy how it all unfolded."

Justin Bowles then grounded out to first base for the first out, moving Wilson to third.

Then a likely hero, catcher Tim Lanier, stood in the box hitting .416 in the CWS with six RBIs, including a grand slam in LSU's opening win over Wichita State. But he struck out on a full count.

It was up to the ninth batter – Warren Morris, a lefty junior walk-on second baseman from Bolton High in Alexandria with no home runs all season. A broken bone in his right wrist, suffered early that season, had hampered him and resulted in surgery on April 24.

But almost magically on the morning of June 8 he felt better than he had since the injury happened on March 6 against Loyola. It was then that he hit the ball off the end of the bat and suddenly had little strength in his wrist and hand.

"After batting practice on the day of the championship game, I stopped Coach Bertman and said my hand felt as close to 100 percent as it had all season," Morris recalled. "For the first time, I could drive the ball and not just slap at it."

Morris had been resorting to bunting and half-swinging since returning to action in the NCAA Regional.

Bertman kept "Merc" in the lineup for his speed, fielding, leadership, intellect and spiritual nature, which grew out of his religious faith. Healthy in

1995 as a sophomore, Morris had led LSU in hitting with a .369 average and had 50 RBIs with eight home runs.

Nicknamed "Mercury" Morris by Bertman after the Miami Dolphins running back of the 1970s, Morris also stole 18 bases in 1995. Late that season, he was selected for the Team USA tryouts for the 1996 Summer Olympics in Atlanta along with LSU shortstop Jason Williams and third baseman Nathan Dunn.

Morris also started in 1994 as a redshirt freshman in left field and hit .284. He remained a preferred walk-on only because he was such an excellent student and went to LSU on a full academic scholarship, graduating in zoology.

LSU, which entered the championship game against Miami at 51-15, was also 21-0 with Morris as a starter that season as he played here and there after his injury occurred. Originally, the injury was misdiagnosed, and Morris vacillated between playing with it and resting it before the correct diagnosis was finally made.

* * * * *

Morris hit his way into LSU baseball history using a new bat. Bertman's daughter, Jodi Bertman, who ran the "Grand Slam" hitting facility in Baton Rouge, flew in with new Easton bats. Naturally superstitious and on a 7-0 run in the NCAA postseason, LSU's other hitters didn't want to use new aluminum bats. But Morris – 1-for-9 in the CWS – took one.

Before he could bat, Morris made a critical play in the top of the third when he threw Rudy Gomez out at the plate to end the inning and keep his team within 2-0. LSU took a 3-2 lead in the third with Morris singling and scoring. He doubled to start a two-run seventh and scored again, helping cut Miami's lead to 7-5. Morris also reached on a fielder's choice after a sacrifice bunt and crossed again in the eighth as LSU scored twice to tie it, 7-7.

Robbie Morrison (4-1, 1.11 ERA, 14 saves) was a first team All-American with 86 strikeouts in 57 innings. A right-hander, Morrison entered with two outs in the seventh, and Miami gave him an 8-7 lead in the top of the ninth on an RBI single by shortstop Alex Cora off LSU reliever Patrick Coogan.

When Morris came up to bat, Morrison's wicked curve had just struck out Lanier. But Lanier gathered himself, and as he passed Morris near the on-deck circle, he said, "Pick me up."

He might as well have said, "Hold the rope," which was always Bertman's teamwork motto. Because Morris grabbed on.

"That was just what I needed to hear," Morris said. "When you can't come through, know that there is a teammate there to hold the rope for you and back you up. It reminded me that this isn't about me. It's about us."

Morris also had a plan.

"I can remember thinking, 'Even if I strike out, I'm going down swinging,'" he said. "I did not want to allow our fate to be decided by an umpire or anyone. My single focus was to stay aggressive. All I wanted to do was hit a solid line drive base hit to score Brad. Hitting a home run was not on my mind."

Morris was 2-for-3 at the time with a double, three runs scored and suddenly a pain-free right wrist. And he was expecting to see a curve ball on the first pitch.

"I knew he was feeling better, and I noticed enough space between second and first because the first baseman was guarding the line," Bertman recalled. "I'm thinking he'll single, and we'll tie it."

Morrison, meanwhile, was fixated on a single statistic that flashed on the scoreboard.

"When I saw Morris had no home runs, I thought we had this thing won," Morrison told the Florida *Sun-Sentinel* eight months later. "A home run is the last thing I expected. There was no way he could win it. I looked in the dugout, and our guys were laughing, telling me they were getting ready to run me over. So, I was thinking once I strike that guy out, I would run the other way."

"I didn't know he came back from wrist surgery. Had I known, I would probably have thrown the fastball because he may have been slow to come around."

The Miami catcher had put his mitt on the ground to catch the third strike from Morrison against Lanier, who swung and missed just as the ball dropped. And the catcher's mitt was headed to the ground again as Morris prepared to swing.

But Morris, a true Bertman believer, had tricked his mind with Bertman's patented visualization technique.

"The pitch almost looked like it came at me in slow motion," Morris said years later. "My mind's eye saw it as a plump pitch right over the middle of the plate. That's what I told reporters after the game. It's amazing how your mind can distort reality to get you to do what needs to be done."

Morris had been *Bertman-ized* and didn't realize it.

"After I watched it on TV, I was like, 'Wait a minute, that was a good pitch.' It was a low curve ball," Morris observed. "Coach always talked a lot with us about the importance of imagery – being able to see yourself in your own mind succeeding."

Or make a pitch seem fatter than it is.

"If you can do this and see yourself succeeding enough times, your mind doesn't know the difference between what's really happened and your imagery," Morris said. "I know it's a far-out thing for some people, and not every player on the team bought into this. But I was totally in, and it made a huge difference."

Bertman's and Morris' imagery simultaneously undershot the reality of

(Continued on page 113)

Coach Skip Bertman talks with catcher Mike Bianco and pitcher Ben McDonald on the mound at Alex Box Stadium in Baton Rouge in 1989.

Tookie Johnson was a great 4-year player for LSU and a member of the 1991 National Championship team. He became a highly successful high school coach and athletic director.

Russell Springer was one of the best pitchers in LSU baseball history. He went on to play in the Major League for 18 years.

Pete Bush stretches to catch the last out in the final game of the 1989 Regionals against Texas A&M.

Chad Ogea pitches in a 1991 game at Alex Box Stadium. A fierce competitor and one of the all-time best pitchers at LSU, he later played pro ball and pitched for the Cleveland Indians.

Ben McDonald, one of the top pitchers who ever graced the mound for LSU, was the 1989 Golden Spikes Award winner. After finishing his college career, the 6'7" player from Denham Springs, La., was the No. 1 pick in the MLB draft.

Pat Garrity makes the game-winning hit against Texas A&M during the 1989 NCAA Central Regional, sending the LSU Tigers to Omaha for the College World Series. A&M and their fans were stunned and deeply disappointed by the loss, as they were No. 1 in the nation going into this series.

Mike Bianco takes a signal from Coach Bertman during a 1988 game in Alex Box Stadium. One of the best catchers in LSU history, since 2000 he's been the highly successful head baseball coach at the University of Mississippi.

Catcher Gary Hymel makes a tag-out in a 1991 game against Nicholls State of Thibodaux, La. Hymel was selected Most Valuable Player of the College World Series in Omaha in 1991, the year of LSU's first National Championship.

Rich Cordani hits a 2-run homer against USC during the 1990 NCAA South I Regional at Alex Box Stadium.

Johnny Tellechea, a member of the 1991 National Championship team, is among the best defensive players ever to wear a Tigers' uniform.

Mike Sirotka, the best left-handed pitcher in LSU baseball history, played in the big leagues for the White Sox and Blue Jays.

Right fielder Lyle Mouton of Lafayette, La., demonstrates his talent as a true power hitter. In a 1991 College World Series game against Florida, in the first inning, he hit a home run estimated at 500 feet deep. In the seventh inning, he added a 390-foot grand slam off the scoreboard in left center for the 8-1 final. Asked what his secret was, in addition to natural talent and strength, Mouton mentioned holy oil: "I put it on my body and my bat."

Coach Bertman gives signals to the pitcher during a 1991 game at Alex Box Stadium, as assistant coaches "Beetle" Bailey and Dan Canevari help out.

Rick Greene, who pitched at LSU from 1990 to 1992, was the closer in the National Championship game in 1991 and was on the 1992 U.S. Olympic team. He was drafted in the first round of the MLB draft by the Detroit Tigers in 1992 and pitched in the Major Leagues.

Armando Rios hits a home run during 1991 Regional play in Alex Box Stadium. He also hit homers in the 1991 and 1993 College World Series, both won by the LSU Tigers.

Ronnie Rantz, a 2-time National Champion, prepares to deliver a pitch during a 1991 game at Alex Box Stadium.

Paul Byrd pitched at LSU for three years and was a major contributor on the 1991 National Championship team. He pitched in the Major Leagues from 1995 to 2009, and was known in the Majors as "the nicest guy in baseball." His career path continued as an announcer for the Atlanta Braves.

Chris Moock was a key player on the 1991 National Championship team. Moock family members played not only baseball but also football in their college days.

Coach Bertman and his players celebrate their 1991 National Championship on the pitcher's mound at Omaha's Rosenblatt Stadium. Skip's wife, Sandy, looks on.

President George H.W. Bush greets and congratulates members of the 1991 National Championship LSU Tigers. The players flew to Washington, D.C., for the White House reception, but Coach Bertman didn't make the trip because he was recovering from hip-replacement surgery.

Todd Walker had the best 3-year run in LSU baseball history – an All-American and National Champion, then a Major Leaguer. He is one of only three players whose number is retired at LSU.

Russ Johnson tags out a runner during the 1993 College World Series, which LSU won. Johnson went on to play Major League baseball for the New York Yankees.

Brett Laxton pitches in the 1993 College World Series in Omaha. He threw a complete game shutout in the title game – an 8-0 win over Wichita State – setting a title game record with 16 strikeouts. Named the national Freshman of the Year, Laxton finished the season 12-1 with a 1.98 ERA.

Jason Williams, a native of Gonzales, La., was arguably the greatest 5-year player in LSU history and a 2-time National Champion, in 1993 and 1996. A steady and consistent player, he is the SEC leader in runs scored, a 1996 Olympian, and a member of the LSU Athletics Hall of Fame.

LSU Tigers jubilation comes with the winning of the 1993 National Championship against Wichita State in Omaha.

*Coach Bertman talks to his team before the start of a game
at Alex Box Stadium in 1996.*

(Continued from page 96)

what was actually happening as the ball soared to right field.

"Watching the batted ball, first I thought, 'We're tied.' But then I thought, 'That has a chance,'" Bertman said.

Morris was thinking just like Bertman.

"When the ball came off my bat, my first thought was, 'double!'" Morris recalled. "So, I was running hard down the line, hoping to get to second. As I'm running, I can see the ball making its way toward the right field corner. As the ball disappears, my immediate thought is, 'I just hit a home run – my first of the season.' It's not until I touch first, turn toward second and see the Miami infielders lying face down that I realize, 'That's not just a home run. We just won the championship.'"

LSU announcer Jim Hawthorne captured the iconic, shocking moment in textbook fashion as he was perfectly informative, spontaneous and dramatic.

"We'll take a base hit, an error, a wild pitch or something," he began. "The stretch by Morrison and the pitch. Swung on and hit to right field. That's way back there. Way back there. Home run! Tigers win! Oh, my! And the Tigers are the National Champions! I don't believe it! His first home run of the year. Holy cow! Oh, my!"

The normally mild-mannered Bill Franques at Hawthorne's side exclaimed, "Oh, my goodness. This is unbelievable! Oh, what a story! You couldn't have written this in Hollywood!"

As LSU's players euphorically enveloped Morris at home, a sudden and strange rash of head and hand injuries spiked across Louisiana and other outposts of the worldwide Tiger Nation like a pandemic.

"I bet you 50 percent of the people that come up to me tell me at some point in their story that they jumped up and either hit their head or their hand on a ceiling fan," Morris said. "It's amazing how many that happened to. It's like a common theme of jubilation. 'I jumped up and hit the fan.'"

* * * * *

Morris has never been the same. The walk-off has forever rotated over his head like a halo.

Morris' older brother, Wally, was watching back home in Alexandria.

"I knew he was going to make contact because Warren hardly ever struck out," he said. "But I was afraid he'd pop up, and he'd have to live with that for the rest of his life. Then when he hit it, I turned to my wife, 'Hey, his whole life just changed.'"

So did Morrison's, the Miami pitcher. He remained a dominant reliever for two more seasons at Miami and was a second-round pick of Kansas City in 1998 before finishing his pro career in Double-A. And he still holds the Miami career record for average strikeouts per nine innings with 13.9.

"But I battled it for years, I really did," Morrison told the Baton Rouge *Advocate* 20 years later when he reunited with Morris and threw a ceremonial first pitch to him before an LSU game.

"I'd say it was three, four or five years before I got over it," he said. "It's something that's helped me as much as it's hurt me, looking back at it now. It was a huge piece in my life."

Former Miami coach Jim Morris suffered nightmares before he finally won national championships in 1999 and 2001.

"I'd wake up in the middle of the night," he told ESPN in 2011. "The game was going on, and I couldn't get out and do anything. I'd wake up sweating. Thank goodness for the fact that we've won two championships since. But I've been asked more about that game than the two championships."

* * * * *

Bertman was coming off a lull, by his standards, in 1994 and '95. After the 1995 season, when LSU was eliminated from a home NCAA Regional for the second time in four years, the Baton Rouge *Advocate* quoted the false prophecy of a radio show caller:

"Looks like Bertman's been around too long. The game has passed him by."

Bertman, who turned 58 in 1996, became one of just six college baseball coaches to win three national championships. He assumed there would be more, but not like this.

"We may win the national championship again, but we'll never do it like that," Bertman stated. "And LSU agreed. It was a bottom-of-the-ninth homer, never happen again, never happened before, 50th year, the whole thing. It was a one-of-a-kind."

By a player out of nowhere who never hit a home run at Bolton High in Alexandria.

* * * * *

Patrick Coogan picked up the win in the title game in relief to finish the season at 6-0 with 95 strikeouts in 80 and two-thirds innings. Junior Kevin Shipp threw the first 5 and two-thirds innings of the game and finished at 5-4 with a 2.63 ERA with a team-high four complete games.

"The pressure was huge, and they handled that," Bertman said. "The injuries – they handled that. I didn't always make the right moves. They handled that, too. Ultimately, it was the leadership of our older players that won it for us."

And Morris was going places now with a healthy wrist and a new halo.

"It was remarkable how quickly he recovered," said Dr. Ronnie Mathews, who performed Morris' surgery at Our Lady of the Lake in Baton Rouge on April 24 and was at the game behind Bertman's wife, Sandy.

"I think that home run was the first time he really had a good, hard, full swing since the surgery," Dr. Mathews said. "He hit it so hard. It was a straight shot. Didn't know if it had enough carry, but the story is that it did."

And it was no fluke. Morris would soon hit a three-run walk-off home run for Team USA to beat Japan, 8-6, in Richmond, Virginia, in preparation for the Summer Olympics. He hit five more homers with 11 RBIs and led Team USA with a .409 average as it won the bronze medal in Atlanta.

A fifth-round pick by the Texas Rangers in 1996, Morris was traded to Pittsburgh in 1998 and finished third for the National League Rookie of the Year in 1999, hitting .288 with 15 home runs and 73 RBIs. He stayed with Pittsburgh through 2001 before finishing off his MLB career in 2002 with Minnesota and in 2003 with Detroit.

Since his retirement from pro ball in 2006, he has been in the front office of Red River Bank in Alexandria. He lives with his wife, Julie, and three daughters in this central Louisiana city where he grew up.

It's been a wonderful life for Warren Morris – a modern-day Jimmy Stewart.

And he never grows weary of people asking him about the home run.

"I can't get tired of that," he said. "It always ends well."

Chapter 12

'Gorilla Ball' and the 1997 National Championship

"I think what you're getting at is really one of the things that makes him one of the greatest coaches, if not the greatest college baseball coach of all time. He evolved. He was always on the cutting edge."

– Ole Miss baseball coach Mike Bianco, a former LSU catcher
and three-time national champion LSU assistant coach under Skip Bertman

During his years as pitching coach and associate head coach at Miami from 1976 to 1983, Skip Bertman was basically a "defensive coordinator," to use a football term.

Through his first 13 years as LSU's baseball coach, including national titles in 1991, '93 and '96, Bertman remained a defensive coordinator – a.k.a. pitching coach – while also running the entire program on and off the field.

No less than 14 of the 21 pitchers Bertman put in the Major Leagues while at LSU played for him from 1984 to 1996. On the 1989 team alone that reached the College World Series, there were six – Ben McDonald, Curtis Leskanic, Russell Springer, Paul Byrd, Chad Ogea and John O'Donoghue – and a team earned run average of 3.63. His 1987 pitching staff of Gregg Patterson, Mark Guthrie, Barry Manuel, Stan Loewer and Dan Kite produced a Bertman-best 3.07 earned run average at LSU.

The bats started getting bigger and more energized in 1996, but Bertman's staff of Eddie Yarnall, Chris Demouy, Brett Laxton, Patrick Coogan and Kevin Shipp kept the ERA at 3.38 – the last sub-4.00 ERA of Bertman's career.

The bat barrels for 1997 were even larger and wider with more explosion.

"Bigger, and just the way the ball bounced off them in '97 – the trampoline effect," said Patrick Coogan, an All-American junior right-hander in 1997 who was 14-3 with a 4.46 ERA.

If you happened to walk by Alex Box Stadium on the way to an LSU football game on an autumn day in 1996, you'd be lucky if you didn't get hit by a baseball.

"We saw it in the fall, man," said Brandon Larson, a transfer shortstop who hit just 10 homers in 1996 at Blinn Junior College in Brenham, Texas. He would hit 40 for LSU in 1997, crushing the school record of 26 set in '96 by SEC Player of the Year and consensus All-American first baseman Eddy

Furniss of Nacogdoches, Texas.

Larson remains one of only four college players to hit 40 home runs. No one has hit more than 34 since as the NCAA has kept the bats smaller and weaker, beginning in 1999.

"I'm going, 'Wow, I'm hitting bombs. And other guys are hitting bombs. This Eddy Furniss guy, he just put one off the scoreboard out there,'" Larson said of the legendary fall practices of 1996.

Bertman noticed the power surge right off.

"By the end of fall, I could see we were different," Bertman said. "The bats were so electric. It was hard to make a pitch to get them out. Fall ball that year was big for me."

* * * * *

Bertman began transitioning from defensive coordinator to offensive coordinator – small ball to home run derby. It was not unlike Alabama football coach Nick Saban realizing defense's days like he knew them were over when he hired passing attack guru Lane Kiffin to run his offense in 2014.

"Early in my time at LSU, I was the biggest of the small-ball coaches," Bertman said. "Then I did what the players showed me I needed to do. Personnel dictated."

LSU's second-year recruiting coordinator/hitting coach Jim Schwanke, formerly of College World Series brand Oklahoma State, had filled Bertman's 1997 roster with beefier, stronger hitters.

In addition to Larson, there were two other junior college transfers: outfielders Danny Higgins of Galveston, Texas, and Wes Davis of Big Spring, Texas. Incoming freshmen were infielder Blair Barbier of New Orleans, infielder Johnnie Thibodeaux of Lake Charles, and Los Angeles catcher Brad Cresse.

The newcomers would join larger upper classmen like Eddy Furniss and infielder Trey McClure, a former quarterback at Central High near Baton Rouge. The only regular position starter returning other than Furniss was fellow senior center fielder Mike Koerner, who had hit 12 home runs in 1996.

"Other than the bats, I saw I had big guys, and we had been weightlifting. But we got more into it going into '97. Guys were going around like this," said Bertman flexing his bicep.

"He was always ahead of his time. It was Skip's instincts. He saw what was coming before anyone else," pitching coach Dan Canevari pointed out.

"There is a foundation," said Ole Miss coach Mike Bianco, who was Bertman's catcher in 1988-89 and an assistant for national titles in 1993, '96 and '97. "A lot of the stuff we do at Ole Miss, like bunt defenses, I learned in 1988 with Skip. But there are other parts of the system that evolved and came full circle with technology and the game changing. Skip was never scared to change. He had guts. He was willing to venture out."

At Anthony's Steakhouse in Omaha in '97, Bertman publicly praised a strength coach during the traditional pre-World Series gathering with players, their families and friends of the program.

"I want to introduce the coach who really made it all happen – Kurt Hester," Bertman said.

"Hester made a difference that year. He made them big and strong. And nobody else was doing that. Again, instincts," Canevari pointed out.

"Skip was the first to really get into the weights," Bianco said. "Now, everybody does. I've got a 9,000-square-foot weight room that's bigger than most football weight rooms. Baseball players lifted weights in the '80s, but not like what Skip started in '97. No one had strength coaches."

* * * * *

By very early in 1997, Bertman's instincts proved spot-on as baseballs started flying out of Alex Box and beyond. There were six home runs by six players in the opening 13-2, 11-5 doubleheader sweep of Baylor. LSU hit a school record-tying seven homers by five players in a 16-2 win over Southern.

Even the cavernous Superdome in New Orleans couldn't contain LSU at the Winn-Dixie Showdown as Tom Bernhardt hit a grand slam in an 11-4 win over North Carolina. Larson followed with an LSU record-tying three homers against Duke, including a walk-off for a 9-8 win. Through eight games, LSU had 25 home runs.

"After the Superdome, I knew," Bertman said. "Everybody was hitting home runs. I went to the team and said, 'Look, we're going to switch to Gorilla Ball all the time. There are no take signals. Nobody will ever have the bunt sign. We're probably never going to steal. If you get picked off, I break your legs. OK? We're just going to let you guys hit.'"

Even junior infielder Casey Cuntz, who entered '97 with one career home run, hit his fifth in a 6-4 win over Virginia Commonwealth in game 11.

"I can't really explain why," he said.

"Thunder sticks," ace pitcher Patrick Coogan said.

The LSU Thors started off 19-0 and would stay No. 1 for eight straight weeks. By May 1, they were 42-8 overall and leading the SEC at 19-4.

The term "Gorilla Ball" went national in 1997 after being coined in 1996 when Bertman wrote one of his patented acronyms on the squad room board about coach Jim Schwanke's hitting approach – "A-P-E" for Approach, Plan, Execute.

"I guess you want us to be a bunch of gorillas," cracked Chad Cooley, who had hit 14 home runs in 1996 as LSU led the nation that year with 131, destroying its school record of 87 from 1994.

In 1997, Gorilla Ball grew gargantuan as LSU broke its record of 131 home runs on April 26 in an 8-0 win over Auburn – with 21 games still to go. On May 2, Larson broke Furniss' school home run record with his 27th in a 13-8 win at Arkansas. Larson hit his 28th the next day over a 40-foot wall in center field in an 11-5 win.

"I hit it over that whole thing, and I knew it as soon as I swung," Larson said. "That was one of the few that I quote, unquote, 'pimped.' I got every bit of it and just stood there and watched."

Bertman was just kind of watching, too, in the most relaxing season of his career, as the bats, the pitching staff, the strength coach, and the power took over.

"They were so good, I just sat there and let 'em play," Bertman said. "I sat on my hands in '97. I didn't give any signals at all on offense. That was the only year."

There were exactly four sacrifice bunts.

"There was no hit-and-run because I wanted the guy to have his rip. If you strike out, you strike out," Bertman said.

"He did something that most coaches don't: He switched over. And you didn't have to get it all with those bats, so the percentages he loved were in his favor," Canevari explained.

"I think what you're getting at is really one of the things that makes him one of the greatest coaches, if not the greatest college baseball coach of all time," Bianco said. "He evolved. He was always on the cutting edge."

The LSU fans loved Gorilla Ball almost as much as football, as evidenced by the fact that Alex Box Stadium led the nation in attendance for the second straight season with an average of 6,484 fans per game.

"I tell people that Alex Box back then, it was an event," Larson said. "It wasn't like going to a baseball game. It was like a concert. People were dog-crazy screaming. And at the old Box (which was replaced by the new Alex Box Stadium 300 yards down Nicholson Drive after 2008), they were right on top of you. After Gorilla Ball came into play, they had signs and yells. They were rabid about the home runs. And we gave it to them!"

And in the end, LSU delivered an NCAA record 188 home runs, which will likely never be broken, towering over the previous mark of 161 by Brigham Young in 1988. The closest any team has come since was LSU itself in 1998 with 157.

LSU averaged 2.69 home runs a game in '97, still the NCAA record. In all, nine players hit double-digit homers: 40 by Larson, 22 by Koerner, 17 by Furniss, 17 by Bernhardt, 16 by Davis, 15 by Barbier, 12 by McClure and 11 apiece by Higgins and Cuntz.

The Tigers hit at least one home run in every game, six in a game twice, five in a game eight times, four homers six times, three in a game 18 times. Larson had nine multi-home run games. Babe Ruth had just 10 multi-homer games when he hit 60 in 1927.

"It was insane," Bianco said. "Now, my coaches or a player will look up and go, 'LSU hit 188? You had a guy hit 40?' Obviously, the bats were zooped, and we weren't the only team hitting them. We just hit more of them than anyone else."

LSU scored double-digit runs in 32 games – nearly half of the 70-game schedule – and finished with a school record 57 wins.

"I really enjoyed never being out of a game. It never mattered what inning or where we were in that lineup – we could get you at any time and have that inning," Barbier said.

"Those offenses were about foot on throat," said Doug Thompson, who finished 12-3 with a team-high 158 strikeouts in 124 innings with a 4.63 ERA. "I never had more fun in my life. I didn't let giving up a couple of early runs bother me. I was convinced it was just a matter of time before we scored a bunch."

No. 4 Auburn (39-7) came to Baton Rouge leading the SEC in ERA and batting average. It fell 7-1 and 8-0 with a merciful rainout as LSU's players – craving more competition – tried to get a rise from the other dugout late in the second game just for entertainment. But Auburn went away quietly.

"It's the first time all year we've been dominated like this," said a disgusted Auburn coach Hal Baird.

"All season, we came on the field and just annihilated the competition," Larson said.

It's hard not to "pimp" a few dozen home runs when you hit 188.

"They couldn't throw at us, because we had nine guys with at least 11 or 12 home runs apiece," Larson noted. "You're going to hit me and pitch to Furniss? Or hit Furniss and pitch to Koerner? Hit Koerner and pitch to McClure? Hit McClure and pitch to Bernhardt, who's the Incredible Hulk in right field?"

Perhaps no LSU team in any sport ever had more sustained, swashbuckling swagger than the 1997 Tigers.

* * * * *

As confident as the Tigers were with their historic home run numbers, gashes in the gladiators' armor appeared late.

There were two losses out of three at Mississippi State in mid-April and a 16-1 shellacking at Arkansas on May 4 that was at the time LSU's worst loss of the Bertman era. The Tigers followed by dropping two straight at Alabama in the last regular season series, including the worst defeat of LSU baseball in 104 years, 28-2, before a record Sewell-Thomas Stadium crowd on May 10.

Starter Doug Thompson, who was LSU's other ace that season, was oddly ineffective in that lopsided loss. He couldn't get an out in the third inning as he allowed seven hits and seven runs in all with a grand slam in the second to Roberto Vaz.

LSU's Gorilla Ball had been tamed, and the Tigers were mired in their worst losing streak since March of 1996 at three with one regular season game left for the outright SEC title.

An angry Thompson wanted to stay in, but Bertman said no.

"You've got to trust me today, Dougie boy," he said. "It's going to be bad today. But listen, tomorrow, I'm going to bring you back to win the SEC."

Alabama sent 15 to the plate and scored 10 in the fourth for an 18-1 lead.

"Skip lit up a cigar during that game," Coogan recalled. "Hadn't seen that before. Then he says, 'Hey, boys, no more hits today. We're going to need them tomorrow – law of averages.'"

Bertman huddled the team in the outfield when the game finally ended. Many Bama fans gathered to rub it in as Alabama was 8-2 vs. LSU since 1995 under Coach Jim Wells – the new Bertman.

"That was embarrassing, guys," Bertman said. "Your families came all the way here on a charter bus for this? But, hey, we've got them right where we want 'em. They're going to be so tired tomorrow from running the bases today that we'll kill them."

The clairvoyant one was right again. Alabama started fast by taking a 3-1 lead in the first inning Sunday and touched up LSU starter Joey Painich for five hits in two and a third innings. But the Tide beached over the final frames with only one hit and lost 6-4.

As Bertman predicted, Thompson won the SEC, relieving in the third and holding Alabama to one run on a hit with five strikeouts to go to 8-3. Furniss' two-run homer tied it 3-3 in the sixth. Conan Horton's solo home run put LSU ahead 4-3 in the seventh, and Koerner's two-run homer stretched that to 6-3.

"It was the greatest postgame speech ever," Coach Schwanke said. "He took all the pressure off."

LSU won three straight in the SEC Tournament with a 12-7 win over Alabama, but lost the title to the Tide, 12-2. Something Coach Jim Wells said after losing the regular season crown, though, would soon prove prophetic.

"LSU has a way of winning when they have to. They'll be there at the end like they are every year," he said. "Bertman Jr." would prove to be clairvoyant, too.

But first the Tigers had to get to Omaha to show off all that offense.

* * * * *

At the NCAA South I Regional at Alex Box Stadium, LSU easily dispatched UNC-Greensboro, 14-0, and Oklahoma, 14-3. The Tigers turned a triple play against the Sooners as McClure fielded a grounder at third, touched the bag for a force out, threw to second to Barbier for a force out, then Barbier completed it with a throw to Furniss at first. LSU hit five home runs in this game to give it 165 for the season.

LSU was in the "marble game," a term Bertman used for the Saturday winner's bracket final in the former six-team, double-elimination format. Win it, and you're one win from Omaha. Lose it, and you have to win three to advance.

LSU lost it, 11-5, to pesky No. 2-seed South Alabama. The Jaguars beat LSU for their 18th win in 19 games in a game that was suspended by rain on Saturday night with USA leading 8-4 in the seventh. The game was completed Sunday, and LSU looked bad, striking out 16 times.

Then LSU suddenly faced elimination Sunday night against No. 4-seed Long Beach State as they trailed 7-6 in the bottom of the seventh.

"I remember looking at Larson and Furniss with all their bombs and thinking, 'Wait, we're going to get beat at the Box? It's going to be surreal if we lose this game with this team,'" Thompson said.

"This great team almost lost," Coogan said. "I'd never experienced the Box like that. The place was on pins and needles from the sixth inning on."

Furniss' full-count, solo home run to right field off All-American closer Ara Petrosian tied it 7-7 in the top of the eighth. But Long Beach State threatened to take the lead in the bottom of the eighth after second base umpire Scott McDougall called a balk on Coogan that put the lead-off hitter on second base with one out.

"Oh, it was a balk, 100 percent," said Coogan, who had relieved in the seventh.

"It was a balk, but they almost never call that in that situation," said Bertman, who proceeded to argue like it was the worst call in history.

Bertman moved as fast as he could to the mound as did Coach Schwanke, who tried to keep Coogan and Bertman away from McDougall.

"How do you make that call?" Bertman yelled.

"Skip was just furious," said Blair Barbier, who ran to the mound from second base. "And the crowd went wild."

Then Bertman flipped the bill of his hat around to get in the face of McDougall.

"That took it to a whole other level. The crowd got electric," Barbier said. And the argument went on.

"What do you do for a living?" Bertman said.

"I sell insurance," McDougall replied.

"Really. Well, I'm sure you do a great job selling insurance, but you suck as an umpire!" Bertman shouted.

And that was it. It was just the second ejection of Bertman's career.

Bertman then retired to his office behind the first base dugout. Bianco and

Schwanke took over the team.

LSU Sports Information Director Herb Vincent was driving east on I-10 for the SEC spring meetings in Destin, Florida, having left the Box with LSU up 6-3 in the top of the seventh. He turned around before getting too far away from Baton Rouge when he heard the ejection from Jim Hawthorne on his car radio.

"I just thought, 'I need to get back and see what's happening,'" Vincent said. "I walked into his office, and there's this huge cloud of cigar smoke."

Before that stogie, Bertman lit a bonfire under his team and the crowd of 5,949.

"We needed that jolt of energy," Barbier said.

"I couldn't believe it," Larson said. "He never does that. He just sat there most of the time that season, patted you on the butt, pulled us together. So, to see that, it was like, 'He's one of us now. We have our own junkyard dog as the coach.' He just waited for the right time to come out and wake us up. He bumped the guy. He turned his hat around. There's no way in hell we're going to lose this game now.

"That Alex Box magic, man, it's real."

Coogan felt that way, too, as he struck out the next two to end the inning. When he fanned No. 3 hitter Izzy Gonzales, who had four hits and three RBIs, for the last out, Alex Box exploded.

"That was the loudest moment I ever heard at the Box," Thompson said. "I promise you, I literally remember feeling the ground shaking. Considering the moment, it was All-American ace-type stuff from Patrick."

Thompson met Coogan at the first base line and picked him up.

"Running off the field after that is probably the most amped up I've ever been," Coogan said. "There was a buzz. It was like the closest I've ever come to playing in Tiger Stadium. The fans absolutely came alive at that moment."

The game went into extra innings tied at 7-7 before LSU erupted for seven in the 11th to take a 14-7 lead as closer Ara Petrosian and the bullpen buckled under the Box magic. Petrosian gave up two bases-loaded walks and two wild pitches that scored runs around a two-run double by Davis and an RBI single by Jeremy Witten.

Coogan finished off Long Beach State in the bottom of the 11th and allowed no hits or runs in four innings with four strikeouts for the win to go to 13-3.

"Skip gave me the biggest hug," Coogan said. "You saved our ass there," Bertman told him.

It was about midnight, and LSU still had to beat South Alabama twice the next day, beginning at 11 a.m. on Memorial Day Monday on one of the most humid days of the year.

South Alabama wilted in the heat from the outset in both games, losing

14-4 and 15-4, with LSU hitting four home runs in each game. The Tigers took an 8-1 lead after three innings in the first game and 11-4 after four as Larson, Koerner, Davis and Higgins homered. LSU scored 11 runs in the fourth inning of the second game with Koerner hitting his 20th and Higgins his 10th. LSU pushed that to 14-1 in the fifth. Larson homered twice in game two to go to 37 on the season.

Before the first South Alabama game, Bertman had a little one-on-one motivational talk with Thompson in the bullpen. Obviously fatigued and sweating while warming up before starting, Thompson did not look like he could last more than an inning or two after throwing six to beat Oklahoma just two days earlier.

"He exhaled his cigar big and I thought he was going to go over the game plan," Thompson recalled. "But he asked me why I came to LSU. I said 'to win a national championship.'"

"Ooh, that's good," Bertman said. "Well, listen, unless you pitch all nine, that's not going to happen this year. It may be 15-11, but I can't take you out. You've got to have as thick a skin as you've ever had, and if you do, we're going to Omaha."

Thompson pitched all nine, allowing six hits and four runs with 10 strikeouts, enabling Bertman to save pitchers for the second game.

"For him to tell me that in that moment, 'This is yours,'" Thompson said. "That's all I needed from him."

Thompson later passed out watching the second game. Barbier cramped up badly, too. Furniss caught the last out and collapsed in full body cramp. Several players on both teams had to receive intravenous fluids in the LSU locker room. As the second game drew to a close, Thompson and Barbier were still being treated in the locker room.

"We've got to get out there," Thompson said. "So, we literally walked arm-in-arm, holding one another up, into the dugout and saw the last out. Awesome feeling."

The dryer, more pleasant heat and cool nights of Omaha awaited.

* * * * *

Bertman's biggest concern was the emotion- and fluid-draining Regional his team had just survived. Such marathons had hurt some of his previous teams in Omaha, particularly in 1989 coming out of Texas A&M.

And would this Gorilla Ball approach work in Omaha?

"Our philosophy is to live and die with the home run," Bertman said at a CWS press conference. "That's tough for an old small-ball coach like me."

But Bertman was enjoying his most stress-free season ever.

"Skip barely ever criticized that team," LSU baseball Sports Information Director Bill Franques said. "Not really. Not with all those home runs, and

Thompson and Coogan were both aces."

No. 2-seed LSU (53-13) with an NCAA record 178 home runs drew No. 7-seed Rice (47-14) with 119 home runs. LSU had Larson, who had SEC records for home runs (37) and RBIs (110) while hitting .381. Rice had Lance Berkman, who was No. 1 in the nation with 41 home runs, 134 RBIs and hitting .438.

Rice also had closer Matt Anderson (10-1, 1.82 ERA, 9 saves), who would soon be the first selection of the MLB draft.

Anderson entered in the bottom of the seventh, retired LSU in order with two strikeouts and went to the eighth with a 4-2 lead. But he walked Barbier. And Larson – who would be the 14th pick in the draft – slammed a breaking ball over the left field bleachers for a two-run home run to tie it, 4-4. Jeremy Witten later put LSU ahead 5-4 with a sacrifice fly.

Chris Demouy shut out Rice in the ninth for the win after relieving Thompson. And LSU was up and away.

"I take a lot of pride in that home run because Skip's scouting report said basically, 'If you get to Matt Anderson, good luck,'" said Larson, who hit just the third homer of the season off Anderson. "The cool thing is every player on our team was wanting the chance to homer off him. None of us were afraid."

LSU's hard work was over. The Tigers breezed into their second straight national championship game, beating Stanford, 10-5 and 13-9. LSU tied a CWS record with five homers in the first win over Stanford.

Larson hit his last two homers for an even 40. Bernhardt, Furniss and Davis homered. Koerner homered twice in the second win as LSU eliminated Stanford.

* * * * *

LSU now had the chance to repeat as National Champions. The matchup would be against a very familiar and formidable foe, Alabama, which had defeated Mississippi State, 3-2, then battled through the loser's bracket with wins over Mississippi State and Miami twice to reach the finale.

It was a classic matchup of the rising pupil, Jim Wells, in his second CWS in just his third year versus the still-rising teacher, Skip Bertman, in his ninth CWS in 12 years. They talked and walked alike and won alike.

But Wells seemingly had Bertman solved as he was 9-4 against him since becoming Alabama's coach in 1995, including the 28-2 and 12-2 blowouts in the past few weeks. The Tide was hitting home runs, too, with 159 to LSU's 186.

"It's great to be in the National Championship game, especially against somebody who means so much to me," Wells said. "It's going to be a very emotional day."

It was a classic matchup of best vs. best as Alabama was No. 1-ranked and the No. 1 seed to LSU's No. 2 ranking and No. 2 seed. LSU won the SEC regular season. Alabama won the SEC Tournament. LSU was 56-13. Alabama was 56-13.

Alabama, though, was missing one of its stars: junior pitcher/outfielder/infielder/DH Roberto Vaz, a rare two-way player who was 4-1 with a 3.40 ERA and eight saves while hitting .400 with 22 home runs, 73 RBIs and 14 stolen bases.

But Vaz broke his right foot just after batting practice before the NCAA South II Regional final against USC in Tuscaloosa when he stepped on a baseball. A teammate had just bunted one that stopped on the white first base chalk line, perfectly camouflaging the ball. Vaz never saw it, and it instantly broke his foot.

Consequently, he missed Alabama's 9-8 win over USC. He would have started or pitched in relief in the National Championship game and surely would have added to his team's offense.

After playing four games in five days to reach the championship, Coach Wells was left to go with mid-week starter Michael Daniel (4-0, 5.53 ERA), a junior right-hander, who had thrown just four innings in the regular season. But Daniel had held LSU to two runs on six hits in seven innings for the 12-2 win in the SEC Tournament final just three weeks prior.

LSU had ace Patrick Coogan (14-3, 4.33 ERA) and ace Doug Thompson (11-3, 4.66 ERA) for relief.

* * * * *

Over the final weeks of the season, Bertman had added a new twist to his motivational videos, which usually featured past exploits. Suddenly they included the current season. There was so much home run footage.

"He stopped showing videos of the '96 team," Larson recalled. "He'd show Higgins or Koerner or me hitting bombs right before the next game. So, we wanted to go out now and make another highlight so we could see one of us the next time. That was some motivation, man."

The bus from the Embassy Suites to Rosenblatt Stadium literally rocked on Saturday morning, June 7, 1997.

The team's Omaha bus ride music for the second straight year was "Keep It Live" by the Dazz Band, and LSU was all that.

"A lot of dancing. We didn't care about the losses to Bama," Coogan said.

"We were so laid back and laughing and cutting up. It was a party," Larson said.

"They're real relaxed. Let them stay that way," said Bertman, who had one more touch in his pre-game speech.

"You represent your family, your school, your Maker ... and a *dynasty*," he said.

And it was on.

"I can't even describe it," Larson said. "Whether it's a video or what he says in the huddle, or one of his stories, he'll make you believe you can do anything."

Danny Higgins led off LSU's bottom of the first with a home run to left. Mike Koerner singled in a run. Tom Bernhardt doubled in two more, and Bama pitcher Michael Daniel was done. LSU batted around. Higgins came up again after one of Alabama's three errors in the game to single in two more, and it was 6-0. LSU went up 9-0 in the second after another two-out error by the tumbling Tide on a three-run double by Wes Davis.

Bernhardt, who hit .615 in the CWS, added a solo home run in the seventh – the Tigers' 188th and final blast of 1997 – to put LSU up 12-4 before it added a run in the eighth for a 13-6 final.

Coogan struck out eight in four and a third, and Thompson finished with seven strikeouts and the win. He fanned Matt Frick to end it and tossed his glove in wild exultation.

"I never thought of doing that," said Thompson, now an analyst for the LSU Baseball Radio Network. "All of that was just sheer exhilaration. What's interesting is if you look at all those clips from the other championships, some of them look similar. And Skip always said the videos are everything because the players see themselves in these moments. It's like you already did it."

And the Tigers had done it again: four national titles in seven years with more drama, swagger and power than anyone before them.

Warren Morris' walk-off, two-run home run with two outs in the bottom of the ninth had more than ended the 1996 national title game, 9-8 over Miami. His suddenly healed wrist bone that flicked his only home run of the season also turned the page to Gorilla Ball.

LSU hit at least one home run in 77 straight games from Morris on Saturday, June 8, 1996, through Saturday, Feb. 21, 1998.

"The Warren Morris walk-off – that's the greatest thing that ever happened to LSU baseball," Larson said. "But I'm going to say '97 was LSU's greatest season. The '96 team captured the moment. They were great. They teed it up for us, and we just drove it out of the park."

If you're scoring at home, they drove it out 188 times, to be exact.

Chapter 13

A fist full of titles
(The 2000 National Championship)

*"They just won't give up. Of all the national
championships, this is the best one."*

– Skip Bertman on Jan. 17, 2000, after winning his fifth title since 1991

The winds of change struck college baseball as the 1998 season whistled to a close. First the weather. Then the bats – the "thunder sticks," as LSU pitcher Patrick Coogan called them.

LSU was still the gargantuan gorilla of the game as it continued its home run flight of 1997 when the Tigers hit an NCAA record 188 homers that will live forever. The Tigers hit another 157 in 1998 to lead the nation.

In its '98 College World Series opener on May 30 in Omaha, LSU set the CWS record for most home runs in a game with eight in a 12-10 win over USC. They also set the CWS record for most players with homers in a game with seven – Brad Cresse with two and Danny Higgins, Cedrick Harris, Eddy Furniss, Clint Earnhart, Wes Davis and Trey McClure with one apiece. They were pictured in a group shot in the Baton Rouge *Advocate* each holding a bat and with Cresse holding two.

And LSU set the CWS record for most homers in an inning with four in the seventh by Harris, Higgins, McClure and Cresse. The Tigers entered the inning down, 10-5, but scored five before a McClure two-run single in the eighth won it.

The *Advocate* sports front page headline said it all: "Going …" under a picture of Davis' home run, "Going …" under a shot of a Cresse homer, and "GONE" under a wide shot of Furniss' homer.

The wind was blowing out of Rosenblatt Stadium, at times at 20 m.p.h., and USC hit two of its own as the teams combined to hit the most home runs in CWS history with 10. All records were still standing through 2021.

Cresse's two-run home run in the seventh that tied it 10-10 remains legend as it cleared the left field sign at 410 feet and the bleachers for an estimated distance of 500 feet. (It even surpassed Lyle Mouton's majestic moonshot to center in LSU's win over Florida in the Omaha opener seven years earlier.)

LSU hit six more home runs two days later in a 10-8 win over Mississippi State to set the CWS record for most home runs in two games at 14. Higgins,

Cresse, Earnhart, Davis and Harris homered for the second straight game, and Blair Barbier joined the barrage party.

Then the wind turned, and the cold came, dropping temperatures from the 80s to the 40s on June 4 before LSU was to play USC again.

"The phone rang that morning," Barbier recalled. "It was Bones (equipment manager Mike Boniol of Alexandria)."

"Hey, wear your sweats," Boniol said.

"Dude," Barbier told roommate Johnnie Thibodeaux. "That's a joke. You know the pranksters on this team. I didn't bring mine anyway."

It was no joke. And Gorilla Ball froze.

LSU still managed home runs by Josh Dalton and Harris for the most in three CWS games at 16, but USC also had two and 11 hits in all for a 5-4 win. The Tigers had a human-like seven hits after 25 hits through their first two CWS games.

It was still cold a day later with the wind blowing in again, and LSU's bats died once more against USC. The Tigers mustered just eight hits and were down 7-0 before getting eliminated, 7-3, from the 1998 CWS.

"They were small-ball games. They were bunting," Barbier said as if describing a contagious disease. "We had to play *their* game."

As LSU flew home from Omaha without a title, the weather grew warmer for bats, and USC beat Arizona State for the championship, 21-14. It was a score that did not sit well with the NCAA baseball powers. Nor did the 39 hits and another nine home runs for second all-time in a CWS game.

* * * * *

For 1999, the NCAA eliminated the pop and size from the bats considerably, and LSU dipped to 104 home runs.

"The bats were clearly weaker," said Cresse, who dropped from an SEC-high 29 homers in 1998 to 10 in 1999 amid injuries that plagued the rest of the team as well.

There was another change, perhaps partly directed at LSU's swath, too. Striving for more parity and different teams in Omaha, the NCAA expanded the postseason from the six-team NCAA Regional to a four-team set, followed by a best-of-three, two-team Super Regional.

So, the NCAA legislated against Gorilla Ball and LSU in a way, and it worked in '99 as the Tigers' third place SEC finish at 18-11 was their worst since 1995. They still reached the Super Regional, but had to travel to rival Alabama, where they were unceremoniously swept, 13-6 and 13-5.

Right-handed ace Kurt Ainsworth, a third-year sophomore who missed virtually all of 1998 after elbow surgery, finished 13-6 with a 3.45 ERA. He led the SEC in strikeouts with 157 in 130 innings and tied for most wins.

A first-round draft pick in 1999, Ainsworth reached the Majors in 2001 at age 22. Of the 40 pitchers drafted out of LSU from 1986 to 2001, Ainsworth was one of only three not to be in uniform at a CWS and the only one of those three taken in the first three rounds.

For the first time since 1995, LSU would not go to Omaha.

Had the new game passed Bertman by? He talked of retirement at this time.

* * * * *

Neither new NCAA rules nor a heart scare would stop Bertman from getting to Omaha one more time.

After a three-game series amid searing temperatures at Georgia in May of 1999, Bertman started passing out, coming to, and passing out while on the plane. And pitching coach Dan Canevari freaked out. He ran to the back looking for a doctor and saw sophomore shortstop Ryan Theriot playing cards with two of his teammates.

Theriot had committed a base-running blunder at Georgia that drew Bertman's ire. Thinking McClure had homered, Theriot trotted home from his lead at third and was in the dugout when he realized McClure did not homer. Theriot was thrown out at third for not tagging up. Theriot still had a ways to go before he "graduated," as Bertman would say.

"I had some learning to do, let's say that," Theriot remembered.

"You did it," Canevari screamed on the plane. "You finally did it, Theriot! He always said you were trying to kill him."

"What!" Theriot exclaimed.

"Skip just passed out," Canevari said. "Then he came to and said, 'That Theriot's going to kill me. He can't run the bases.' And then he passed out again. And then he came back to, yelling at you."

Luckily, a doctor was on the plane. An ambulance picked up Bertman at the Baton Rouge airport, and his cardiologist met him at Our Lady of the Lake hospital. Bertman had an irregular heartbeat, but was soon fine after some medication, diet adjustments and fewer cigars.

The health scare forced Bertman to miss his first game anywhere ever – a 6-5 loss at Northeast Louisiana on May 11 in Monroe.

"Man, it's hard not to have any input," Bertman said after listening to the radio call of Jim Hawthorne and Bill Franques. "Jim and Bill do a great job, but I can't stand waiting out each pitch without seeing it. I'm anxious to get back."

Retirement was the last thing on his mind now as Bertman returned for the next series. When 1999 ended, he was like many of his players: After spending time on the disabled list, he went into the new millennium on fire.

Bertman had won championships as a "defensive coordinator" in small ball with bunts and as an offensive coordinator in Gorilla Ball, or "big ball," as he called it, with homers. But as the game changed back, so did Bertman.

The game wasn't passing him by. He was staying ahead of it and getting better and better like fine wine.

"He trusted us and didn't micro-manage," said Blair Barbier, who was a freshman second baseman with the 1997 champions. "But I didn't see a big layoff from '97 to 2000. Same coach. Still so engaging with the unbelievable ability to motivate. He was in his prime. He was just on it.

"And he had this Sunday Speaker Series for us with CEOs from all over the country. He'd use what they said to set up the next games. And his videos! I mean it was amazing to watch him work."

Bertman was more grandfatherly, but still doing the work.

"He had relaxed a little bit," said Bill Franques, LSU's baseball Sports Information Director since 1989 who was also an administrative assistant in Bertman's later years. "But he was still on it like when he was younger. He wasn't as concerned with curfews, but that 2000 team policed itself. I will say, though, one of my jobs was to sit outside a classroom to make sure a player was in class. He was still having his staff do that in 2000."

* * * * *

All of Bertman's toil came to fruition one more time in 2000 – his wisdom, his speeches, the Speaker Series, the sports psychologists, the music, the visualization and, especially, the videos.

"Skip was really into the videos," Barbier recalled. "Kevin Wagner (LSU video director) and others were always shooting for Skip's coaches' shows and for us. It was amazing because before our games, not only would you get Skip's speech, but you'd also get a pump-up video with "Thunderstruck" or "Welcome to the Jungle" right before you'd play. You were ready to run through a wall. Sometimes he'd tie in what the Speaker Series person on Sunday had told us. This guy was just on it."

One of the 2000 team's favorite movies was DreamWorks Pictures' "Gladiator" with Russell Crowe as Maximus that came out in early May of 2000 just as LSU was nearing postseason.

"Strength and honor," Maximus says before battle. "At my signal, unleash hell."

With arms wide, Maximus peers at a packed Colosseum in Rome – like Alex Box Stadium in Baton Rouge – and famously yells, "Are you not *entertained*?" after just slaying several with his sword, then tosses it to the crowd.

A similarly built Barbier or Cresse could have hollered the same line after a home run in an NCAA Regional in 2000 A.D., then flipped the bat.

Bertman would have one of LSU's videographers splice Maximus with a sword with Cresse hitting a home run.

Or they would do the same thing with "Braveheart," a 1995 film in which Mel Gibson plays 13th century Scottish warrior Sir William Wallace, who says, "Are you ready for war?"

"The players would say before a game in a Scottish accent, 'Are you ready for war?' Then they'd go nuts," Canevari recalled.

The players also saw historical Major League videos. They learned who Sandy Koufax was and Joe DiMaggio and Ted Williams.

"I worked hard at all the video stuff. I'm very proud of that. I made the time. I had time for everybody and everything. A lot of coaches work hard. I just used the 24 hours differently," Bertman explained.

Bertman's visualization teachings were the cornerstone of the 2000 team and previous ones. He would tell them to see movies of themselves in their heads getting the winning hit or striking out the last batter before they would actually do it.

"Be the star of your own movie," he would say.

Some would think about it as they closed their eyes to go to sleep.

"A-V-C was a thing for us," Barbier said. "Analyze, Visualize, Concentrate. It's just how we were coached up. It was really big for the pitchers, but we all knew we had to see ourselves there. We'd talk about it all the time – the power of visualization. And we still do this in our professional lives today."

When the final credits rolled, this would be one of Bertman's best-ever teams – balanced, well-rounded, adaptable to the NCAA's smaller swords, visualizing success, veteran-laden, deep, and flat tough as the Tigers overcame both lingering and sudden injuries.

* * * * *

As the 2000 season began, there were questions. Who would replace Ainsworth as the ace? Who would make up the rest of the pitching staff?

There was junior Brian Tallet, a native of Oklahoma City who looked the part at 6-foot-7 and 193 pounds, and he was left-handed. But Tallet had not found it yet after arm surgery that made him redshirt in 1998. He was just 3-4 with a 4.01 ERA in 1999.

There was also a tall right-hander from Big Spring, Texas – 6-3 senior Trey Hodges. He was trying to come off two surgeries on his right arm from the previous July – a partial bicep tendon repair and bone spurs in his shoulder. He was 3-2 in '99 with a 7.08 ERA in 34 innings.

Hunter Gomez of Ponchatoula, La., had the best numbers of the returnees at 4-3 with a 4.38 ERA and seven saves in his junior year in '99.

"I kept waiting for Tallet," Bertman said. "You had to give players time to develop. I was patient."

And it happened in 2000 as he became one of the best pitchers in the SEC at 15-3 with a 3.52 ERA and 134 strikeouts.

Gomez also came through, finishing 9-1 with a 4.04 ERA. Weylin Guidry, a sophomore who pitched just seven innings in 1999, became the closer with seven saves and a 2.68 ERA. The third starter was supposed to be Hodges, but he was slow to find his groove after his injuries. Senior Ben Saxon and freshman Bo Pettit combined to start five SEC games, while Hodges logged four.

Most of the position players were back: three seniors in Barbier at third, Cresse at catcher, and right fielder Jeremy Witten; two juniors in Cedrick Harris in center field and Brad Hawpe at first base; and sophomore Ryan Theriot at shortstop.

Two prized freshman recruits rounded out the lineup in second baseman Mike Fontenot and left fielder Wally Pontiff, who was converted from a backup third baseman.

Jeremy Witten, who was a punter on the football team from 1996 to 1999, already had two national championship rings as he red-shirted in '96 and played in 1997.

"We knew we were going to have a really good offense," Barbier observed.

He was right, as the Tigers led the SEC with a school record .340 batting average, which was still standing in 2021. Other LSU records set in 2000 that stuck through '21 are hits (864), hits per game (12.5), singles (558), doubles (194) and road wins (24 along with the 1989 team).

Hawpe led the nation in doubles with an SEC record 36 that remained in 2021, and Tallet's three shutouts still ties him for the LSU record with Aaron Nola in 2013, Ben McDonald in 1989 and Randy Wiles in 1970.

Cresse led the nation in home runs with 30 and in RBIs with 106, while LSU led the SEC in RBIs (598), slugging percentage (.542), runs (652) and – for balance – strikeouts pitched (574).

The 2000 team also remains the only one in LSU history to go undefeated all postseason at 13-0 – 4-0 in the SEC Tournament, 3-0 in the NCAA Regional, 2-0 in the Super Regional and 4-0 in Omaha.

But the Tigers started a mediocre 6-5, including the worst non-conference weekend in school history with 10-2, 11-7 and 10-2 losses to No. 10 Houston. The Cougars were the first non-SEC opponent to sweep three from LSU at home since 1969.

LSU had lost to Arizona State and McNeese State at home just before the Houston series, so that was five straight losses at home for the first time since 1978.

In a staff meeting, Bertman pointed out that the Tigers' batting average for the season was below their opponents' average.

"That's the sign of an awful team," he told hitting coach "Turtle" Thomas, pitching coach Dan Canevari and third base coach Bill Dailey. "This team is playing *awful*."

The bats soon came alive, though, building to .340 for the season and cutting the opponents' average to just .272. And LSU won 12 of its next 15. After losing the first two of its opening SEC series to Georgia at home on March 10 and 11, LSU never lost more than one at a time and finished 41-9 from that point.

The Tigers finished second in the SEC at 19-10, then won the SEC Tournament in Hoover, Alabama, while barely breaking a sweat in disposing of Georgia, 11-3, Alabama, 18-12 and 6-5, and Florida, 9-6.

But the most important development of what is an NCAA warm-up was something that happened in that 18-12 win over Alabama. For the first time since 1998 at Blinn Junior College in Texas, Trey Hodges felt like he was a complete pitcher again.

The slider – his main pitch – was as sharp as ever as he struck out five in five and two-thirds shutout innings around three walks and four hits. He retired the side in every inning with runners on, including in the ninth.

"I came in, and very differently, very obviously – felt it," Hodges would say 21 years later. "I knew it at that point that I was 100 percent. It was like a light bulb went off, and I was healthy again."

Bertman saw the light. He had another pitcher just in time. LSU was on its way. The Tigers destroyed Jackson State and Louisiana-Monroe, coached by former LSU assistant Smoke Laval, by 19-1 and 21-0 scores in the NCAA Regional at the Box before advancing with a 5-3 win over ULM.

It turned out that Bertman didn't even need Hodges – yet.

* * * * *

For the Super Regional, the No. 4 Tigers (46-17) would host No. 14 UCLA (38-24) in the best-of-three series.

Trey Hodges was scheduled to start the third game after Tallet and Gomez, but they never got to him. LSU swept the Bruins with ease, 8-2 and 14-8, to reach the College World Series for the fourth time in five years. The Tigers out-hit UCLA, 21-12, and the Bruins committed six errors. It was like they were never there.

Barbier and other LSU players tailgated with some UCLA players afterward.

"As soon as they announced we were going to LSU on ESPN, I looked around and could see our guys were down," one of them told Barbier.

"They didn't want to come," Barbier said. "We were such benefactors of what Skip built – how tough it was to play at the Box as a visiting team. We really got the benefit of the 'bricklayers' of his first teams."

LSU led the first game 5-0 by the fifth and by 10-0 in the fourth of game two.

"By the time you looked up after all the fans' rowdiness and the barbecue wafting across the field had settled down, it's the fifth inning and we're blowing them away," Barbier said. "That intimidation factor was there, and it played for us. That stretch of baseball at the old Box with the atmosphere was so special, and how the fans were right on top of you. Remember how close? You couldn't hear in the dugout talking to each other. I mean I get chills thinking about it now."

UCLA's players who were graduating or going to pro ball were told by UCLA coach Gary Adams that they could stay and tailgate with the LSU fans. And, boy, did they! Adams had a blast as did players from both sides.

* * * * *

The Super Regional with UCLA started a string of LSU mastery over present or future first-round draft choices that would stretch through Omaha in the coming weeks.

In the 14-8 clinching win, LSU scored five earned runs on five hits and four walks off UCLA starter Josh Karp, who didn't get out of the fourth in taking the loss to fall to 10-2. In 2001, Karp would be the sixth player taken in the first round of the draft. UCLA also had second baseman Chase Utley, who was only 1 for 8 in the two games with a home run. He would be selected in the first round of the 2000 draft a week later.

Texas right-hander Beau Hale, who would be the 14th player taken in the 2000 draft, was waiting for LSU in Omaha for a World Series opening round game.

* * * * *

LSU had last met Texas in the CWS in 1989 and was eliminated, 12-7. Texas was now coached by "the Skip of the West," Augie Garrido, who had won three national championships at Cal State-Fullerton to Bertman's four. Garrido, a year younger than Bertman, won his first title in 1979. He went to Texas in 1997 and was in Omaha with the Longhorns for the first time.

At Cal State-Fullerton, it was Garrido who handed Bertman his two worst postseason losses ever – 11-0 at the NCAA South Regional in Alex Box in 1992 and 20-6 at the College World Series in 1994. Both eliminated LSU, with the latter marking the only time Bertman went 0-for-2 in Omaha. Garrido was known for bunting and manufacturing runs like the old Skip.

It was Baby Steps Ball vs. Gorilla Ball remnants. Texas had 126 sacrifice bunts entering the CWS. LSU had 16. Texas shortstop Todd West had recently set the NCAA record for sacrifice bunts with 29. Texas had 31 home runs. LSU catcher Brad Cresse had 30 of his team's 86 home runs so far and zero sacrifice bunts.

Everything's big in Texas, but the Longhorns' offense was a little light in the cleats.

Bertman did practice his bunt defenses, but as the end of the week neared he was tired of hearing about the bunt from the media, or as comedian George Carlin liked to say in a mocking high voice: *the sacrifice.*

"Everbody's talking about how much Texas bunts," Bertman said from his desk before leaving for Omaha. "I'm not afraid of the sacrifice bunt, OK. Texas bunts, so we'll field it and throw them out. Let me tell you something: We play our game. No one can get into our head by doing something like the sacrifice bunt. We've been practicing the same bunt defense we always have."

Bertman also did not believe in working too hard on something that was not a strength.

"We didn't work a lot on bunt defenses, or bunting, or first-and-third offense," Barbier said. "We just took more BP (batting practice). We took more ground balls. We would break out new bats, and we would have home run practice. He wanted us to really work on the things that we were going to be, as opposed to being good at defending the bunt or first-and-third. Not that we didn't practice all that, we just didn't overdo it."

And the best bunt defense can be a home run offense.

Barbier hit a two-run homer in the first inning off Beau Hale to give LSU a 4-0 lead over Texas and added a solo homer in the fifth for a 6-2 advantage before Mike Fontenot's solo home run in the seventh put LSU up 13-3. And this was against the nation's No. 1 earned-run-average staff at 3.12.

Texas never got a bunt down and fell, 13-5.

"If you work too much on your weaknesses, next thing you know, you lost your strength," Barbier said. "The bad thing may improve, but you're worse overall. Think how many times Skip's teams were not really that good everywhere in the field. Some of those guys were there to drive in runs."

Bertman took a full swing after the game as well.

"We were practicing a first-and-third bunt defense the other day," he mused. "And I told the boys they might not ever get first and third. We get some runs, and they're not going to bunt."

LSU met a future first-round draft pick two days later in USC right-hander Mark Prior. Prior no-hit LSU through five and had a 3-0 lead in the sixth until Theriot singled to left with one out. Then Fontenot singled, and Hawpe launched a three-run home run to tie it, 3-3.

Theriot's RBI single put LSU up 4-3 in the seventh, Hawpe homered again, and the Tigers went on to a 10-4 win. Prior allowed four hits and five earned runs in all for the loss.

Hodges threw six innings in relief and held USC to four hits and two runs with three strikeouts for the win.

Hodges relieved again three days later in the ninth for the save in a 6-3 semifinal win over Florida State, putting LSU in its third championship game in five years. The Tigers scored three in the eighth with a two-run single by Cedrick Harris for the win. Weylin Guidry got the victory by getting two outs in the eighth as Bertman used five pitchers in all, saving Tallet for the title game against Stanford.

Stanford reached the title game by beating upstart Louisiana-Lafayette in the Cajuns' first Omaha appearance, 19-9, in the other semifinal round.

Bertman told Hodges he was going to need him for the third time in six days in relief after Tallet.

To win his fifth title in 10 years, Bertman would have to get by another first-round pick: Stanford ace junior right-hander Justin Wayne (15-3, 3.04 ERA). There was also junior right-hander Jason Young (9-1, 3.71 ERA), who would be picked in the second round of the draft.

*	*	*	*	*

LSU, as usual, took an early lead in the second inning, off Jason Young. Wally Pontiff led off with a double and scored on a Cedrick Harris single. After Jeremy Witten singled, the Tigers showed their balance with a sacrifice bunt by Ray Wright to move the runners to second and third. They manufactured a run when Theriot pushed a groundout to second, scoring Harris for a 2-0 lead.

"Hey, we knew how to bunt," Barbier said. "We just didn't do it a lot."

Unknown to the CBS cameras, other media, and almost everyone in LSU's dugout, the Tigers suffered a significant injury in that inning.

Harris, a right-handed hitter, had squared around to bunt before his single. When Young's fastball ran up on his hands, it caught the index and middle fingers on Harris' right hand and broke both of them.

"The fingers had started turning colors. Skip had come out, and we were telling the ump, 'Hey, look.' But they didn't give me a base," Harris recalled vividly.

After Bertman and third base coach Bill Dailey looked at Harris' fingers, he took some warm-up swings, clearly holding his first finger straight up off the bat and his middle finger closer to the bat but loose as he swung. But he stayed in.

"Luckily, he threw me a fastball away, and I was able to hit a line drive to right center, holding the bat with my bottom two fingers," Harris said.

Harris, briefly, was feeling no pain.

"That was a very exciting moment," he said. "It gave us the lead. The adrenaline got me through that. The pain really set in after that. My fingers were throbbing, throbbing."

After LSU batted, trainer Shawn Eddy quickly taped the two fingers together, cut a hole in Harris' batting glove for the two throbbing, purple fingers, and gave him three Advil.

"I just didn't want to come out," Harris said. "I wanted to help win this championship. I just said I can deal with two or three hours of this and stay out the way a little bit. From that point, it was mind over matter."

Harris, who came to LSU in 1997 as a pitcher, also had to adjust his throws and hope he didn't have to throw to the plate or to third.

"I used the bottom two fingers and basically threw changeups," he said. "Just anything to stay in the game. I was like, 'Two more hours, and I'm good.'"

Harris also kept it secret just how bad his fingers were.

"I knew they were broken, but nobody else did," he said. "And I made it a point to not tell anybody. If they knew two fingers were broken, they might take me out. I couldn't bend them at all, but I wasn't coming out of that game. And whatever they had in that medical box, I was going to use it."

On the other hand, Harris was also still dealing with the same hamate bone surgery in his left wrist that Warren Morris healed from four years earlier in time to hit his walk-off home run that beat Miami in the championship game.

Harris had the hamate surgery shortly after suffering his injury on March 4 at Central Florida. He returned to action just four weeks later at Auburn, but he wasn't healed. He just had the trainer wrap it, and he played through it, as Morris did, by slap-hitting and bunting.

Harris and his mummy hands finished 1-for-4, but he hit two balls well to the outfield that were caught. He never left the game.

"I was still in pain from the hamate, but I definitely didn't feel it as much as the broken fingers," he said. "I just really was trying not to think about it."

Stanford took a 4-2 lead in the fourth when Craig Thompson hit a one-out grand slam to left field. Brian Tallet gave up another single, but he regrouped to retire the next two batters.

Earlier, in the third inning, a Stanford batter hit an apparent two-run home run to right field. But LSU right fielder Ray Wright jumped into the stands, full of LSU fans who had the awareness to give him room to make the catch.

By this time, even LSU's fans had one of Bertman's patented coaching acronyms down. In this case, HWA – How-to-Win Awareness. The LSU fans were paying attention and instinctually did not go for the souvenir ball as fans do so often regardless of the situation. And they helped their player win.

"Ray Wright was an infielder playing outfield because we needed him," Bertman said. "He was just an all-around athlete and a great effort player. He didn't always make plays like that, but he sure did that day. That's what it's all about."

Tallet gave up a two-out single in the fifth, but got out of the inning. Then the ninth batter singled to lead off the sixth on Tallet's 109th pitch.

Bertman looked over to Trey Hodges.

"Hey, Rutledge, get loose," he said to Hodges.

It was Bertman's way of getting Hodges ready for the moment by loosening him up mentally as well as physically. When Hodges first got to LSU in the fall of 1998, Bertman mistakenly referred to him as Trey Rutledge, a reliever on the Tigers' 1993 National Championship team.

And Bertman just kept calling Trey Hodges by Trey Rutledge's name, either by accident or design as a joke.

"It was probably the biggest moment of my life," Hodges said. "The only reason I came to LSU was to win a championship. I didn't come to LSU because I loved the purple and gold, or whatever. And what he did changed my focus. Instead of me worrying about going into this championship game, I'm thinking, *Hey, can you just get my name right?* He's brilliant."

Hodges had pitched six innings for the win over USC five days earlier and threw two-thirds of an inning two days earlier for the save against Florida State.

"My arm felt like a pile of mush," he said.

And thank goodness, the trainer had packed enough Advil.

"I never would do this, but that day it felt so bad, I took three Advil," Hodges said.

Hodges replaced Tallet and looked like mush. On his first pitch to the second batter, he balked, and the base runner on first went to second. He did get the second batter to ground out to second before the next guy popped up a bunt for the second out. But Hodges walked a batter and gave up an RBI single, and LSU was down, 5-2.

Still mushy, Hodges hit the next batter to load the bases. And the Tigers were in trouble.

The next man up hit a screaming bouncer down the third base line for what looked like a sure double. But Blair Barbier dove to his right and smothered the ball against the ground with his glove and came up firing. Hawpe caught it without a hop on a perfect stretch to end the inning.

Barbier's play was reminiscent of LSU third baseman Chris Moock's stab and throw in the eighth with a runner on third and LSU leading Wichita State 6-3 in the 1991 national championship game. If Moock doesn't make that play, it's 6-4 and the tying run comes up for the Shockers. LSU won that one, 6-3.

Naturally, Barbier had seen that play many times on the TVs in the team room.

"There was rarely regular TV on in our squad room," Barbier recalled. "It was always videos of LSU teams that won the World Series. We were constantly watching that on a loop, and you wanted to pretty much be like those guys."

While Hodges pitched lights-out after the Stanford run in the sixth, LSU's offense was dying a slow death. The Tigers had no hits since Witten's single scored Harris in the second inning for the 2-0 lead.

Stanford ace Justin Wayne took the mound to start the fifth and dealt a wicked slider. He retired the side in order, striking out a confused Mike

Fontenot looking, then got Brad Cresse swinging with three straight sliders. After walking Hawpe and hitting Barbier in the sixth as it began raining, Wayne struck out Pontiff on a slider, got Harris looking on a slider, and struck out Witten on three pitches.

LSU reverted to the bunt in the seventh, but Wright was thrown out. Then Wayne got strikeouts six and seven out of 12 on Theriot swinging and Cresse looking.

Cresse, the nation's leader in home runs with 30 and RBIs with 105, was 0-for-2 with two strikeouts and 1-for-12 for the series. Theriot was 0-for-4 at lead-off. Hawpe was 0-for-2 with two strikeouts and a walk at clean-up. Barbier was 0-for-2 with a ground out to the pitcher and another one into a double play – and growing angrier each inning.

"Those two pitchers were shoving it, and we were down," said Barbier, the team captain. "It wasn't real rowdy in the dugout like it normally was. There wasn't a lot of energy. The day was gloomy. And I just couldn't take it anymore. I didn't want to be on the first team that lost a championship game under Skip."

And Barbier called everybody up on the edge of the dugout as the Tigers prepared to bat in the bottom of the eighth, down 5-2. They had never trailed by so many so late in an Omaha championship game.

Barbier was taking "ownership," a term that football coach Nick Saban introduced at his introductory press conference the previous November. But Bertman had been preaching it for decades.

Barbier was on the steps with fellow senior Jeremy Witten slightly above everyone else. Only Barbier was talking like the former high school quarterback he was.

"I laid into them," Barbier said. "It was expletive-filled. 'We need to get up now. Quit feeling sorry for yourselves. We're playing for the national championship, and *this* is the game we're going to be ho-hum?'"

No one said anything.

"I was literally yelling at them," Barbier said. "I could see, though, that it was not that we didn't want it. We just couldn't grasp the momentum. I said, 'Look, we're still in the game. We need to show up and go for it.'"

Then Barbier realized he was on deck. And Hawpe popped up to the catcher on a full count to start the inning. Stanford was five outs away from becoming just the second opponent to hold LSU to two runs or less over the previous 39 games.

"I didn't even have my right glove on," Barbier recalled. "And then, before I looked up, it was 1 and 2."

Barbier had taken a ball and fouled two pitches hard down the third base line.

"I stepped out of the box, thinking to myself, *You just yelled at them like that, and now you're going to strike out on four pitches? You need to pick your ass up,*" Barbier said. "I gave myself the same speech I just gave them. I was really motivated, because the last thing I could do was strike out after saying that."

Barbier fouled two more down the third base line. Then he launched one to left field, 325 feet, but it was foul, just as he had done in the sixth. He took a ball for a 2-and-2 count.

"The LSU fans are just desperate for something to cheer here in the eighth inning," said CBS' Greg Gumbel, who, like Barbier, was born in New Orleans.

Barbier fouled one back and dug in for the eighth pitch of the at-bat. Up to this point, he had seen only fastballs or sliders.

Then Wayne threw a changeup for the first time all day. It was low, but across the middle of the plate.

"And it tailed right into me," said Barbier, who went down a tad to get it.

"I liked it low. Up here, I couldn't really handle it," he said, pointing to his mid-section. "Down low, I could really get good rips off."

And it was gone. It cleared the 332-foot sign in left field, just fair, cutting Stanford's lead to 5-3 and giving LSU its first hit since the second inning.

"It was super-emotional when I got to home," Barbier said of his ninth home run of the season – the 46th of his career.

Pontiff then walked on a full count. After Harris and his broken fingers and hurting wrist flew out to right, eighth batter Jeremy Witten stepped up, hitting only .154 so far in Omaha.

Wayne left a 1-and-2 slider up a little, and Witten crushed it over the 360 sign in left-center to a wild bunch of LSU fans. Witten rounded third and signaled No. 1 with his seventh homer of the season and 20th of his career. And Rosenblatt – Alex Box Northwest – exploded.

"When Witten hit his, I'll never forget that feeling," Barbier said.

"Once Witten hit that two-run home run to tie it, it was over," Cresse said.

Wright hit a hard liner to left, but it was caught.

"So, all that happens, and we went from feeling sorry for ourselves to like we're the '27 Yankees!" Barbier said.

Amazingly, Bertman had, in a way, already called Witten's shot and Barbier's. At the press conference the Friday before the game, he foretold the future again.

"When you're here in Omaha and playing for the national championship, you don't go up and check-swing," he said. "You get up and you whale at it. Anything can happen. If it's your turn, you'll win. We don't get many home runs out of somebody like Jeremy Witten, but he could hit two tomorrow."

Bertman said the same thing to his team just before the game and instead of closing with his usual, "Let's play like a champion today," he fired, "Let's be a champion today."

The players erupted from the huddle.

"It was the best speech I ever heard," pitching coach Dan Canevari said. "I loved the part, 'You don't come to Omaha to check-swing or be tentative and hold at third.'"

Hodges was still hearing the speech and feeling his Advils in the top of the ninth as he retired the side on 12 pitches in a five, four, three countdown.

"I was almost like possessed at that point," he said.

Hodges struck out one batter on five pitches, got another on four with a shallow fly to right, and got another on three pitches with a fly to Harris in center.

Hodges worked extremely fast in between pitches for what was a five-minute inning.

"It was just the adrenaline, the focus, and almost that feeling of invincibility," Hodges said. "I don't know how, but I probably could've pitched another five innings. Maybe the Advil kicked in."

Hodges ended up winning his second game in the CWS to go with a save and was named the MVP. Not bad for part of a rehab season as he finished 5-2 with two saves and a 5.25 ERA.

"To end up in the situation I ended up – how fortunate, how blessed, how lucky," Hodges said. "It's almost like things are out of your control."

The Advil, meanwhile, was wearing off Harris' broken fingers fast.

"They were throbbing bad," he said. "Trey and I were walking wounded, man, but we could smell that victory."

It was time for the bottom of the ninth, and Barbier picked up his speech where he left off in the eighth.

"Do you believe?" he asked players one by one in the dugout. "That was the shortest speech ever. Just a quick look at everybody," Barbier said.

"He'd just made the rah-rah speech, then backed it up with a home run," Cresse said, laughing. "If you can't believe after that, then what are you doing?"

Bertman had also predicted on Friday what was about to happen here.

"Don't worry if you don't do well on your first two or three at-bats," he said at the press conference. "But make sure you get that last one. And you don't stop at third. You're here to score and win it."

Theriot was 0-for-4, but he singled on the first pitch, between third and shortstop, bringing up Fontenot.

CBS analyst Jerry Kindall, a former Arizona baseball coach, said it was an obvious bunting situation. But he didn't know LSU. Fontenot, who had one sacrifice bunt in 292 at-bats on the season, was whaling away and eventually drew a walk, which was like a bunt but without the sacrifice.

"Skip always said in Omaha, 'We didn't come here to play it safe,'" Barbier said.

This brought up Cresse – 1-for-12 in Omaha with eight strikeouts.

One of the sports psychologists Bertman had used during the regular season had called Barbier and Cresse's hotel room the night before to talk to Cresse. Barbier answered, but Cresse refused the call.

Cresse already had his own sports psychologist with a concentration on visualization: Skip Bertman.

"He preached that all the time," Cresse said. "Close your eyes and put yourself in the moment. We had seen so many reps of that. Visualizing the pitch, visualizing the moment. I went to bed envisioning getting in the batter's box in that moment with the crowd roaring, the game on the line. I envisioned hitting a homer."

Barbier was standing near Bertman in the dugout.

"We're going to bunt him here, right?" he asked Bertman.

"Oh, good one," Bertman said and cracked up laughing.

Brad Cresse had exactly one sacrifice bunt in four seasons at LSU as he stepped up to the plate. The bunt sign was not on. He took the first pitch for a strike, then laced the next one by the shortstop to left field for a walk-off RBI single – if Theriot could score, that is.

Theriot was just stepping on third when the Stanford player fielded Cresse's hit in left field, but it would take a great throw to the plate to get the speedy Theriot. There was no stop sign at third, but it didn't matter. Theriot wasn't going to hold up anyway.

The throw was far to the right of home plate, and a sliding Theriot scored easily for the 6-5 win – and Bertman's fifth national title in 10 years.

* * * * *

LSU's players were already on the field as Theriot scored because of the "Hold the rope" belief system. There was no waiting to see if he scored. They knew it would happen. They had already seen it.

"In the dugout, we knew," Barbier said. "If the ball made it through, they would have to throw Ryan out. Good luck with that. Everybody in the dugout was up, and knew he was coming. And I will tell you this, none of the coaches and nobody on the team was worried whether Brad Cresse was going to show up that day or not after his slump."

The rest of the team held the rope until Cresse could.

"We knew he'd eventually come through," Barbier said.

Just like Bertman said, it wasn't how Cresse did on his first three at-bats. It was "that last one."

This amazed Stanford's pitcher.

"Cresse didn't really seem to have an idea what was going on with my sliders," Justin Wayne said. "Then all of a sudden, he does."

Then Theriot got up and, as if on cue, tossed his helmet – in similar fashion to Armando Rios' toss in the 1993 World Series after scoring the winning run in the bottom of the ninth on Todd Walker's single to beat Long Beach State, also 6-5. (That win put LSU in the national title game, where the Tigers beat Wichita State, 8-0.)

"I try not to exaggerate, but I saw that Armando Rios play at least 50 times," Theriot said. "Just in different clips and highlight videos LSU would put together. That was always one of the clips. And I saw it when it happened on TV when I was 12. So, all that stuff played into that moment, tossing the helmet."

"Be the star of your own movie," Bertman always said.

"I didn't plan it. It's not something you think about at all," Theriot said.

At least not consciously.

"It just happened. It was one of those deals, man. You've seen it so much," Theriot added.

He had already seen it in his mind's eye.

"I visualized Brad getting a hit in the ninth," Bertman said. "It's a belief system. It's real important. This stuff really works."

Another thing that really matters in baseball is tenacity.

"They just won't give up," Bertman said. "Of all the national championships, this is the best one."

Chapter 14

2001: A Skip odyssey
The final season

"Anyone who's ever been to Omaha would die to get back there. Once you experience the magic there – just the way the grass smells, the way the dirt plays, and the 25,000 every day – it becomes a part of your being, a part of your soul. And you'd give anything to get back there."

– Wally Pontiff on June 3, 2001, after LSU failed to return to Omaha
because of a 7-1 Super Regional final loss to Tulane

And then it's all over.

"We were a great team in 2000," senior catcher Brad Cresse said. "That was really apparent in the locker room after the championship game, seeing not only me but all the guys in tears – in ecstasy."

That feeling flowed on at Barrett's Barleycorn Pub & Grill in Omaha – the official LSU party spot before, during, after, and long after national championships.

"I remember going to Barrett's and having a bottle of champagne, probably up to the ceiling," said Cresse, who delivered a walk-off single for the 6-5 win over Stanford that afternoon and Skip Bertman's fifth and final national title.

"We all had a sip from it. And we were all there together celebrating. That's the sad part of baseball, though. Everything ends suddenly," Cresse said.

This was Cresse's second title in four years, the first being in '97 when he was a freshman.

"Guys were getting drafted, returning to college, going to Cape Cod or Alaska for summer ball, so you really just had that night," Cresse said. "For some of us that was the culmination of our college careers – we got that night at Barrett's. I wish it could've been a month or two."

Then there was the plane ride home and the celebration at LSU.

"We still keep in touch, but it was never the same," Cresse said. "We go from being together seven days a week for nine months to celebrating, and the next day you're all over the place. It was an exciting time to be going to pro ball, but it was extremely sad in another respect. I get teary-eyed sitting here talking about it 20 years later."

Bertman spent part of that last night in Omaha with his wife Sandy and four daughters, Jan, Jodi, Lisa and Lori. They watched a replay of the game at the Omaha Marriott restaurant bar. During the game, he waved to granddaughter

Sophie Guirard (Lori's daughter) in the crowd.

"We'd like to spend more time traveling and seeing our children," Sandy said as they left. "Sometimes I think I'm getting too old for this, but I'll let him decide whenever. We're all together here."

The whole family often reunited in Omaha – sort of a summer Christmas. They were all there in 1996 when Jodi, who operated the Grand Slam batting cages in Baton Rouge, delivered a new bat to World Series hero Warren Morris.

"I'd be just as happy if he stayed for 10 more years," Sandy said. "I love it. I love it. It never gets old."

And Skip loved that last championship team.

"It was the tightest unit of any team and a lot of fun to be around," said pitching coach Dan Canevari.

"What if I get another bunch like this? How do you walk away from this? I wouldn't want to miss this," Bertman said. "And it was an easy year, too. We had very few problems."

But three weeks later, on July 6, the Baton Rouge *Advocate* broke the story that the 2001 season would be Bertman's last and that former assistant Ray "Smoke" Laval would leave the Louisiana-Monroe head coaching job to be a coach-in-waiting assistant during Bertman's last season. Laval would take over in 2002.

To finish his career appropriately in Omaha one last time, Bertman would have to replace top pitchers Brian Tallet and Trey Hodges. And Cresse, the stud catcher who led the nation in home runs (30) and RBIs (106) in 2000 and led LSU with a .388 average.

Also gone was third baseman and 2000 title game dugout orator and team captain Blair Barbier, who hit .338. Gone were first baseman Brad Hawpe, who led the nation in doubles with 36 and hit .362, center fielder Cedrick Harris (.370) and outfielder Jeremy Witten (.343).

Eight were drafted from the 2000 national champs that June – Tallet (2nd round), Cresse (5th round), backup catcher Ryan Jorgensen (7th round), Harris (10th round), Hawpe (11th round), pitcher Heath McMurray (12th round), Hodges (17th round) and pitcher Billy Brian (25th round). Barbier signed with the Chicago Cubs organization. Tallet, Jorgensen, Hawpe and Hodges would reach Major League Baseball.

The 2001 team would struggle to find the camaraderie of the 2000 team, but it did return top position starters such as junior shortstop Ryan Theriot, who was voted team captain; sophomore second baseman Mike Fontenot; sophomore Wally Pontiff, who moved from the outfield and designated hitter to third base; and outfielders Ray Wright, a senior, and Dave Raymer, a junior. Reserves Johnnie Thibodeaux, a senior, and junior Victor Brumfield were back and easily could've been starters elsewhere.

Experienced pitchers who decided to put off pro ball were back: closer Weylin Guidry, Bo Pettit, Shane Youman, Tim Nugent, Jason Scobie and Billy Brian.

And recruiting ace Turtle Thomas had been recruiting from coast to coast. He pulled in two switch-hitting transfers with power: outfielder Todd Linden from the University of Washington and catcher Matt Heath from the Florida Gators. And he nabbed three more strong hitters from junior college: outfielder Sean Barker and first baseman Zeph Zinsman from California and first baseman Bryan Moore from Florida. Another Californian was shortstop Aaron Hill, one of the nation's top prep recruits, who would be an outfielder/designated hitter and a freshman All-American.

Bertman himself recruited left-handed pitcher Lane Mestepey from Central Private High near Baton Rouge. Mestepey had attended Bertman's off-season camps while a youngster, and Bertman noticed his talent early. He would become the ace and pitch at LSU for four seasons. Canevari and Thomas recruited freshman pitcher Brian Wilson of Londonderry, N.H., and Mississippi Gulf Coast Junior College transfer Roy Corcoran. Wilson would become the closer by season's end, and Corcoran would become a vital member of the rotation.

Bertman at 62 had LSU at the height of its assembly line to Major League Baseball. Returnees to the 2001 team who would be drafted that June included Fontenot, Theriot, Scobie, Youman and Brian. Pettit and pitcher Brad David would be drafted in 2002 along with Pontiff and Pettit again in 2003.

On a typical summer night in 2001, 16 former LSU Tigers were playing in Major League ballparks – a testament to the Bertman touch from 1984 to 2001.

* * * * *

The Tigers opened the 2001 season at No. 3 in the nation by Baseball America and Collegiate Baseball and promptly went 12-2, including a 10-0 run. Everything seemed to point to a proper Skip send-off in Omaha at the College World Series.

And the season had a carnival parade and rock concert atmosphere to it as Bertman took his farewell tour – not unlike Los Angeles Laker Kareem Abdul-Jabbar's in 1989 – with sellout and record crowds home and away.

"LSU baseball was at the height of excitement in the 2001 season," said Baton Rouge business magnate Richard Lipsey, a close friend of Bertman who helped start the baseball Coaches Committee to help the program.

"We'd just won the fifth national championship. Our Coaches Committee was never stronger," Lipsey said. "I wanted Skip to keep coaching for obvious reasons, but I understood. He was ready."

Old friend and rival coach Ron Polk had retired from Mississippi State in 1997, but he came back and was in his second season as Georgia's coach.

No. 2 LSU (12-4-1) opened the SEC season there on March 9, leading the league in hitting at .356. But LSU was No. 11 in earned run average at 5.08 with 15 errors in the previous five games.

Georgia won the opener, 8-7, in 11 innings on Friday. LSU then won 5-3 in 11 innings before losing the series finale, 4-3 – also in 11 innings for the third straight time.

"Nobody's played three straight extra-inning games in the SEC," Polk said as he puffed a Honduran cigar. "No one. That's a record that will go down in infamy. And it's fitting that the last three games of me and Skip went down like that."

Bertman, the still engaged rock star, and his No. 2 Tigers (25-9-1) helped set the Louisiana record for attendance at an outdoor baseball game on April 11 in a 7-6 loss to No. 16 Tulane at Zephyr Field in Metairie in front of 11,669. Tulane had already beaten LSU previously that season, 13-3, at the Box. The Tigers would hear more from the Wave, which was coach Rick Jones' best team yet and was standing at 29-7.

For the series opener against Ole Miss at Alex Box on April 13, new Ole Miss coach Mike Bianco went all out. He had to. He was Bertman's catcher at LSU in 1988 and '89 and an assistant for national titles in 1993, '96 and '97. LSU teammate Pete Bush told him he'd better bring his A-game.

"This is his Kareem tour," Bush told Bianco, who had nothing special planned as he was engrossed in the series for first place between No. 2 LSU (25-10-1, 10-5 SEC) and No. 18 Ole Miss (26-10-1, 10-5 SEC).

"It's bad enough, you've got to go to Alex Box Stadium and play the Tigers," Bianco would say 20 years later. "And you've got to play Skip Bertman. But now, you've got to give this big speech beforehand. I told my team, 'Hey listen, I'm about to say a lot of really nice things about this man, and I mean all of it. But we're still here to kick their butts.' I was so nervous."

Then Bianco's team gifted Bertman with a 15-2 LSU victory before 8,413 – the second-largest crowd in Alex Box history. Ole Miss won game two, 23-10, scoring the most runs by an opponent in the history of Alex Box (built in 1938). But LSU took the series with a 6-3 win on Sunday, regaining first place in the SEC at 12-6.

* * * * *

The Skip Farewell Tour flamed out temporarily somewhere near Bunkie, La., on Interstate 49 three days later because the bus to Northwestern State in Natchitoches broke down. So, if you happened to be driving on that afternoon of April 18, you may have seen a man in full LSU uniform navigating the deep brush between highways. That was Bertman, and his No. 2 team was stuck in the bus playing cards, watching movies and yelling, "Watch out for snakes, coach."

Another bus picked up the team and got it to Natchitoches in time for the 7 p.m. first pitch. But Bertman had a speaking engagement at 5 on campus. More than 300 fans had paid $50 apiece to hear the five-time national champion legend.

So, Northwestern State coach John Cohen made the 90-minute drive down to Bunkie. Following Bertman's directions, Cohen pulled over on the I-49 shoulder after passing an exit by about 300 yards.

"I'm just sitting there, man," Cohen said 20 years later. "I'm looking for the bus across the median, which is wide and deep. It's not drivable. The grass is higher than your car. And here comes Skip. He's got a coat under one arm, a briefcase under the other. And he's walking across, high-stepping."

The speed limit was 70, but Cohen noticed people fully stopping as they noticed Bertman.

"And they're doing this double take. 'Hey, that looks like Skip Bertman. That *is* Skip Bertman,'" Cohen said.

Bertman tried to clean his shoes and boarded Cohen's vehicle, which Cohen backed up 300 yards on the interstate to the previous exit, saving 20 to 30 minutes. And they made it to Natchitoches by happy hour for the speaking engagement.

"And, of course, he was great," Cohen said. "The fieldhouse was jammed with people. Skip was phenomenal. We made a lot of money off it for the program."

Then Northwestern State won, 10-8, before the largest crowd in Brown-Stroud Field history at 4,214. Skip the Rock Star left them all happy.

"It was a day I'll never forget from start to finish," Cohen said. "Skip didn't have to do that. He didn't have to bring his team here, but he's a great ambassador for baseball in this state and in the country."

It was a day Bertman would never forget, either. It wasn't his first bus breakdown.

"Bus rides are what made me an athletic director," he said. "It'll get people out of coaching."

With a better tour bus, LSU started rolling again and won eight straight from April 21 to May 1 to reach No. 1 in the nation in the ESPN coaches' poll. The Tigers (36-13-1) were alone in first place in the SEC at 17-7 after their first three-game sweep at Alabama since 1988.

Lane Mestepey was masterful in the opener in Tuscaloosa in a complete-game, four-hit, 4-2 victory to go to 8-1 on the season with six strikeouts in front of 6,190 – the largest crowd of the season at Sewell-Thomas Stadium.

Before the second game, Alabama coach Jim Wells – an LSU assistant from 1987 to 1989 – gave Bertman a bottle of Crown Royal and an Alabama No. 1 jersey encased in glass with a memorable inscription:

"To Skip Bertman, you're simply the best. The best there ever was. The best there'll ever be."

Wells went on to compare Bertman to former Alabama football coach Bear Bryant, who won six national championships, and to UCLA basketball coach John Wooden, who won 10 in 12 years.

"I've learned a lot from him," Wells said. "Every pitch counts. Everything counts."

Wells got tossed from the game in the fifth inning after pitcher Mark Carter hit – some say intentionally – LSU batter Bryan Moore. Carter said he was angry about LSU's previous batter, Todd Linden, showboating after a home run when he flipped the bat and pointed. Both teams rushed the field.

That day, Linden became the first LSU batter in history to hit home runs from both sides of the plate in an 8-7 win.

LSU was on fire. Before a 12-1 win at the University of New Orleans two days later, former UNO athletic director and baseball coach Ron Maestri gave Bertman a $750 crystal cup for what he did for college baseball in Louisiana. It was a classy gesture by Maestri, who was the first coach to take a Louisiana team to Omaha when his Privateers reached the CWS in 1984 – the year of Bertman's first season at LSU.

*   *   *   *   *

Bertman was on the verge of his first SEC title since 1997 as the Tigers headed to Fayetteville with Arkansas last in the West at 8-16 and 24-26 overall. Razorbacks' coach Norm DeBriyn gave Bertman a plastic Hog hat before Friday's game.

It was a practical gift for Bertman as the sky would soon be falling.

Then someone left another gift on the dugout Sunday: a broom. Arkansas swept LSU, 8-1, 5-4 and 4-3 as the Tigers committed five errors and fell from No. 1 to No. 7 in the ESPN poll and to eighth and ninth in the other polls. LSU had not been swept in three games in the SEC since 1996 at Florida.

The Tigers regrouped and beat a mediocre Auburn team, 20-5, in the opener of Bertman's last home regular season series. It was a great night all the way around. Before the game at home plate in front of 7,885, LSU's assistant coaches gave Bertman tickets for a Caribbean cruise.

"Our league is so much better because of Skip," Auburn coach Steve Renfroe said. "And the rest of the country is trying to catch up. There are stadiums popping up everywhere. His legacy will not only be the five national championships. It's going to be the total package."

But LSU proceeded to lose the next two, 7-5 and 9-7, to a team that finished 15-15 in the SEC for eighth. LSU committed another five errors on the weekend for an anticlimactic last regular season hurrah by Bertman. Then he rode off into the sunset with Sandy on Sunday in the beautiful 1957 Chevy Bel Air convertible used in the movie "Everybody's All-American," which was filmed at LSU in 1988.

But LSU was running on empty with five losses in six games and fell from first to third in the SEC with Ron Polk's Georgia Bulldogs winning the league.

LSU regrouped to reach the SEC Tournament title game before falling to Mississippi State, 4-1, on just four hits. But the regular season slide was too damaging, and LSU was not awarded a top eight national seed, which meant no home Super Regional should the top seeds advance.

After winning the NCAA Regional at home, LSU (43-20-1) had to venture to Zephyr Field in Metairie to play No. 5 national seed Tulane (53-10) in a best-of-three Super Regional.

"We didn't host because we got swept at Arkansas," Bertman said. "If we had beaten Arkansas, we might have had it."

But suddenly, it was clear this team did not have it.

"We had some dudes, but in order to win it takes more than that," Theriot explained years later. "A team has to gel and create a winning culture: Never say die! It just didn't happen – the locker room chemistry and makeup. Major League general managers scout character and makeup."

Theriot would know. After parts of five seasons in the minors, the third-round pick of the Cubs in '01 would play in the Majors for eight years on four teams, including two World Series champions.

After scoring the winning run in the 2000 national title game for LSU, he would help the St. Louis Cardinals win the World Series in 2011 by hitting .271 with 47 RBIs. Then he would sign a one-year contract in 2012 with San Francisco, where he would win another World Series in remarkably similar fashion to LSU's 2000 title as he scored the go-ahead run in the final game to beat Detroit.

"I didn't think about that until somebody said I scored the winning run for LSU in the World Series, too. I said, 'Wow, that's cool,'" the three-ringed Theriot said. "But I do remember thinking, 'It takes more than great players to win it all.' 2001 was just different. Blair Barbier wasn't there anymore. And Cedrick Harris wasn't there. And Cresse, Hawpe, Hodges and Tallet weren't there. The list goes on. We were super-talented in '01, but I didn't like the vibe. Neither did Skip."

Bertman saw it happening before it happened, as usual. There were too many transfers and not enough Barbiers.

"There are a lot of great players that I had, but they weren't always competitive," Bertman said in a 2021 interview. "That kind of stuff means a lot to me. Those guys – winning every pitch meant something to them. Guys like Mike Sirotka, Chad Ogea, Brett Laxton and Blair Barbier. Every pitch meant something. Every at-bat meant something to Barbier. He didn't give any away."

Bertman may have said it best after a home, three-game sweep of Florida on March 18 that followed a 1-4 slump, including the first-ever loss to cross-town Southern, 11-6.

"We have a Forrest Gump team," he said. "You know, a box of chocolates. We never know what we're going to get."

* * * * *

In the opener, LSU got a classic, 4-3 win in 13 innings over Tulane before 11,719 – the largest crowd ever in Louisiana at an outdoor baseball game. A sacrifice fly by David Raymer in the top of the 13th put LSU ahead for good.

Freshman closer Brian Wilson shut out Tulane in the 11th, 12th and 13th for the win on three hits and a walk with two strikeouts. (Wilson would be picked by San Francisco in 2003, and he became Bertman's 20th of 21 pitchers to reach the Majors from 1987 to 2006. The heavy-bearded Wilson would become the MLB saves leader in 2010, contributing to the Giants' first World Series title since 1954.)

Freshman starter Lane Mestepey was another hero as he threw a career-high 10 innings, allowing three runs on 11 hits with but one walk and six strikeouts. Tulane reliever Barth Melius also dazzled with eight strikeouts in seven innings of relief around six hits and two runs in taking the loss to fall to 10-2.

Wally Pontiff, who had been teammates with Melius at Jesuit High in New Orleans, hit an RBI single in the seventh off him to tie the game 3-3.

"It's hard to imagine something like that until you're actually out there. It was an incredible game," Melius said.

"It was a marvelous game," Bertman said. "We battled and battled."

And the Tigers were one win away from a return to Omaha. But the dramatic, breathtaking, exhausting win over Tulane before a fitting record-breaking Louisiana crowd would be Bertman's last – No. 870.

The "Forrest Gump" team just up and stopped running the next day and the next, and a spent LSU fell, 9-4 and 7-1.

And Tulane reached Omaha for the first time in history.

Johnnie Thibodeaux flew out to Tulane right fielder Matt Groff at 3:44 p.m., and Skip Bertman had coached his last game: No. 1,203 at LSU.

* * * * *

"He thanked us all for the wonderful years," Thibodeaux said. "He got a little emotional back there. We're going to miss him a whole lot."

Bertman still bowed out with one more record as 11,870 showed for his last stand, breaking the record of Friday that broke the previous record set by LSU and Tulane in April for largest attendance at an outdoor baseball game in Louisiana. The individual game attendances and the three-game total of

35,268 were more than any other Super Regional.

And Bertman wasn't done coaching either. He gave one more inspirational speech about Omaha to a baseball team: the one across the diamond from his.

Bertman approached Tulane coach Rick Jones, who had finally slayed the LSU dragon, becoming the first coach ever to beat LSU in a game that would have sent LSU to Omaha with a win. The Tigers were 11-0 in such games going back to May 25, 1986.

"Let me talk to your team," Bertman said to coach Jones.

"What?" Jones said.

"Let me talk to your team about Omaha," Bertman said.

"Sure, sure," Jones said.

And there was Bertman's No. 15 in the Green Wave's post-game huddle.

He looked at Tulane shortstop Andy Cannizaro, who finished as the Wave's leader in stolen bases with 52 and with a .395 batting average.

"Cannizaro, the bases are 90 feet apart in Omaha. You can steal just as well in Omaha or better."

He looked at Jake Geautreau, who finished with 21 home runs and 96 RBIs. "Jake, the right field fence is much shorter than this one. Take your cut, Jake."

Tulane did win a game in Omaha and would return in 2005.

"I just wanted a Louisiana team to have a chance," Bertman explained two decades later. "It stunned Tulane people."

LSU fans were stunned, too. Some of the older players, like Theriot and others, thought it might happen, but that did not soften the sting, particularly for Wally Pontiff, who delivered one of the most emotional, sincere and stirring postgame epitaphs in LSU baseball history.

"Anyone who's ever been to Omaha would die to get back there," said Pontiff, who had been once – the year before when LSU won its fifth national title under Bertman. "Once you experience that magic there, just the way the grass smells, the way the dirt plays, and the 25,000 every day, it becomes a part of your being, a part of your soul, and you'd give anything to get back there."

* * * * *

There would be LSU fans in Omaha as they had already purchased tickets and hotel rooms a year in advance, but there would be no LSU.

"When you don't get there, it feels like part of you dies a little bit," Pontiff said. "I'm dying on the inside right now, and I can't imagine not going. I don't want to go to summer ball. I want to go to Omaha."

But he would never play in Omaha again.

After telling Tulane not to check swing in Omaha and to whale at it, Bertman felt the end, too. After a few weeks off, he would take over as LSU Athletic Director, on July 1.

"I'll miss these guys and all the players," he said with watery eyes. "I'll miss you people. Yeah, I'm going to miss it."

And his voice broke.

"Yeah, there are going to be some times that will be tough," he said.

One of those happened just over a year later, on July 24, 2002, when Wally Pontiff died in his sleep at his parents' home at the age of 21 of an undetected, abnormal heart condition. This included a narrowing of the small arteries and a floppy heart valve. He had been drafted the previous June by Oakland in the 21st round.

"He was everybody's All-American," Bertman said in one of the eulogies at New Orleans' Jesuit High before a capacity crowd of 1,500 in the chapel. "How could a 21-year-old touch so many people? Because he was that kind of person. He personified perfection on and off the field. He had a perfect swing since he was 8 years old. He was a terrific student. He always gave himself up for the team. He had grace, honesty and dignity. Sleep well, we love you."

LSU lost another member of the 2000 national champions just three years later, on June 17, 2005, when Johnnie Thibodeaux died in a car crash in his hometown of Lake Charles at age 28.

On June 14, 2012, Skip and Sandy lost their daughter, Dr. Lisa Jo Pate, to cancer at age 44, leaving husband Dr. Drew Pate and sons Sam and Ezra. She had a PhD in clinical psychology from LSU and was on the faculty at Tulane and Harvard.

"When these kinds of things happen, all you have is your faith. And I need a lot of it," Bertman told LSU senior associate athletic director Verge Ausberry at the time.

Tragedy again struck Bertman's last national championship team on April 4, 2021, when center fielder Cedrick Harris' 14-year-old son, Cedrick Harris Jr., died after an accident in an all-terrain vehicle in Arkansas. Harris Sr., who played from 1997 to 2000, and his wife, former LSU women's basketball and WNBA star Marie Ferdinand, met at LSU.

"Wally, then Johnnie, Lisa Bertman, Ced Harris' son – it's devastating," catcher Brad Cresse said. "Way too young. Couldn't happen to nicer people. God has a plan, but I don't understand."

Cresse and eight teammates from the 2000 team took a private plane to Harris' son's funeral in Arkansas. Others drove or flew. Among the former players in attendance were Blair Barbier (1997-2000), Patrick Coogan (1995-97), Brad Cresse (1997-2000), Chris Demouy (1996-98), Jamin Garidel (1998-2001), Weylin Guidry (1999-2002), Randy Keisler (1998), Jeff Leaumont (1998-99), Trey McClure (1996-99) and Doug Thompson (1997-98), as well as equipment manager Wes Penn (1996-2000).

"Some guys drove in from all over the country. It just shows the true bond," Cresse said.

Cedrick was shocked at the number of former teammates at his son's funeral.

"That was very special to me," he said. "Their support that day meant more than any championship. That was just a testimony to that team and to Skip. When I saw those guys, it really comforted me. It really helped me and Marie. Seeing those guys walk through that door and be there for me, I'll never forget it."

Cresse was nearly crying again.

"It wasn't just four years of baseball," he said. "I can't put into words what Skip built – the band of brothers. That will never change."

Chapter 15

Shifting gears:
From baseball coach to Athletic Director

"You don't understand, Skip. You're just a coach"
– LSU Athletic Director Joe Dean

Hiring and retaining the right athletic director at LSU in the 1980s proved to be anything but a boring administrative matter. And the same held true two decades later when Skip Bertman was being considered for the job.

Indeed, in the fall of 1985, *Sports Illustrated* declared on its cover that these were "Crazy days at LSU." The magazine was referring in part to the emerging story of then-Athletic Director Bob Brodhead being under pressure to resign due to alleged financial mismanagement.

Brodhead was being accused of making improper payments and incurring questionable expenses in the line of duty. Earlier, he had pleaded guilty to Federal charges of electronically eavesdropping on an NCAA investigation into LSU football. The fallout from all of this included Brodhead's resignation in the fall of 1986.

But Joe Dean came to the rescue as the new athletic director in 1987. He had been a marketing executive with Converse athletic shoes and a former LSU basketball player and SEC basketball announcer. He quickly restored credibility and fiscal responsibility to the Athletic Department. He was also friendly, open, and charismatic.

But he hired two head football coaches with questionable records from smaller-time schools, both of whom failed – Curley Hallman of Southern Mississippi after the 1990 season, and Gerry DiNardo of Vanderbilt after the 1994 season. Hallman had a losing season in 1989 at USM even with future NFL quarterback Brett Favre. And DiNardo actually was hired after his team lost 65-0 to Tennessee to finish 5-6 in 1994.

"How about that? He loses 65-0 and gets a new job," Alabama coach Gene Stallings said at the time.

In another low-light of his time as AD, Joe Dean was at the center of an embarrassing Title IX discrimination lawsuit for several years, initiated by five former LSU women's soccer and softball players in 1994. LSU would pay approximately $2.1 million to settle the case in 2001.

But near the end of Dean's term, in 1999, he was credited with an assist in one of the greatest hires in LSU history: football coach Nick Saban.

After first objecting to LSU Chancellor Mark Emmert's decision to fire DiNardo, who was 2-8 in '94, Dean helped connect Emmert to blossoming sports agent Jimmy Sexton of Memphis. One of Sexton's clients was Saban, who was coming off a breakthrough, 9-2 season in 1999 at Michigan State.

Considering Dean's failed hires of Hallman and DiNardo, Emmert took over the search for a new football coach. Working with him were Stanley Jacobs and Charles Weems from the LSU Board of Supervisors, and former Tiger Athletic Foundation president Richard Gill of the Fortune 500 Shaw Group engineering firm in Baton Rouge.

But Dean stayed involved on his own anyway.

"You had Joe Dean interviewing people over here, and Mark Emmert interviewing the real people over here," explained LSU deputy athletic director Verge Ausberry, who was with the Tiger Athletic Foundation fundraising arm at the time. "They were sending Joe out on ghost trips. Whatever Joe was saying about Mark Richt (Florida State offensive coordinator) or Phil Bennett (Kansas State defensive coordinator), Mark Emmert had a whole other agenda."

In the end, Saban was hired at the then-astronomical price of $1.2 million a year.

* * * * *

For much of the 1990s, LSU football and basketball suffered. Each had six straight losing seasons – football from 1989 to 1994 and basketball from 1993-94 through 1998-99, including the last four years of the otherwise very successful Coach Dale Brown, who retired in 1997. He had taken LSU to a school record 10 straight NCAA Tournaments from 1984 to 1993, plus to two Final Fours and two Elite Eights in the '80s.

New coach John Brady had two losing seasons to start off, but he would take LSU to the Sweet 16 in 2000 and the Final Four in 2006.

But for most of the 1990s, baseball was all that LSU fans could get excited about, as far as major sports were concerned.

"Baseball was the constant. Baseball was always the one that won and won consistently and won big. And the crowds kept getting bigger, and they kept building more on the stadium," said SEC associate commissioner Herb Vincent, who was LSU's Sports Information Director from 1988 to 2000.

"Skip's teams made up for that and gave hope," said Richard Lipsey, a Baton Rouge businessman and LSU financial supporter who became friends with Bertman shortly after he moved to Baton Rouge from Miami in 1983.

"Baseball brought morale back to LSU. The football team had six straight losing seasons. The basketball team slumped during the 1990s. But baseball gave LSU fans a sense of winning. It gave them something to look forward to."

Under Joe Dean as athletic director, Bertman won all five of his national championships, in 1991, '93, '96, '97 and 2000. But Dean often opposed Bertman on funding for enhancements and additions to Alex Box Stadium and to the program overall. That included Bertman's dream of a new Alex Box Stadium, something he would later see through as athletic director. Because of Bertman, the state-of-the-art facility opened in 2009, a block or so from the original one, with a 9,200-seat capacity, concourse sports bar and suites. By 2011 the capacity had grown to 10,326.

"You don't understand, Skip. You're just a coach," Dean would tell Bertman from time to time.

"And I'd say, 'Joe, I really do understand,'" Bertman said. "That wasn't just Joe. At the time, a lot of people would align a coach with an eighth-grade physical education teacher. See, not with a biology teacher or a college professor."

Bertman actually did teach P.E. at Miami Beach High in the 1960s and '70s, but he also keenly observed and studied as the baseball coach how LSU's Athletic Department worked – and sometimes didn't work so well.

"Skip always had a grasp on what was going on in the Athletic Department," Herb Vincent recalled. "There were a lot of times when Skip was coaching, and we'd sit and talk in the dugout for a long time after games about what was going on in the Athletic Department. Skip always had a good idea about tickets and promotions and compliance and what was going on here and there. Sometimes, he was kind of critical. We had a lot of conversations."

* * * * *

During his final years as baseball coach, Bertman occasionally expressed a desire to be LSU's Athletic Director. But originally he balked at the idea of taking the job.

This was just after rising Oregon State Athletic Director Mitch Barnhart, 41, turned down the chance to replace Dean as LSU's athletic director in December of 2000. Bertman, 62 at the time, had announced the previous summer, following his fifth national championship in 10 seasons, that 2001 would be his last season as baseball coach. At the time, he was no longer interested in being AD, or so he thought.

"I don't have enough experience," he said on Dec. 21, 2000. "There was a time when an athletic director played golf and raised money. It's a much more complex job now. You have to wear a lot of hats."

Would Bertman be *just a coach* after all?

"Skip wasn't interested in the job," said Bertman's friend Stanley Jacobs, a former member of the LSU Board of Supervisors as well as a former TAF president and Athletic Council chairman. "He said he didn't want to be an administrator."

Mitch Barnhart, who had built a reputation as a fundraiser, was hot at the time. He had long been Chancellor Emmert's first choice to replace Joe Dean, who turned 70 in 2000. Emmert wanted an experienced, sitting athletic director.

Several Board members were still miffed at Emmert for alone hiring Nick Saban and wanted to make this hire someone with strong LSU ties. They did not want an outsider like Barnhart.

The Board's preferred candidate was East Baton Rouge Parish District Attorney Doug Moreau, an extremely well-respected and personable former LSU football star. He had been a district court judge in Baton Rouge and was in his fourth decade as a color analyst on LSU football radio broadcasts. But he had no athletic department experience.

"A group of us – the old-timers on the Board – wanted an LSU person, all things being equal," Jacobs explained. "Someone who understood the culture as well as being a sharp athletic director. We thought Doug Moreau – University High in Baton Rouge, Miami Dolphins, judge, district attorney, bright, knew everything about LSU, media savvy – would be great. We weren't going to bend. And Mark wasn't going to bend either."

The Emmert-Board battle grew so intense over the summer and fall of 2000 that it scared away Barnhart, and he withdrew his name from consideration.

So, Emmert had to compromise. He targeted someone with the coveted LSU ties, but also with the athletic department experience, albeit by one degree of separation: Skip Bertman. Bertman had experience working for, with, and sometimes against LSU's Athletic Department. He knew the place inside and out – good and bad.

On Saturday, Dec. 30, 2000, Emmert, who was on a holiday trip with his family on the West Coast, called Richard Lipsey. (It was Lipsey who 19 years later would help to push out embattled LSU Athletic Director Joe Alleva and usher in Texas A&M Athletic Director Scott Woodward, who had strong LSU ties. A Baton Rouge native and LSU graduate, Woodward was Emmert's right-hand man as director of external affairs from 2000 to 2004.)

Emmert: "Richard, what do you think about Skip being the athletic director?"

Lipsey: "I think it's a wonderful idea. Skip knows how to lead people and how to hire the right people. He'd be great."

Emmert: "Let me think about it."

Lipsey then calls Stanley Jacobs.

Lipsey: "Would Skip be acceptable to the Board?"

Jacobs: "You better believe it. But I already thought of it. He's not interested."

The next day, Dec. 31, 2000, Emmert calls Lipsey again.

Emmert: "I'm in Dallas on the way home. I've made a decision. It ought to be Skip. I'm going to land in Baton Rouge at 3 p.m. Could you have Skip at your house at 4 p.m. so we can talk privately?"

Lipsey calls Bertman, who arrives at his home at 3:45 p.m.

"Mark pulled up at 4 p.m. on the dot," Lipsey recalled. "I took them to my library and closed the door. Thirty minutes later, they came out and shook hands. Skip's only reservation was he wanted to talk to his wife, Sandy. Did he really want to get back in the fire? He told Mark he'd call him."

Mrs. Bertman initially did not want Skip to take the job.

"We wound up with an excellent combination," Emmert said. "Skip has decades of experience as a college coach, has proven to be an excellent fundraiser, and knows how an athletic department works. Skip brings to the table all the purple and gold you would ever want. He is extremely visible and well-liked in the community and the state."

Before the athletic director offer, Bertman was going to see his annual salary package dip from $450,000 ($200,000 base) in his last year as baseball coach in 2001 to $150,000 a year for two years as an assistant athletic director, but with a lot of income expected from speaking tours. His new athletic director job would pay him $400,000 a year ($350,000 base). But the money was not the only reason Bertman took it.

"We said, 'We need you. Please, help us,'" Emmert recalled. "I shamelessly appealed to his understanding of how important the job was and how important LSU athletics was. I tried everything and anything to get him to say yes. Not everybody thinks that's a dream job. He had just retired and had lined up a whole bunch of speaking tours."

Bertman was impressed.

"They need me," he told friends. "And I thought I could help. There are a lot of athletic directors who don't understand coaches. I felt I understood coaches. And I knew what to do."

LSU's Board of Supervisors unanimously approved Bertman as athletic director on Jan. 19, 2001, but he wasn't present for the vote. Already multitasking, he was speaking at a previously scheduled baseball clinic in Columbus, Ohio.

"I'll be shifting gears," Bertman told the Baton Rouge *Advocate* by phone. "It's a great challenge, and I think it's something I can do for my school. I feel I understand the needs of the coaches. I think I could go four to six years. I'm looking forward to it. It's going to be fun. It could be difficult, but it can be incredibly rewarding."

Bertman already had a plan.

"I remember being at home in early December of 2000," said Bill Franques, who became LSU baseball Sports Information Director in 1989 and was still on the job in 2021.

And the phone rang.

"Bill, I'm coming by to pick you up. We've got to go to the office. I need a media guide from every sport," Bertman told him.

"He hadn't been announced as athletic director yet, but he wanted to research and learn every sport – the coachs' bios, the athletes, the history of the programs," Franques said. "Even then, he was preparing himself to be AD. I thought that was pretty significant."

Bertman wanted to learn his new roster.

"The first thing I'm going to do is talk to every coach and every administrator I can and find out where they're at and what their needs are," he said. "Then I'll come up with a list of priorities."

Bertman would not begin that process until July of 2001. He still had to coach his baseball team for one more season, and he had a talented team with which to defend his fifth national championship.

In the meantime, Emmert and company began assembling the makings of an all-star team for Bertman, the AD.

• There was **Scott Woodward**, an Athletic Department and State Legislature liaison as LSU's Director of External Affairs. (He would become the University of Washington's athletic director in 2008 and Texas A&M's athletic director in 2016 before coming to LSU as AD in 2019.)

• There was **Jerry Baudin**, who was LSU's Vice Chancellor of Finance before becoming interim athletic director in December of 2000 to ease Bertman in.

• There was associate athletic director for business **Mark Ewing**, who also came over from the university, where he was the budget director for the entire LSU campus.

Bertman, with the help of Woodward and Baudin, soon began putting his own athletic director team together while still coaching his baseball team. Often, Bertman would be at his desk at Alex Box meeting with various LSU officials by day. And by night, he would switch the tie for the cap and become baseball coach.

In May of 2001, Bertman tapped American University Athletic Director **Dan Radakovich**, a former South Carolina associate athletic director who got his MBA degree at Miami while Bertman was there. Radakovich became Bertman's top assistant as senior associate athletic director.

In August, Bertman and company hired two more associate athletic directors in Texas Women's University Athletic Director **Judy Southard**, a former women's basketball coach at Marshall, and **Verge Ausberry**, a former LSU linebacker from New Iberia who had worked at the Tiger Athletic Foundation and at LSU's Academic Center for Athletes.

"Jerry Baudin and I and some other people made sure that Skip had a good team around him," Woodward said. "Verge was one of the key persons to come in and really help. Dan Radakovich and Mark Ewing were great in the transition process. And so, we had the waterfront covered. Verge understood the place. Radakovich understood athletic departments. Baudin understood higher education finance as well as anyone I've ever been around. And Mark Ewing understood budgets as well as anyone on campus."

In the summer of 2002, Bertman hired an associate athletic director of communications in **Herb Vincent**, one of the very best sports information directors in the nation.

In December of 2003, Bertman and company hired **Chris Howard** from the NCAA's enforcement division to be LSU's associate director for compliance. He replaced **Bo Bahnsen**, who was promoted to Associate Athletic Director for Internal Relations. Bertman also hired **Eddie Nunez** in 2003 as Assistant Athletic Director for Game and Event Management from the same job at Vanderbilt.

"We were all polished to be executives and administrators," Ausberry said. "But Skip taught us people skills."

LSU needed all the teamwork it could muster and all the leadership Bertman had to offer as soon as he officially took over in the summer of 2001 after narrowly missing a 12th trip to Omaha.

The athletic facility arms race had dawned in the 1990s, and LSU was late to the game.

But Skip Bertman would be calling the pitches now and making them.

Chapter 16

Athletic Director,
but still hawking tickets

*"We're going to put in a seating licensing plan,
and they're going to fire me."*

– Skip Bertman to Herb Vincent in 2002, while trying to hire him
away from a sports cable company in Birmingham to work for LSU

I t wasn't the bottom of the ninth, but the late innings were upon LSU in early 2003 when it finally decided to enter the athletic facilities arms race with a ticket licensing program. It was all the rage with virtually all the other major college sports programs around the country.

"We were so far behind. We were an outlier," LSU's Athletic Director Scott Woodward said in a 2020 interview. Previously, from 2000 to 2004, Woodward was Chancellor Mark Emmert's right-hand man as his director of external affairs.

Former Athletic Director Joe Dean had a history of resisting ticket price increases. And he was not in favor of the ticket licensing programs, known as PSLs (Personal Seat Licenses), that were being used throughout pro sports and beginning to spread through college football. Fans had to pay hundreds or thousands of dollars up front just for "the right to buy tickets."

"What Skip did was he recognized the top programs in the SEC had something in common," said former LSU Board of Supervisors member Stanley Jacobs. "They spend money, they price-scale their stadiums, and they put a surcharge – or fee – on the tickets. Skip came to me with the idea."

Jacobs did not think it would work.

"Skip, you're telling me that you're going to put people out who had great tickets who have been supporting LSU forever? You're going to take their tickets away and put them in the end zone? And he says, 'That's the only way it can be done. It's an economic war if you want to compete,'" Jacobs recalled.

It was time for LSU to join the financial fray whether LSU's largely old-school fan base wanted to or not. And Bertman was the pitchman.

"A lot of people had had season tickets for 50 or 60 years," Bertman pointed out. "The older people said, 'You can't do this.'"

When fans got too old to go to the games, the rules said they could pass the tickets only to their heirs.

"It was like something out of Shakespeare," Bertman laughed. "It was unreal. Only a direct heir could take the throne and get the tickets! There were some families that had like 10 or 20 season tickets for decades."

It was clear that Berman and his staff had to come up with a plan to take most of the pain out of this transition.

Bertman may have been 63 when he took over as Athletic Director in 2001 from Joe Dean. But he was young-at-brain while Dean was old-school in his thinking.

Deputy Athletic Director Verge Ausberry explained it this way:

"Skip was old, but Skip got it because he was a coach. He knew what it took to win. And he was all about winning. And when Mark Emmert was chancellor, he wanted to win everything. That's why we had to get the ticket licensing going."

A transfer period of the precious tickets was planned for January through April of 2004 in which LSU's 45,000 season ticket holders could place their tickets under someone else's name, whether a family member or not. Those tickets not transferred or purchased would become the property of the Athletic Department and would be available for resale.

"If you wanted to give them to Fred or sell them to Fred, you could," Bertman explained. "If you wanted to keep them, keep them. That transfer period was very successful. What it did was shrink the number of tickets some people had from 22 or so to maybe 10."

In just over a year, Bertman had gone from baseball genius to ticket titan. He was no mere placeholder Athletic Director after all. By the spring of 2003, he knew nearly as much about PSLs as he did about Omaha.

"He understood the ticket licensing viscerally," NCAA president Mark Emmert said in July of 2019. It was Emmert who, as LSU's chancellor, hired Bertman as Athletic Director in December of 2000.

"He's got a great business head on his shoulders. You know the beauty of baseball coaches is they learn how to manage money – especially back then. Because they didn't have much of it back in his day like now," Emmert added.

When Bertman interviewed Herb Vincent in the summer of 2002 to hire him back to LSU from College Sports Southeast cable television in Birmingham, he wasn't talking baseball.

"As a matter of fact, he was explaining everything LSU was going to do about the tickets," Vincent recalled. "He said, 'We're going to increase the prices, and we're going to build this.' And he showed me the diagram of the new west upper deck at Tiger Stadium, and where the new baseball stadium was going to be."

But it wasn't going to be easy.

"We're going to put in a seating license plan," Bertman told Vincent. "And they're going to fire me."

Vincent took the job anyway, and he went to work with Ausberry and Associate Athletic Director Dan Radakovich.

"Those three guys plus me convinced people that we needed this," Bertman said, making it clear that this was a team sales effort.

"Herb and I did scour the countryside to figure out how we were going to sell that," Radakovich said. "At the end of the day, we made the financial case for the dollars that LSU was not getting that some of the other SEC schools were. It was a compelling case, and we were able to sell it to Skip, who sold it to TAF president Ron Richard and to Mark Emmert."

Timing is everything with Bertman, who repeatedly preached "timely hitting" when he was a coach. And he and his sales team could not have timed the public presentation of LSU's new ticket licensing plan – expertly dubbed the "Tradition Fund" – more perfectly.

Of course, hawking tickets was something he had already done on a smaller scale – like having his players stand on the corner of Nicholson Drive and South Stadium Drive (now Skip Bertman Drive) or go to LSU-Kentucky home basketball games in full baseball garb to sell baseball tickets.

"Skip just had this vision," Vincent said. "He knew things would happen before they would happen. 'This guy's going to pop out to second base,' he'd say. Or, he'd tell a player, 'You may not get a hit your first three times up. But in the eighth, oh!, something's going to happen.' Sure enough, it would. He always knew what was going to happen."

Bertman imagined Alex Box Stadium finishing No. 1 in attendance every year when he took the job in 1983. And LSU did exactly that for nearly a quarter of a century, starting in 1996.

"Even before it was filling up in the '80s, he'd want to build more stands," Vincent said. "We're like, 'What do you want to build more stands for? You're not filling the ones you've got.' Well, pretty soon, they filled up. He was always staying ahead with bigger concession stands and adding to the stadium. He just knew. Somehow, he just knew."

* * * * *

Financing the expansion of the football stadium, which had 91,600 seats in 2001, would be an even bigger challenge than growing Alex Box with its 7,760 seats.

This was beyond the reach of the baseball Coaches Committee and the Tiger Athletic Foundation. A new west upper deck for Tiger Stadium would cost $60 million. There was also a new stand-alone, Pentagon-like, football-only operations center nicknamed "Saban Land" in the works for $15 million that would connect to the indoor practice facility. And there was another $7 million needed for various other Tiger Stadium improvements and additions.

An earlier ticket licensing plan was scratched in 1999 under the previous administration because of poor marketing. So, Bertman felt he had to make this work.

The Ticket Licensing Plan was steadily worked on for 18 months by Bertman, Woodward, Radakovich, Vincent, Ausberry and others. It was unveiled at a press conference on August 13, 2003, with the season opener less than three weeks away.

"We timed it so the announcement would be right before the season," Vincent said. "That's when people are most excited about LSU football. Less time to complain, most optimistic."

It did not go over well in all circles as the new prices were staggering. And Nick Saban was coming off his worst season at LSU: 8-5 overall in 2002 with a 2-4 finish. That was disappointing following the SEC title in 2001.

The Bertman Ticket Doctrine would not go into effect until the 2004 season. The base ticket prices would rise from $32 to $36 after the 2003 season. But the required fee for the right to buy the tickets – cleverly labeled a "donation" to the Tradition Fund and packaged with an 80 percent write-off on itemized tax returns – rose from $25 or $50 to as much as $400 for sideline seats between the 25-yard lines.

Chairback seats in the new west upper deck between the 25s would cost $150 before the ticket price. Field box seats carried a $100 fee before the ticket; end zone seats and upper deck seats from the 25s and in were $85 before the ticket. The new west upper deck would also include 3,255 club-level seats, as opposed to only 807. The overall seating capacity grew from 91,600 to 92,400.

And in all, LSU expected to make $14.5 million a year on the new seating licenses – if the Board of Supervisors approved it.

"It was seen as a radical thing at first," Woodward pointed out.

"Don't forget, at that time the Board was a bunch of good ole boys," Jacobs recalled. "Tickets at those prices was a foreign concept to them. A lot of us thought it was going to be a nasty scene. But Skip educated them. 'There's a market there,' he'd say. Skip worked on it for nearly two years before he brought it to the Board. I mean, he had power point presentations. It was well organized."

Opposing the new ticket plan, LSU fan Maria Carruth spoke at the Board meeting on Aug. 21, 2003.

"The Athletic Department has lost the concept of what college athletics is all about," she said, explaining she would have to pay five times as much for her two sideline tickets in 2004 as compared with 2003, a jump from $164 to

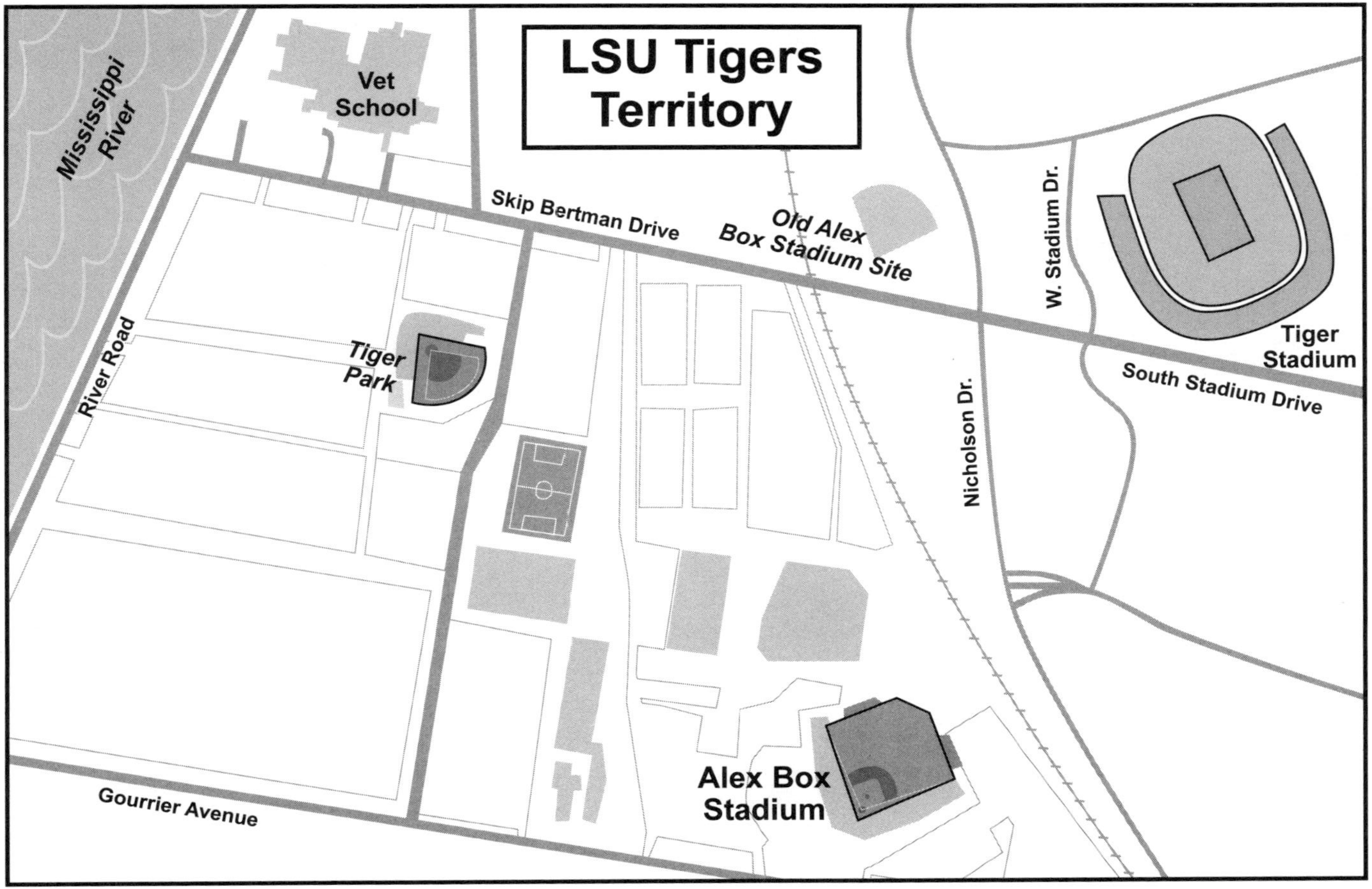

The new 9,200-seat Alex Box Stadium opened in 2009. Skip Bertman oversaw the $38 million project as Athletic Director and had been working toward it since his coaching days at LSU.

LSU Tigers Territory

Mississippi River

River Road

Gourrier Avenue

Tiger Park

Vet School

Skip Bertman Drive

Old Alex Box Stadium Site

Alex Box Stadium

Nicholson Dr.

W. Stadium Dr.

South Stadium Drive

Tiger Stadium

$872.

"According to this plan, I am becoming disenfranchised," she said. "I can't squander $800. I can't afford it."

Carruth was speaking for many fans.

"It was unpopular, no question about it," Woodward said. "But Skip was a hell of a salesman and understood it. And people trusted his vision, including everyone around him. He sold it properly. He explained it well."

He didn't get fired. Bertman, who was just three years removed from his fifth national title, saw his popularity beat the new plan's unpopularity.

"We had no shortage of challenges, but having someone with Skip's credibility was just incredibly useful because people love him. And they know he only wants the best for LSU. He made it a lot easier for all of us," Emmert said.

"Skip understood the program inside and out. That was big. He was right there with us formulating the ideas. He got it. He was committed to it. When you're committed to a cause, you become very passionate about it. Skip knew it was the right thing to do at the right time for LSU athletics," Radakovich explained.

In the end, the Board of Supervisors approved the Tradition Fund ticket plan, 15-1.

* * * * *

On Aug. 30, 2003, LSU opened the football season with a 49-7 win over Louisiana-Monroe. It finished 13-1, took the SEC at 7-1, and won its first National Championship in football since 1958.

"Winning has a good way of curing a ticket price increase," Woodward said. "It was like we kept waiting for this uproar about the ticket licensing, and it never happened because everyone was so elated about LSU winning a National Championship. Good timing. I remember thinking, 'Oh boy, this is beautiful.'"

Good thing they didn't try to push it through the year before. LSU was shut out for the first time since 1996 - 31-0 at home to Alabama. And the Tigers dropped the Cotton Bowl to Texas, 35-20, to finish 8-5.

"It was announced in August of 2003. The team wins the National Championship the following January. And the invoices go out two weeks after the game," Radakovich said. "That sure didn't hurt."

Summing up the impact of the Bertman Ticket Doctrine on LSU sports in general, Stanley Jacobs put it this way:

"Skip's ticket plan is what brought us into the 21st century."

* * * * *

Though Bertman was a detail person to the max, he was a big believer in delegation of tasks and responsibilities to those who worked under him.

"He'd often say, 'I've known you for a long time. You've known me. You know how I work. I trust you to do the job. You don't have to check with me on everything. You know what I like. If you do something wrong, I'll let you know. But I trust you to make decisions,'" recalled Herb Vincent, an associate athletic director under Bertman.

Bertman continued to come up with his own ideas as well. As he did when he was baseball coach, Bertman started scheduling the football team against in-state opponents – which had been considered taboo for decades.

Under Bertman, LSU played Louisiana-Lafayette in 2002 for the first time since 1938. The Tigers played Louisiana Tech in 2003 for the first time since 1941, and Louisiana-Monroe in 2003 for the first time ever.

"It was a waste of money to pay hundreds of thousands of dollars to bring a small school in here from far away when we can bring in a better team from right next door," Bertman reasoned. "More of the fans from in-state schools will come to the game. It's great for them and for us. We keep the money in the state, and we can showcase our stadium and campus to people from Louisiana."

* * * * *

Radakovich remembers another shrewd strategy of Bertman's that parked more dollars in the Athletic Department's lot. Where some athletic directors saw parking for huge motor homes and recreational vehicles (RVs) as a headache, Bertman saw dollar signs.

"Skip just loved parking," Radakovich mused. "And he really liked motor home parking. That was such a big deal for him."

Bertman figured that fans with huge vehicles had large discretionary income. So, he planned to give them the choicest parking spots on Tiger Stadium's south side at a hefty price.

He wanted to more than triple the price of RV parking, from $1,500 a year to $5,000. But instead of just shoving it down the big-ride folks' throats, Bertman invited a couple dozen ticketholders who had RV parking spots to a meeting with him, Radakovich, Ausberry and Vincent. This was so that he could explain the plan.

"He's giving a little talk, and everybody starts getting a little restless about a price hike," Radakovich recalled.

And then Bertman points at Radakovich, Ausberry, and Vincent.

"These guys want to charge you $10,000 to park," he says as he raises both hands to show 10. "*Ten thousand dollars. Ten!*"

Bertman pauses and lowers his voice.

"But you're my people, and I'm going to charge you *five* thousand."

And Bertman gets a standing ovation from a group of people who would leave the building with $3,500 less than they had when they came in.

After the meeting, Radakovich and Ausberry and Vincent walked up to Bertman and spoke in unison:

"What the hell are you doing?"

Bertman just smiled.

"Learn. Learn from that, grasshoppers," he said like Master Po in the *Kung Fu* television series of the 1970s.

They had just witnessed Bertman Economics 101.

* * * * *

Bertman knew about "fan experience" before it was a corporate marketing buzzword. He routinely sent Athletic Department employees to other SEC schools to see how they worked as far as ticket sales and game management.

"He always said, 'We're the Walmart employees,'" Ausberry recalled. "You take any call no matter how good or bad. You say, 'Yes sir. No sir.' If they're complaining about their hot dogs being cold, you sit there and listen. You say you'll check on it. If their seats are broken, you'll fix that."

Everything mattered, particularly the little things.

"Certain items were incredibly important to him," Radakovich said. "One was customer service – making sure people got calls back, facility functions. He had just a laser focus to make sure people enjoyed their experience at your athletic events."

He was ahead of his time.

"The 'fan experience.' It's cliché now," Radakovich said. "He had that in the '90s at the old Box, and he carried it forward into his day-to-day work at the Athletic Department before it was a term. That's probably one of the bigger things I've taken from him."

Radakovich brought Bertman's philosophy with him to athletic director jobs at Georgia Tech, Clemson and Miami.

"Treat people with respect and make sure you listen," he said. "He is a great listener and just wanted to learn and understand. He liked to ask, 'Why are you thinking that way? Tell me why you're thinking that way.'"

Ausberry tries to maintain the Bertman philosophy at LSU today.

"Don't be apathetic. That's what he taught us," he said. "If you don't have the passion, then you've got a problem, and then you become immune to everything. Skip kept us motivated. We still tell Skip stories."

Chapter 17

More than 'just a coach'

"I never thought Skip was a 'reach-hire' as Athletic Director."
– LSU Athletic Director Scott Woodward

Skip Bertman played a major role in not only five National Championships, but in nine. Besides the five his baseball teams won, four others were won by coaches he hired in various sports when he was Athletic Director.

In just seven years on the job, Bertman hired four coaches who went on to win National Championships – Les Miles in football in the 2007 season, Dennis Shaver in women's outdoor track in 2008, Paul Mainieri in baseball in 2009, and Chuck Winstead in men's golf in 2015.

"You look at it across the board what we did here," said Associate Athletic Director Verge Ausberry. "We were up there every year in all sports. Coaches felt like they mattered. Skip talked to them as a coach. He knew what they were going through. At a lot of places, the administration thinks it's above coaches. Skip set out to reverse that, and he did."

Under Bertman as Athletic Director from 2001 to 2008, LSU had success in virtually all sports, which had rarely been done in the school's history. In the 2006-07 sports season, the Tigers finished with a school record 12 teams ranked in the top 25.

The football team won SEC championships in 2001 and '03 and the national title in the 2003 season under Nick Saban. After Bertman hired Les Miles from Oklahoma State as football coach in 2005, the Tigers won the National Championship again in the 2007 season; won two SEC championships, in 2007 and 2011; and had another national championship game appearance in the 2011 season before losing to Alabama and Saban.

The men's basketball program under Coach John Brady won the SEC West in 2005 and reached the NCAA Tournament, then won the overall SEC title in 2006 and reached its first Final Four in 20 years. Brady's record of 65-30 overall and 34-14 in the SEC from 2003 to 2006 was the best in the SEC over that span. But following a signficant dip over the next two seasons, Bertman fired Brady.

The baseball team reached the College World Series in 2003 and 2004 under Ray "Smoke" Laval, a former LSU assistant whom Bertman hired to replace himself. Bertman then fired Laval after a disappointing season in 2006 and hired Notre Dame coach Paul Mainieri, who reached Omaha in his second season, in 2008.

The women's basketball team reached the Elite Eight in 2003, then went to five straight Final Fours from 2004 to 2008. The last one was under Coach Van Chancellor, a four-time WNBA championship coach whom Bertman hired after the 2006-07 season. The University fired the vastly successful Pokey Chatman in 2007 because of an alleged inappropriate relationship she had with an LSU player.

The gymnastics team made it to the Super Six – equivalent to a Final Four in basketball – for the first time in 2008.

The women's track team won three straight indoor national championships from 2002 to 2004 and took outdoor national titles in 2003 and 2008. The men's track team won indoor national championships in 2001 and 2004 and an outdoor title in 2002.

Dennis Shaver, the coach for both track programs, was promoted from assistant coach to head coach by Bertman in 2004, and he won the 2008 women's outdoor national title four years later.

Shaver had the women's team ranked No. 1 for the last month of the season in March of 2020 as it prepared for the NCAA Indoor Championships in Albuquerque, N.M., as the favorite to win it all. The spread of the coronavirus (Covid-19) ended all remaining NCAA events, however. Shaver was later named the women's indoor national Coach of the Year by the U.S. Track & Field Coaches Association.

The softball team reached the College World Series in 2001 and '04 and won SEC championships in 2001, '02 and '04. The women's golf team reached NCAA postseason play in 2006 and 2008.

Bertman fired men's golf coach Greg Jones after the 2005 season and hired former LSU golfer Chuck Winstead of Ruston. Winstead went on to win LSU's first national championship in golf since 1955 in 2015. LSU's soccer team reached NCAA postseason play for the first time in 2007.

The men's tennis team reached NCAA postseason play eight times, from 2001 to 2008, while the women's team made it to the NCAA's seven times over that span. The women's swim team reached the NCAA postseason in 2001, 2002, and 2007, while the men did in 2001 and 2003.

The volleyball team's entry into NCAA play in 2005 was its first since 1992, and it repeated in 2006, '07 and '08.

"Skip's era – it was the greatest era of LSU athletics so far," Verge Ausberry said. "Nothing better. Two football championships, Final Four in men's basketball, five Final Fours in women's basketball, men and women track national championships. Baseball went to the World Series, and so did softball." *(Continued on page 193)*

*Coach Skip Bertman talks strategy on the mound
with Tim Lanier and Kevin Shipp during a 1996 game.*

Patrick Coogan pitched in the 1996 and '97 National Championship games in Omaha. He won 23 games over a 3-year period while at LSU.

Young Patrick Coogan, who aspired to be a baseball player at LSU, poses with Coach Skip Bertman during a youth baseball clinic in Baton Rouge in 1985. Patrick's dream came true.

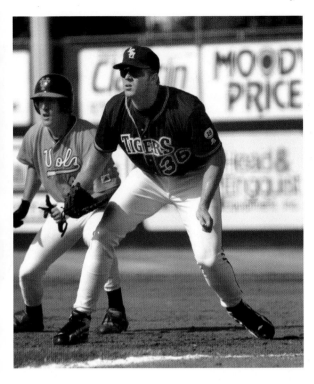

Eddy Furniss, among the best 4-year baseball players in LSU history, is one of only three players whose number has been retired at LSU.

Brandon Larson, who had arguably the best year ever of any LSU batter, hit 40 home runs in 1997, leading the Tigers to the National Championship that year.

Second baseman Warren Morris hits the game-winning home run in the bottom of the 9th inning with two outs as LSU defeats Miami for the National Championship in 1996.

Blair Barbier, one of the all-time great team captains and leaders of LSU baseball, was a 4-year starter who contributed significantly to the Tigers' 1997 and 2000 National Championships.

Brad Cresse, who played for LSU from 1997 to 2000, was a hero of the 2000 national title game. That year he led the nation in home runs with 30 and RBIs with 106.

The LSU Tigers defeated Miami in the College World Series to become National Champions in 1996. The final game ended in spectacular fashion with Warren Morris' legendary home run in the bottom of the 9th.

Having captured the National Championship for the second year in a row, the 1997 LSU Tigers enjoy the post-game celebration at Rosenblatt Stadium in Omaha, Nebraska. They beat the Alabama Crimson Tide.

Ryan Theriot scores the winning run against Stanford in the bottom of the 9th to win the 2000 National Championship. Theriot is the only player in baseball history to score the winning run in both a college national title game and in the Major League's World Series.

Cedrick Harris, a vital cog on LSU's 2000 National Championship team, was one of the greatest center fielders in LSU history. A quiet and respected leader, he was one of the toughest competitors to ever wear the Purple and Gold.

Discussing strategy during a 2000 game at Alex Box Stadium are, left to right, Coach Bill Dailey, Coach Dan Canevari, and Coach Skip Bertman.

Trey Hodges pitched for LSU in the 1999 and 2000 seasons. He was named Most Valuable Player of the 2000 College World Series as he picked up two wins, including one in the national title game.

Wally Pontiff, a member of the 2000 National Championship team, was a terrific student and a great athlete. His untimely death at age 21 from an undetected heart defect was deeply felt by those who knew him, on and off the baseball field. He died in the summer of 2002. Skip Bertman said of him: "He had grace, honesty and dignity. He always gave himself up for the team. He was everyone's All-American."

The 2000 National Championship was the last of Coach Bertman's five, and the team celebrated with gusto after the big win in Omaha.

Accompanied by his wife, Sandy, Coach Bertman talks to fans at the ceremony naming the field at Alex Box Stadium for him: Skip Bertman Field. The event took place on the final weekend of the 2013 regular baseball season.

Skip Bertman bids farewell to fans after his final game as LSU's coach. ▶
The game against Tulane was played at Zephyr Field in Metairie in 2001.

Skip Bertman talks to fans at Alex Box Stadium in Baton Rouge following his last home game, in 2001. The huge sign in the background, known as "The Intimidator," shows a key part of Skip's LSU legacy: five National Championships. (The sign, which has been known to actually intimidate some competitors, serves to remind visiting teams that when they play here they're playing one of the nation's best.)

Coach Bertman walks with new LSU baseball coach, Paul Mainieri, at Alex Box Stadium before Mainieri's first home game, in 2007. Following in Bertman's footsteps, the new coach would go on to win the 2009 National Championship with his high-spirited Tigers.

Only a month after coaching his last college baseball game, Skip Bertman officially took over as Athletic Director at LSU, on July 1, 2001.

(Continued from page 176)

"Skip was always more than a baseball coach," said Stanley Jacobs, a former member of the LSU Board of Supervisors. "He understood every aspect of being an athletic director. When you think about it, for an athletic director, you want a likeable, personable guy out of the community. Mark [Emmert] saw it in Skip."

In the end, LSU Chancellor Mark Emmert hired a legend who was still hitting home runs.

"If you watched him at a football game when he was AD, he was always walking around, mingling with everyone, going into the crowd, sitting with the media," Jacobs said. "He'd say, 'Take a walk with me.' He'd go around just greeting people. He'd go to the concession stands. 'That coffee hot?' He just has great people skills. You go to a restaurant with Skip still today, he's a rock star."

LSU's latest rock star athletic director, Scott Woodward, formerly of Texas A&M and Washington, pointed to Bertman in the audience and called him his mentor during his packed introductory press conference at LSU's Manship School of Journalism on April 23, 2019.

"I did that because he's always been one of my mentors, absolutely," Woodward said later. "He'll shoot you straight. You can always talk to him. I never thought Skip was a 'reach-hire' as athletic director. I view talent differently."

Woodward learned that from Chancellor Emmert, who took a chance on Bertman after first seeing him as a compromise.

"Skip had never done a job like that before, but he's got just great common sense," said Emmert, who has been president of the NCAA since leaving Washington in 2010. "He thinks well, and he's great with people. He knows how to manage folks and run a team. So, he had a lot of things that recommended him naturally. Plus, everybody knew and loved Skip."

Emmert left LSU in 2004 to become president at the University of Washington, his *alma mater.*

"I felt really good about walking away and leaving it all in [Skip's] capable hands. The beauty of Skip was you always knew where he was. He always had the best interest of the University at heart. He always knew what it took to make a great athletic program. And he knew that it was his legacy, too. Not just baseball – the whole athletic program," Emmert said.

"If you hire smart people like Skip, they're adaptable," Woodward said. "And if you have someone who really has savvy and understands what they're doing, like Skip, and then they hire smart people around them – that's the key to success."

Chapter 18

Nick Saban should have listened to Skip

"If there was one thing professionally that I would do over again, it would've been to not leave LSU."

– Alabama football coach Nick Saban
at the SEC Spring Meetings on May 29, 2019

From his first days on the job as Athletic Director, Skip Bertman coached the coaches regularly – even one making millions more than he did.

"Oh, I loved him," Alabama football coach Nick Saban said in an exclusive interview at the SEC Spring Meetings in Destin, Florida, on May 29, 2019. "Skip was a little different because most of the guys who had been athletic directors where I coached had not been coaches. Maybe they were coaches for a while, but never head coaches like Skip."

Bertman is 13 years older than Saban, who tends to respect his elders, and both are "old school" in a good way.

"He had a unique perspective on what it was like to be in that chair," Saban said. "He had a lot of infinite wisdom about little things that he could help you with."

Bertman, for example, told Saban to smile more and tell a joke here and there.

"Even if they were public relations-type things, or maybe managing a certain kind of situation," Saban said. "It was a learning experience for me."

Bertman knew not to try to micro-manage Saban.

"He was great because he left you alone," Saban said. "He didn't try to tell you what to do or how to do it, and he let you run your program. But he was very helpful with some of his insight."

Bertman would often counsel Saban or basketball coach John Brady and other coaches when they got upset about something in the newspaper concerning their team or themselves.

"Hey, forget about it. It's just one day. There'll be another paper tomorrow," Bertman would say.

LSU's Sports Information Director for football, Michael Bonnette, usually took the brunt of Saban's temper.

"And I said, 'Mike, he wouldn't treat you like that if he didn't want to make you better,'" Bertman told Bonnette.

Associate Athletic Director Verge Ausberry saw Bertman and Saban as very similar and in the mold of former LSU football coach Bill Arnsparger, whom Ausberry played for as a freshman linebacker in 1986.

"They were the same kind of coaches," he said. "There were some egos, but Skip knew Nick was the best. He'll always tell you that. And Nick respected Skip. Both were like Arnsparger in that they weren't going to compliment you. I could deal with it because Arnsparger didn't give you compliments. It was what you were supposed to do."

Bertman knew Saban was the "best" even when Saban was not so great, such as in 2002 when LSU finished 8-5.

"Blair Barbier and I and Skip were at Mansur's restaurant in Baton Rouge after that season," former LSU pitcher Doug Thompson said. "And LSU fans were like, 'Who's this Saban guy?' So, we asked Skip what he thought. And Skip goes, 'Oooh, listen, this guy is going to go down as the greatest of all time.'"

"You mean at LSU?" Thompson asked.

"No, no, no," Bertman said. "I mean, like John Wooden and Bear Bryant. They're going to erect statues for him – the greatest of all time. He's got a system like ours."

"Back in the car, Blair said, 'Skip's really losing it, huh? The guy was just 8-5. Greatest of all time?' And the next year, he wins it all," Thompson said. "It's always kind of spooky to look back and realize how much Skip told the future."

Bertman also correctly predicted Saban's future when he left LSU after the 2004 season to be the Miami Dolphins coach in the NFL. Saban did not enjoy himself there in 2005 and '06 as he lost more than he won for the only time in his career, and later wished he had listened to Skip.

Just before Christmas Day in 2004, while still LSU's coach, Saban had an offer of $6 million a year from Miami Dolphins owner Wayne Huizenga to leave his $2.3 million LSU job and become the Dolphins new coach. But he had a hard time making up his mind – partly because the No. 1 and No. 2 recruiting classes in the nation he signed in 2003 and '04 would be blossoming in 2005.

"It's always hard because of the relationships you have with players to just walk off and leave them," Saban said. "I thought, too, we had one of the best teams ever coming back the next year, in 2005.

"Of course, Hurricane Katrina probably disrupted that team's ability to be successful. A lot of those same guys won the National Championship in 2007. Wayne Huizenga was a pretty good recruiter, and I was really torn about what to do."

Shortly before leaving for the Capital One Bowl in Orlando, Florida, Saban met in Bertman's office with Bertman and Richard Gill, a top executive at Shaw Industries in Baton Rouge and a former president of the Tiger Athletic Foundation.

"I remember Skip saying, 'Nick, you've just got to decide what you want your legacy to be,'" Saban said. "He said, 'Do you want it to be as a college coach? Or do you want to try to make a name for yourself as an NFL coach?'"

The question cut to the heart of Saban's decision.

"I really wanted to be a college coach, but I had it in the back of my mind all the time that the ultimate thing that you could accomplish in the profession was to be a head coach in the NFL," Saban said. "Don't ask me why, but that was just kind of there."

Saban had turned down the Chicago Bears head coaching job just days after beating Oklahoma, 21-14, on Jan. 4, 2004, in the Superdome for the BCS National Championship.

"They tried to hire me, and I wasn't really interested," he said. "And I thought because of Mr. Huizenga the next year, the Dolphins were the right one. Skip understood that. As it turns out, what I learned from that experience in hindsight was that *it was a huge mistake to leave college football.*"

Saban struggled to relate to professional players as Miami's head coach, though he did that well as an NFL assistant at Houston in 1988-89 and at Cleveland in 1991-94.

Still, after inheriting a 4-12 team at Miami, he won his last six games in his first season with the Dolphins in 2005 to finish 9-7 and narrowly missed the playoffs while contending for AFC Coach of the Year honors.

But he didn't enjoy it.

Then he slipped to 6-10 in 2006, and wanted out.

"I was fortunate to get another opportunity to be a college coach at Alabama," he said.

He landed at Alabama in 2007, and six national championships followed, in the 2009, 2011 (over LSU), 2012, 2015, 2017 and 2020 seasons.

Had Saban listened to Bertman, he might still be building such a college legacy at LSU.

"I know a lot of LSU fans think I left for whatever reasons, but I left because I wanted to be a pro coach," Saban said. "*We loved LSU.* We worked hard to build the program. *If there was one thing professionally that I would do over again, it would've been to not leave LSU.*"

Saban left a natural, geographical recruiting advantage at LSU that he has not seen at Alabama even with his success there.

"You had … a better recruiting base at LSU, especially in the state," Saban said. "And you only had one school."

Bertman chose LSU over South Alabama for the same reason in 1983. While Alabama has historically been the top school in its state, Auburn has reigned at times and is a consistent threat to Alabama more than any Louisiana school is to LSU.

"So, even if we had as many prospects in Alabama as Louisiana does, you're battling somebody else all the time to try to get them. So, it has been more challenging in recruiting here, no doubt," Saban explained.

Bertman understood this, and he understood coaches, because he was more than "just a coach."

Bertman sensed that Saban's taskmaster coaching style would be best in college because Bertman coached the same way – which was one reason why he never pursued coaching in Major League Baseball.

"I said, 'Mr. Huizenga, you're making a big mistake,'" Bertman recalled. "This Saban guy's not going to be successful in the NFL, although he's the greatest. The professional players won't listen to him.' And he just laughed. I think he figured I was just trying to keep our coach. 'You don't understand. You're just a coach.'"

Huizenga, who passed away in 2018, was the one, like others, who didn't understand – until Saban left the Dolphins after two seasons.

Chapter 19

Skip's secrets to success

*"I was always most concerned with the law of averages
and large numbers in our favor."*

– Skip Bertman, Dec. 11, 2021

Former LSU pitcher Chad Ogea remembers the day he came to the realization that Skip Bertman had a special gift.

This epiphany occurred in Ogea's sophomore year, in 1990, when he was well on his way to becoming a prized Bertman pupil.

The Tigers were on the field at Alex Box Stadium, and Bertman told outfield coach "Beetle" Bailey to move right fielder Harry Berrios over a few steps. And he did immediately.

"The pitcher throws. *Whack!* Ball's hit right to him," Ogea recalled.

Bertman turned to Ogea with a big smile.

"You see, 35 years," Bertman said, though he had been coaching for longer than that.

Clay Parker, a punter on LSU's football team from 1982 to '84 and a talented pitcher, was amazed at Bertman's ability to predict where batted balls would go.

"That's scary," Parker said one day in the dugout.

But he believed and went 8-2 in Bertman's second year at LSU, in 1985, before getting drafted and reaching the Majors.

"He just had a feel for the game that nobody else had," Ogea said. "He knew what pitches were coming. He knew where the ball was probably going when he called the pitches. I mean, he's unbelievable. He'd seen it so much. He wasn't right all the time, but he played the percentages. He'd always talk about that."

So begins "Skip's Success Laboratory." He did not necessarily invent the following principles and practices nor was he the only coach to use them, but he mastered them like perhaps no other:

1. The Law of Averages

"The law of averages says that if I have more guys who can steal home than the other team, and I practice with them, let's say five guys, one day it

199

may win for us," Bertman said. "Because the law says so. It's like the lottery. Most people never win, but there's always one person that wins, because it's the law."

Bertman rarely called a steal of home.

"But I want that bullet just in case," he said.

It was there if he needed it, like the bunt defenses or pick-off plays he practiced with his team and "the Grand Illusion" hidden-ball trick. This trick worked beautifully against Wichita State in the College World Series on the way to Miami's first national title, in 1982, when Bertman was associate head coach/pitching coach at Miami.

"I was always most concerned with the law of averages and large numbers in our favor," Bertman said. "If one guy's missing, *it matters*. If one guy doesn't practice well, *it matters*. If one guy has problems with a girlfriend or has bad grades and isn't paying attention, *it matters*. In baseball, everything matters."

Throughout his coaching career, the law of averages was important to Bertman, and he taught the law to his players. They received a steady diet of videos of high- and low-percentage plays to the tune of The Bobby Fuller Four's 1966 classic, "I Fought The Law (And The Law Won)."

Bertman remains No. 1 in NCAA postseason career winning percentage as LSU's head coach at .754 with an 89-29 record. In this regard, he was above the law, so to speak, as he won all five National Championship games he reached in 1991, '93, '96, '97 and 2000.

"You figure you might lose one," he said. "I had some good fortune, and I had great players. And maybe if I was a better coach, we would've won more earlier on."

When he says he should have won eight in all, as he often does, he is thinking also of the 1987, '89 and '98 teams he took to Omaha.

Bertman also finished his career at 15-0 in Alex Box in games played with advancement to Omaha or to the Super Regional on the line. (His team was eliminated from NCAA Regional play in Alex Box in 1992 and in '95, but that was before the championship round – not in a game that had LSU won, it would have advanced.)

Bertman has been playing the percentages since he coached at Miami Beach High from 1965 to '75 and at Miami from 1976 to '83 and at LSU from 1984 to 2001.

In another life, Bertman could have run a Las Vegas casino. In fact, when LSU played at Nevada-Las Vegas in 1991, he told the team, "Guys, Las Vegas is going to win."

He was referring to the casinos.

"They don't care if you walk away with a bunch of money, because over the long haul, Vegas wins, " 1989-91 pitcher Paul Byrd remembers Bertman saying.

"Same thing's true when you pitch. If you get ahead of the hitter, you'll win," Byrd said. "You may have a bad game, but over the long haul, you'll win. An 0-2 hitter is drastically different than a 2-0 hitter. The importance of putting the percentages in your favor cannot be overstated. He pounded that into us."

"Skip was the first to make me realize that when the four-hole hitter is 0-for-4 in the bottom of the ninth with the bases loaded, buckle up," said Doug Thompson, who pitched on LSU's 1997 National Championship team.

"He's due, Skip would say," Thompson recalled. "That's how he saw the game. Most people would say, 'He's having a bad night. Strike him out again.' That's when you give up the home run."

Thompson always wanted to throw a changeup while at LSU, but Bertman agreed only if he could get it over the plate seven out of 10 times in the bullpen.

"It's a law," Bertman said.

"It's not a real pitch to Skip unless you can throw it where he wants it seven out of 10 times," Thompson said.

Thompson never hit seven, but Bertman let him try a couple changeups outside of Omaha.

"Both were absolutely annihilated," Thompson said.

Oklahoma's Justin Elsey hit a two-run home run off a changeup in LSU's 14-3 win in the NCAA Regional in 1997. And Bertman couldn't resist:

"You happy now, Dougie boy?"

For Bertman, playing the percentages added up to five titles.

"It's not a theory," he said. "It's not a principle. It's a real law. There's no question about it."

2. The Pitching Lab

Patrick Coogan, a right-handed LSU ace on the 1997 National Championship team, was Bertman's ultimate laboratory pitcher rat. At age 8, he met the coach in 1983 before Bertman ever coached a game at LSU.

When he was 12, Coogan was on the cover of Bertman's book "Youth League Baseball," which used Coogan and other members of the Millerville League 11- and 12-year-old team as models.

"I went to all his camps since I was little," said Coogan, who signed with Bertman out of Baton Rouge's Catholic High in 1993. "When I got to LSU, he changed my delivery a little. He'd essentially crafted it since I was 12."

Coogan went 2-0 with 27 strikeouts in 19 innings as a redshirt freshman in 1995, 6-0 with 95 strikeouts in 80 innings in 1996, and 14-3 with 144 strikeouts in 125 innings in 1997.

"What I learned from Skip was how to correct pitches," Coogan said. "When you miss your location, why did it go there and how do you fix it?"

Bertman taught Coogan and others to bite their shirt – figuratively speaking – at the shoulder opposite of the throwing arm when their fastball missed high on their throwing arm side.

"When pitchers really want to gas up, their front shoulder sometimes goes out too far," Coogan explained. "So, your arm gets on a different path and misses high on your throwing arm side. If that happened, he'd make you bite your shirt, so you would keep your shoulder in and drive the ball to the plate. It worked."

And if you didn't correct the pitch, you didn't pitch.

"That's how you got to pitch at LSU: if he could trust you," Coogan said.

"I know their hitters. I'm going to call the pitches that will get them out," Bertman told his pitchers. "But if I can't trust you to be able to execute what I'm calling, you can't pitch for me."

When pitchers executed under pressure, Bertman said they "earned their diploma."

"If you couldn't do certain things, you weren't ready yet," Coogan said. "You had to graduate. You had to repeat it multiple times to be able to pitch for LSU."

And soon, most LSU pitchers reciprocated that trust wholeheartedly. And the ones who were a little short on the God-given fastball in the 90s would have thrown a pitch to center field if Bertman had called one.

Hunter Gomez, who transferred from UNO for the 1999 season, was one of those. He went 4-3 with seven saves with 90 strikeouts and 25 walks in 98 innings as a junior. He made the weekend rotation the next year and went 9-1 with 113 strikeouts and 28 walks in 113 innings on the 2000 National Championship team.

"I could develop talent, especially pitching," Bertman said. "But not at the Big League level. At the college level, I could take a kid that's not even a pro prospect and help him win."

LSU pitching coach Dan Canevari saw this frequently.

"Skip had a system," he said. "When Hunter Gomez went to the mound, he believed he couldn't be beaten because Skip was calling the pitches. Total belief guy. Never got drafted. He threw 85 m.p.h."

Then when someone with more natural talent like Coogan or Thompson also believed, Bertman grew All-Americans.

"The emphatic trust that all of us who pitched had for this guy – surrounded by 16 different documents and music stands full of data, stats and information on the hitter in the dugout – was just unwavering," Thompson said. "So, when Skip says, 'Fastball away,' you say, 'Yep.'"

Bertman was an expert at calling pitches. He had been doing it since his coaching days at Miami Beach High when few did such a thing. He read the swings. At Miami and LSU, he learned hitters from film or pitching sheet study.

"If it's 3-and-2, can I call a breaking ball low and away, likely a ball, so the kid will swing at it? You would know if a player was going to swing at ball four," he said.

"He had a philosophy of pitching patterns," said Rick Greene, a closer from 1990 through 1992 who was LSU's career saves leader with 29 until 2011. "When to be aggressive, when to pitch off the plate or over the plate, when to attack certain hitters. Don't walk a guy with 60 stolen bases. A lot of mental preparedness and positive visualization."

Greene reached the Majors in 1999 with Cincinnati and pitched professionally through 2001.

"The knowledge Skip had based on the percentages and the tendencies was really a pleasure to be around," Greene said.

"From a purely baseball perspective, he absolutely, positively was the best at coaching you through how to pitch to a hitter and how to utilize certain sequences to get him out," said Mike Sirotka, who pitched at LSU from 1990 to 1993 and later for the Chicago White Sox for six seasons.

"He taught things to look for in a swing and how to see them," Sirotka said. "He was constantly teaching us. 'Hey, watch this guy swing. We're going to throw him a curveball here, and he's going to hit it to the shortstop.' He was the best at teaching you how to improve the odds of being successful."

This helped Sirotka exit the Minors after just one full season.

"There's no doubt that the pitchers he put in the Majors were just light years ahead of the rest of the pro guys from a mental perspective in how to approach the game," Sirotka said.

Bertman didn't just say not to walk anyone. All coaches say that. He taught a way to avoid a walk on a 3-and-2 count.

"A lot of pitchers say to themselves, 'I don't want to fail,'" said Trey Hodges, who won Bertman's last National Championship game in 2000 and reached the Majors in 2002 with Atlanta.

"That's a negative thought," Hodges said. "He taught us to say, 'What can I do to control my success?' Well, at 3-and-2, all I can do is pound the zone and whatever happens, happens. Most guys get out 70 percent of the time, so throw a strike."

Ogea, who won Bertman's first National Championship game in 1991 as a junior, felt he had an edge as he quickly reached the Majors with Cleveland in 1994.

"I understood hitters going into pro ball," he said. "I was way ahead of a lot of the guys in the Minors. They wanted to rare back, throw it hard, and hope for the best. Skip had me hitting spots, throwing in when I needed to, throwing away."

Paul Byrd, who was 17-6 in 1990 and still holds the school wins record for a season, was not a power pitcher, but he was a third-round pick in 1991 and stuck in the Majors for 14 seasons on seven teams. He credits "the Bertman Pitching Lab."

"We would have classroom talks at LSU," he said. "Now, schools have a pitching lab. We already had that. We would just talk numbers. It was like a pitching clinic every day. When I got to the Big Leagues, we didn't do that. Now, we'd go over a scouting report, but it was nothing like being at LSU. He made us read certain stats like what hitters hit on certain counts. That became my game."

Byrd was LSU teammates with seven pitchers who reached MLB: Greene, Ogea, Sirotka, Curtis Leskanic, Ben McDonald, John O'Donoghue and Russ Springer.

"Pitching at LSU was more of a school," Byrd said. "And I learned a lot about baseball during those classes with Coach Bertman. That's something that I've always taken with me."

Byrd, a fly ball pitcher, still could hear Bertman's teachings during games deep into his career after an opposing batter just missed a home run.

"I'd have this voice go off in the back of my head, 'Warning track fly balls are the kiss of death for hitters,'" Byrd said, repeating Bertman. "And I would just smile and walk off the mound."

Byrd can still hear Bertman's voice as he announces the Braves' games on television.

"He taught me how to think, and that's as important as a trick pitch or whatever," he said. "He taught me a mindset and how to play the percentages. Even now when I broadcast, I'm able to understand the game better."

3. The Yellow Book

Skip Bertman taught his players how to win, literally. Much of the material he taught them could be found on the pages of the playbook he wrote himself: The Bertman Yellow Book.

It was a yellow binder covering the fundamentals and chock full of rules and instructions on what to do on the field in almost every situation imaginable. It was a training manual. Every player had his own copy and was expected to study it and to follow its instructions.

"It was everything Skip knew about pitching as far as tendencies, percentages, batting averages against certain counts," pitcher Rick Greene said.

"The Yellow Book had a lot about pitch execution," said 1998-2001 pitcher Shane Youman, who pitched for Pittsburgh in 2006 and '07. "Where you needed to put the curveball. Learning how to think about the game in certain situations and execute pitches was huge for me. When I was out on my own and had to make those decisions, that Yellow Book helped me get to the next level."

Yellow Book meetings were often on Friday nights during fall camp and before the season, and it wasn't just pitching. There were lots of meetings.

"It was basically 50 pages of almost anything that could happen in a game," Patrick Coogan said. "You had to learn them and repeat them. So, Friday nights in the fall, we'd have Yellow Book meetings at 7 p.m. You weren't going out."

4. The Shake Off

"If Skip says, 'Shake,' you shake," Doug Thompson said.

This is subtle trickery – a mind game played by LSU pitchers in obvious pitch situations, such as a two-ball, no-strike fastball; a three-ball, no-strike fastball; or a no-ball, two-strike waste pitch outside.

He learned this from Max Sapper, his longtime mentor back in Miami.

Sapper: "If it's two balls and no strikes, what pitch are you looking for from your pitcher, Skip?"

Bertman: "Fastball."

Sapper: "You're right, and so's the hitter. So, before you call the fastball, give the pitcher a signal to shake his head as if he's shaking off the pitch."

Bertman: "Why?"

Sapper: "The batter's going to start thinking about what's coming. And then you call the fastball."

Bertman, who always played catcher as a young man, taught this to all his catchers and pitchers.

"Whenever there was an obvious pitch, this signal was given," Bertman said, shaking his head no. "This meant the pitcher should shake off the catcher. Doesn't mean a hard shake-off. Just a little shake."

It gives the hitter a little something to think about.

"If it's a 2-and-0 count, the hitter's ripping up," Bertman said. "Dead red, they call it, for dead ready. If the pitcher shakes off, and I'm the hitter, I might be thinking curveball now or he's going to throw another pitch other than a fastball. But even if he isn't thinking that, you get him thinking something. That helps. Now, I don't have an algorithm or any statistics on it, but it puts a little doubt in the hitter's mind."

It's another bullet for the LSU pitcher.

"It takes a half calorie to shake," Thompson said. "When you're 2-and-0 or 3-and-1, and the hitter's dead red, and you shake, maybe he swings a little bit later and grounds out to the shortstop instead of getting a hit, or he takes a pitch he should've hit."

LSU pitchers gladly took orders for the Skip Shake Off for decades.

"And someone would ask me, 'Why the hell did that guy take that 2-and-0 fastball right down the middle?' And I'd say, 'Well, I don't know,'" Bertman said, shaking his head.

5. Batting practice versus a lefty

The greatest inventions, such as the cellular phone, tend to be incredibly obvious and have people asking, "Why didn't I think of that?"

Bertman always tried to have at least a couple of left-handed pitchers on his roster as most coaches do. But Bertman also was hell-bent on having a left-handed assistant coach who could throw batting practice to his team regularly. So, his hitters – particularly the left-handers – could routinely be prepared for left-handed pitchers as there are not nearly as many of those as there are right-handers. According to *Scientific America*, 70 to 95% of people are right-handed.

Many coaches don't always think of that.

A coach doesn't want to waste a lefty pitcher at batting practice, so Bertman tried to make sure he had left-handed assistant coaches. The unsung hero of LSU baseball's five national titles from 1991 through 2000 under Bertman was pitching coach Dan Canevari, who arrived in 1991.

A former left-handed pitcher for Bertman at Miami from 1977 to '79, Canevari prepared LSU hitters for the left.

"Plus, Cano threw a good curveball, and he threw strikes," Bertman said. "And he could go for 40 minutes. If you wanted it outside and off the plate to teach our hitters to see the difference, he could do that. He was accurate."

Bertman credits Canevari with keeping some of LSU's greatest left-handed hitters sharp, guys like Eddy Furniss, Todd Walker, Mike Koerner, Justin Bowles and Warren Morris.

"Eddy Furniss' father would've paid money for Canevari to pitch to Eddy. He didn't, but we made sure Eddy got plenty of cuts against Cano. It helped him immensely," Bertman said.

"Most kids don't see enough lefties," Bertman said. "Our hitters didn't know what was coming from Dan. It was high-class BP, and it worked. He'd throw three times to a guy, and they'd be better. They'd learn what to take. They'd make the pitcher throw it over, and they'd hit it."

It worked so well that when Bertman was the coach of the 1996 U.S. Olympic team and Canevari was unavailable because he was running Bertman's summer camps at LSU, Bertman had to act fast.

"I realized all the other Olympic coaches were right-handed, so we went into the community and got some left-handers from the high schools," Bertman noted.

6. 'The inevitable two'

Prepare for the worst early. Bertman called this "the inevitable two," as in two runs by the other team in the first inning.

"The opponent is going to inevitably score two runs in the first inning for a couple different reasons," Coogan said. "They're energized. They're playing LSU. If we're at home, it may be their first time in Alex Box. Their parents may be in the stands. They're going to swing harder. The strike zone may be tighter. And our pitcher's not ready yet.

"So, be ready, and deliver that pitch to get the double play and get out of it before too much damage."

Of course, "the inevitable two" is just a metaphor, Bertman says. However, the first inning of any game is hard to pitch, he adds.

7. Play the best nine, not the nine best

When Blair Barbier, a two-time national champion at LSU in 1997 and 2000, went on his recruiting visit to LSU in 1996, he was taken aback at first by something Bertman said.

Barbier had asked Bertman if he would start or be redshirted, and Bertman was rarely one to promise a starting position to a recruit. Unlike other coaches, he would not say, "You're the missing piece." Instead, he often said this:

"Whether you come here or not, we're going to win the national championship. If you'd like to be a part of that, you can."

He told Barbier point blank:

"Look, big guy, I play my best nine, not my nine best. And if you're in that mix, you will play. And if you're not, you won't. I know all the other guys are telling you you're going to start next year. I don't know if you're going to start at L-S-U. To answer your question, I don't plan to redshirt you yet, but I might."

What Bertman was telling Barbier was that he will play the nine players who best form a team, not necessarily the nine most talented players.

"It was about fitting into the team and finding your place," Barbier said. "It was the first I ever heard of that. And then I noticed it's a sign in the locker room."

Former Long Beach State coach Dave Snow, who had epic battles with LSU in the 1993 College World Series and the 1997 NCAA Regional at Alex Box, was a fan of this Skip-ism.

"He had a great belief that really had an impression on me as a coach," Snow said. "It's not the nine best players that win. It's the nine players who play together the best to form the best nine that win."

8. Don't over-coach

As soon as Bertman saw Todd Walker, Russ Johnson, Eddy Furniss, Joey Belle and Wally Pontiff swing, he signaled a permanent message to his assistant coaches.

"It was the 'Don't coach them' signal," Bertman said. "The reason is, they had perfect swings. Walker especially. And they also hit to the opposite field. They already did that. What are you going to teach them?"

Bertman said that in his patented extremely high voice for emphasis.

"Todd Walker and Russ Johnson weren't big guys, but they could hit home runs," he said. "They did great things for us. Todd's swing was so perfect. I didn't do much for Todd other than bat him third. I told him, 'Don't let anybody fool with your swing.' He was just too good. He was the best. Walker was the best three-year hitter I ever had. He was unreal. He was always going to hit. And he hit left-handers."

Bertman called Furniss the best four-year hitter he ever had.

"Albert Belle, who was Joey Belle when he was here, was another one of our greatest hitters," he said. "He could have played anywhere in college and still been a Major League starter. I could tell in a second he could hit, but he didn't know how to play baseball yet.

"Mike Sirotka was the best four-year pitcher I ever had along with Brett Laxton."

9. Give up something now for later – as in Omaha

One trait of Bertman that many failed to understand even after he began to pile up three and four national championships was his willingness to sacrifice a non-conference win to find out who could pitch under pressure.

Many coaches were afraid to do this then and now because they want to win as many games as possible to stay in the rankings for seedings and, thus, the ability to host in the postseason. That's great, unless you run out of pitchers. Bertman rarely ran out of pitchers because he tended to have a deep roster of those who had tasted pressure.

Such was the case on the night of March 3, 2000, in Orlando, Florida. LSU led Central Florida, 10-5, after six innings, and Bertman had more than enough veteran pitching to close out the game with a win. Instead, he threw four inexperienced pitchers: sophomore Shane Youman, junior college transfer Heath McMurray, sophomore Weylin Guidry, and freshman Bo Pettit. And he lost, 14-13.

Youman allowed three runs on two hits with a walk. McMurray gave up two runs on four hits with a walk. Guidry allowed two runs with two walks. And Pettit allowed two runs on two hits with a walk for the loss.

"They were unable to get their diplomas at that time," Bertman said. "I was giving a lot of guys a chance to see who could go in there with the pressure on."

That's because he never wanted to throw a green pitcher in an NCAA Regional or in Omaha.

"That has to do with making the kid a better pitcher or player for the next game," Bertman said 20 years later. "Or, more importantly, for the national championship game."

Youman, Guidry and Pettit all later got their diplomas in the 2000 season and were instrumental in the Tigers getting to and winning the national championship. Youman finished 3-0 with a save. Guidry became the closer with seven saves and finished 1-2 with a team-best 2.68 earned run average along with 45 strikeouts in 40 innings. Pettit finished 5-3 with 52 strikeouts in 47 innings.

"Baseball's like that," Bertman said. "See, you can give something up for the future in baseball because you can't win them all. The law doesn't allow you to do that."

And you also don't need to win them all. Bertman won his last national championship in 2000 without winning the SEC. He reached Omaha in 1987, '89, '94 and '98 without winning the SEC and tended to lose a lot of mid-week, non-conference games.

"The law doesn't say I have to win *today*," Bertman said. "It's about winning in the end."

10. Preparation

The reason for all the practices and the videos, all the time in the bullpen and the lab, and the Yellow Book was so Bertman and his team would be more prepared than the opponent.

"It's amazing how lucky you get when you're prepared," Bertman likes to say. "I wanted every advantage, see. And my thing was to show the players that the person with the most information wins in life. The team that has the most information usually wins."

Patrick Coogan carried that into his professional life in business.

"Definitely always have a plan," he said. "Not just a hope, a wish, a dream, but a real plan that you can execute and build upon. He preached that."

The right plan can be worth two or three runs.

"We won some games before they started," Canevari said.

"We always felt confident because we had Skip in our dugout," Warren Morris said. "We knew he was prepared, and we knew he had us prepared."

And Bertman did most of his preparation for much of his career the old-fashioned way – without computers.

"He was way out ahead of everyone at using data to make decisions," pitcher Doug Thompson said. "Rarely would he make gut decisions. If Skip Bertman had access to data through computers that there is now, he would be winning championships still."

11. Work Ethic

Skip Bertman's staff included his wife, Sandy, and their four daughters, Jan, Jodi, Lisa and Lori.

"He was always coaching baseball, but whenever there was a serious thing, I always had them call their dad," said Sandy, who taught school while Bertman coached. "He knows the right thing to say at difficult times."

The couple celebrated their 60th wedding anniversary on Feb. 11, 2022.

"I've always given him his space," Sandy noted.

"Sandy was a great coach's wife and rooted me on," Bertman said. "Understood the game, loved the players, knows most of them. She always had a hot dinner ready for me. She ran the concession stands all the years at the camps. With four daughters and my being away at times, she was always there for our girls."

Bertman needed a lot of space on the clock to finish all his work, particularly in his early years at LSU.

"Every day was a reckoning," he said. "I'm going to be in the bullpen 40 times with this guy. And I'm going to know what he can throw, and we're going to go over it. And then I'm going to be there right before the game – maybe eight minutes before. That's what you had to do to call the pitches."

And he didn't just watch the pitchers. Bertman had a chair custom-made for his bullpen view that was higher than normal.

"I had to see his delivery and where the pitch was going," he said. "I would make him bounce it in if I wanted."

Bertman worked with the hitters, too.

"Everybody took 10 swings," he said. "Well, this guy took 20, because he needed it, and I was there at the cages. When they pitched, I stood or sat behind them. When they ran the bases, I was at first, second or third."

Players remember Bertman frequently coaching on the field still wearing a dress shirt and tie he had put on for a speaking engagement or a fundraiser.

"We had really long practices," said infielder/outfielder Pat Garrity, a key member of the 1991 National Championship team. "Bunt defense, pick-off plays, first-to-third plays. We went over everything. Everything was competition at practice, so when we got to the game, it just carried over."

And they got home late.

And Bertman got home late.

"I coached everything, and I coached long," he said. "I practiced longer, harder, but efficiently. I had been doing it since I was 15. I had a mentor – Max

Sapper, who taught me. I read every book. I spoke to every person. I knew what had to be done.

"And Sandy would call, and I'd say, 'Honey, it's not American Legion baseball. I've got to do this. We've got four daughters. They've all got to go to college.' It was hard."

LSU's video people helped Bertman, but he made a lot of his own inspirational videos for players by taping parts of Ken Burns' PBS "Baseball" documentary.

"We had a video made for them every game," he said. "It took a long time, and it cost a lot of money in those days. I watched a lot of video at the time. Or I spoke to coaches on the phone to get information on opponents."

Former LSU assistant athletic director for television and video operations Kevin Wagner would call other teams for video. LSU baseball Sports Information Director Bill Franques would get Bertman a list of all the televised games around the country.

"Or someone knew a guy in California," Bertman said. "We'd get game tape from all over the country."

Bertman spent many hours of his work week speaking to groups to spread the word about LSU baseball and to raise money. He'd often carry season tickets in his suit pocket to sell. He learned from working under Miami coach Ron Fraser.

"I learned how to ask for money, which Fraser was really good at, and that's the hardest thing in the world," Bertman said. "One thing that helped was I could remember the names of about 1,000 people – business people around Baton Rouge we'd meet through the Coaches' Committee."

At Coaches Committee gatherings, guests from the business community would put their names on stickers on their shirts or coats.

"I'd memorize the name with the face. That was really important to me, and people like that," he said.

Bertman and the Coaches Committee raised a lot of their own money. They made the contacts for the construction of coaches' offices, the addition of fence signs, the installation of sprinkler and drainage systems, and other stadium improvements, including dugouts and parking lots. The process would be streamlined and the projects completed much quicker than if the university took it over.

Bertman himself improved the baseball media guide by bidding it out and having it made larger and more attractive with color pictures.

"He understood the value of raising money for the right reasons so you could pay for projects yourself," Canevari observed.

With every new season, there was something new at Alex Box from scoreboards to ceiling fans and bleachers.

And LSU had one of the few baseball programs in the country that actually made money, particularly after the Tigers began hosting NCAA Regionals routinely – every year from 1990 through 2001 under Bertman.

"One of the greatest contributions Skip made was he taught people how baseball works," Canevari said. "He showed athletic directors that you could make money. He would get calls from ADs around the country all the time, 'Hey, how do you do this?' Why are you full?' "

To Bertman, the fans were not just fans.

"We serviced customers," he said. "That's what we tried to do. We worked for them."

Within weeks of his first day on the job as LSU's baseball coach, in the summer of 1983, Bertman contacted Chamber of Commerce offices around Louisiana and got a list of 50 various Rotary Clubs and other civic groups so he could speak to them. Sometimes he'd wear his LSU uniform and bring some season tickets in his pocket to sell.

"Some of them thought I was nuts," Bertman said.

"But he made people realize there was something about to be going on here," Canevari said.

And before the Yellow Book, there was the Yellow Sheet. Three months before Bertman would coach his first game at LSU, he wrote a lengthy memo on yellow, legal-size LSU letterhead to assistant athletic director for facilities Bill McClure, dated Nov. 14, 1983:

> Here is the list of items either in the process of being completed or not yet started that we talked about doing at the baseball stadium or practice field. I realize that nothing can be started, of course, until after you have finished in the football stadium next week.

Bertman then listed 60 to-do items:

> Paint bathrooms, add waterproof tile, install soap dishes, repair or install shower heads, install equipment shelves, install lights for batting cage and bullpen, need new weight scale for locker room, need water fountain for locker room, new toilet for coaches' shower, picnic tables for right field, new foliage for the ticket office, repair and paint bleachers, install lights in parking lot across street.

One-by-one, he crossed them off as they were accomplished, but this didn't happen overnight.

"The place was a disaster," he said. "I had to convince people that I was serious about being LSU's baseball coach."

12. Story time

One of the more amazing things about former Green Bay Packers coach Vince Lombardi was his uncanny ability to routinely come up with something different to tell his team for motivation or inspiration.

And Coach Bertman had that same ability.

"Every day, he had something to tell us," Blair Barbier said. "Think about that. Not only in the squad room after the game strategy, but during the week."

Each Sunday, Bertman had a professional in business or some other field speak to the team as part of the Sunday Speaker Series.

"He would always tie things back into it," Barbier said. "And we were highly motivated individuals to begin with. Then he could bring it to a whole other level and make you even better than you thought you could be. Collectively, you get a lot of people thinking like that who have some talent, and you saw what happened."

LSU players got so much more than the fundamentals. They got the "feeling" that John Matuszak passionately cries out for in one of the greatest sports movies ever made, "North Dallas 40" in 1979. After a loss, one of Dallas' assistant coaches is criticizing players in the locker room. And Matuszak, a former Oakland Raider and Washington Redskin defensive end portraying a lineman, loses it.

"To you, it's just a business. But to us it's still got to be a sport. I want some *feeling*. I want some (expletive deleted) team spirit," Matuszak says.

"Skip gets a lot of credit for everything he's done, but he probably deserves more for how he always gave us the edge," Barbier said. "He was the best at motivation from the inside – not just a fiery speech. From the Sunday Speaker Series to him every day, I mean, priceless. This guy was amazing. Every day, there was something in your locker that matched the speech that he or the speaker gave, and it eventually tied into the game with a video."

Baton Rouge businessman Eric Lane was a Sunday speaker and received an autographed baseball from some of the players that said, "Thanks, LSU baseball."

In the latter months of 2021, Bertman was in Lane's office and saw the baseball in a glass container.

"The boys gave him that some 20 years ago, and that thing was sitting on Eric's desk," Bertman said. "You see, that meant something. The Sunday Speaker Series really worked for us."

Bertman spoke the other six days. He would tell his team about Ted Williams or Joe DiMaggio from baseball, but also about the first man to run a mile in less than four minutes.

"You can do anything if you put your mind to it," Bertman said.

There were stories about Greg LeMond, who won the *Tour de France* in 1986, '89 and '90, and Michael Johnson, who became the only male athlete in history to win the 200 and 400 meters in the same Olympics, in 1996 in Atlanta.

Or he would tell his players how much easier they have it running laps than POWs did in Vietnam.

"Of course, he'd be blowing cigar smoke out the window of his town car while he drove by us running in the heat," Barbier said, laughing.

"Everybody talks about what a great in-game strategist he was, which he was," said former pitcher Paul Byrd. "But to this day, he's the best motivational speaker in baseball that I've ever been around. And I played for Bobby Cox, Terry Francona, Joe Maddon and Mike Scioscia – some of the greats. But if you're talking about a pure, raw, motivational speaker, Skip was the best – every day, every game."

Before Byrd visited LSU during his recruitment out of Louisville, Kentucky, he thought he was going to Arizona State. Then he talked to Bertman.

Byrd's parents feared he had gotten talked into something he really didn't want to do or shouldn't do.

"I can see him sitting there right now like the Godfather," Byrd said. "And within 10 minutes, I had committed to LSU. My parents panicked. They said, "You got talked into something, and you haven't looked at all your options.'

"But Skip had said, 'Hey, big guy, I need you. We'll win anyway, but I need you here.' He has a presence. I owe a lot to Skip for helping make me a better speaker and announcer."

Many of Bertman's stories involved those who could perform under pressure.

"A lot of people couldn't play for Skip, if I'm going to be honest, because it was such an adjustment of pressure," Byrd pointed out.

"Skip always said, 'A diamond is created from the pressure placed upon it,'" said former pitcher Trey Hodges. "He can be a very tough coach, which is great, because you don't just get lucky for 10 years with five titles. The pressure makes you better."

* * * * *

The speakers, the speeches, the videos, the pitches, the secrets, the work ethic, the coaching, they were all about one thing: winning at LSU and beyond.

"I hear from people all the time, 'Oh, we met Coach Bertman. He's such a sweet man. It had to be so much fun to play for him,' " said former pitcher Doug Thompson. "And it *was* the most fun time of my life. But a *sweet man*?"

Not while in lab mode.

"He was trying to do one thing: win," Thompson said. "Skip was the most competitive coach. The man wanted to win. It was his job. It's all he thought about when he was in coaching mode.

"What other detail could he focus on that could help us win? What could he say? Who could he get to speak to us. What video would get us fired up?"

All of this mattered. What Skip knew for sure, and what his players learned along the way, was that everything matters in baseball.

Afterword

'Holding the Rope' in LSU baseball

"All he wanted to do was play ball, ... but his avocation became his vocation. If you get paid for what you want to do, then you're one of the luckiest people on earth."

– Skip Bertman's older sister, Marlene, in the Baton Rouge *Advocate's* March 8, 2001, special section, "Skip Bertman: Architect of a Baseball Dynasty"

Stanley "Skip" Bertman moved twice in his life – from Detroit to Miami Beach in 1942 when he was 4, and from Miami Beach to Baton Rouge in 1983 when he was 45.

Soon after moving to Baton Rouge, Bertman made a quick trip back to Miami to retrieve the rest of his family's belongings. He packed them into a trailer that he pulled behind a rental car as he drove back to the city where he would soon begin his new life as LSU's baseball coach.

On that drive, he spoke into a tape recorder to practice a speech he would give his first LSU baseball team that fall.

He still has a copy of that speech, written on legal-size yellow paper on the back of his list of 60 things-to-do for LSU, dated Nov. 14, 1983.

"I'm very happy and excited to be here," Bertman began in a grimy Alex Box Stadium locker room, speaking to his new team.

"I'm a very lucky guy. Always wanted to coach in college. I was here in 1977 (with the University of Miami), and LSU beat us 4-1. I always liked the facility and the school.

"It was a great job at Miami – a great place for me to coach baseball. I had some offers – maybe six or seven SEC schools. But this school is special! Many things will be done. There will be new locker rooms, more equipment, a bigger budget.

"We're going to have 100 chairback seats. I know a year from now, there'll be new dugouts and 300 chairback seats and outfield fence advertising instead of a chain-link fence. There'll be new paint, foul poles, maybe a scoreboard, new offices here in the stadium and many other improvements."

Soon, it all happened and before long Alex Box Stadium started to glimmer with capacity crowds.

But not without difficulty. In the fall before his inaugural season, Bertman held his first baseball clinic at Steinberg's sporting goods store off Nicholson

Drive near the LSU campus. He and several of his players, all dressed in their baseball uniforms, headed for the store.

"The parking lot was packed, so I thought we were going to draw a big crowd," Bertman said.

But nearly all the crowd of about 300 were there for a different event: a turkey-call demonstration, which featured legendary turkey caller Ben Rodgers of Coffeeville, Alabama. Only three had come for the baseball clinic:

"A man, his son and a dog," said Richard Lipsey, owner of the store, friend of Bertman's and longtime supporter of LSU athletics.

"That was his first baseball clinic," Lipsey added with a smile.

"I knew we had a lot of work to do," Bertman acknowledged.

"It was brutal," recalled Pat Cuntz, one of the players on Bertman's first LSU team. "Basically, we just stood out there in our uniforms. There were only a handful of kids for the clinic."

It wasn't long, though, before Bertman and his team won their first SEC West championship. It happened in Bertman's second season, in 1985.

* * * * *

Soon after his arrival at LSU, Bertman began asking his players what teammate they would want to hold one end of a rope if they were clinging to the other end while hanging from a cliff. Most picked one of the top players on the team. Bertman told them they were wrong.

"The person you want holding the end of the rope, I don't care who it is," Bertman explained in the 2021 SEC Network documentary titled "Hold The Rope." "As long as he's a teammate of mine, I know he'll never let go – because we're one."

On May 5, 1985, pitcher Stan Loewer was on the mound at Auburn trying to get the last out for a 4-3, SEC West-clinching win when he heard pitcher Robbie Smith yell from the dugout, "Stan! Hold on to the rope!" LSU held on.

"That changed everything for us and became somewhat of a motto," Bertman said.

"'Hold the Rope' is what LSU baseball is all about," said Bhrett McCabe, an LSU pitcher from 1992 to 1995 who became a sports psychologist.

The rope held on after Bertman retired and became LSU's Athletic Director following the 2001 season as longtime assistant "Smoke" Laval became coach and won the SEC title in 2003 with trips to Omaha that season and in 2004. Paul Mainieri, who followed Laval after the 2006 season, won the only non-Bertman baseball national title at LSU in 2009 as he caught on to the rope as well.

"Skip suggested to me to have the pitcher coming out of the game hand the ball to the next pitcher, as his pitchers always did, instead of me or the pitching coach taking the ball," Mainieri said. "It creates a feeling of holding the rope.

I thought it was a good idea.

"And when you're *the greatest coach in the history of the game*, and now you're athletic director and you hire me, I'm going to do what he asks."

When Mainieri, who reached the College World Series five times, retired after a Super Regional in 2021, the rope was passed to Jay Johnson, a former Arizona head coach who was introduced as LSU's new coach in front of Bertman on June 28, 2021.

"I look at this man, and I see the John Wooden of college baseball," Johnson said. "This is the greatest college baseball coach of my entire lifetime. Five national championships in a 10-year period is legendary."

When he was an assistant coach at a Division II school in San Diego and Bertman was in his last season, in 2001, Johnson bought Bertman's coaching tape, "Motivation and Teamwork: Winning The Big One."

"I can't tell you how influential that was in my development as a coach," said Johnson, a California native who twice took Arizona to Omaha.

"I used your speeches and your motivational sheets and all these things you utilized to motivate your players to do amazing things," Johnson went on. "The 'Hold the Rope' story was told to me in a small town in California 20 years ago, and I believe that was the start of my journey to here. So, Coach, thank you for showing me exactly how this is to be done."

* * * * *

Bertman still credits his mentor, Max Sapper, a retired lawyer who was director of baseball at the Miami Beach Recreation Department from the 1940s to the early 1960s. Bertman was just 10 and a member of the first Miami Beach Little League team in 1948 at Flamingo Park when he met Sapper.

"Max Sapper was a professional role model for Skipper," Bertman's older sister, the late Marlene Levin, said in a 2001 interview with the Baton Rouge *Advocate*. "He influenced Skip a lot."

Sapper saw something in Skip and let him start coaching teams of 12-year-olds when he was only 14.

"Max loved Skip, and Skip loved Max," Bertman's childhood buddy Louie Hayes said in 2001. "Max was always amazed at the questions Skip would ask when he was just 10 or 11. Even then, we knew."

So did Skip. He kept helping Sapper coach while a catcher and offensive lineman at Miami Beach High. After hitting two home runs off a stud Key West High pitcher, Bertman told *Miami Herald* writer Ed Storin that he was not interested in pro ball. And he still wasn't interested when the Milwaukee Brewers offered him $4,000 to play Class D ball.

"I can remember him in the outfield shagging fly balls with us when we were kids," said Richard Berger, who grew up a few blocks from Skip and went on to play basketball at Tulane before becoming a cardiologist.

"We were all talking about being Stan Musial or Ted Williams or Wilt Chamberlain," Berger said. "And I remember Skip saying, even at that age, he wanted to coach."

After graduating from Miami Beach High in 1956, Skip received a baseball scholarship to the University of Miami. And he kept coaching with Sapper.

"Skip and Max would sit and talk for hours and hours," Berger recalled.

Skip graduated from Miami in 1961. When Sapper died in 1962, Skip replaced him as director of baseball for the Miami Beach Recreation Department.

"Max taught me the very fiber of what I did at LSU," Bertman said. "He was all about teaching. I learned how to be a teacher from him."

Bertman learned salesmanship from his father, Louis Bertman, a businessman who managed and owned the Prince George Hotel in Miami and opened a health food restaurant.

"Be nice to people. Say 'please' and 'thank you,' " he told his son.

"That was one of our big rules at LSU," Bertman said. "Sign those autographs and be nice to people. My dad taught me that. I'm blessed."

Louis Bertman died in 1964 of a heart attack at 60 – too young to see his son's greatest accomplishments as a coach at Miami Beach High, at Miami and at LSU. Just the previous year, in '63, Skip took the first job he always wanted: Miami Beach High baseball coach. And he was off.

"All he wanted to do was play ball when he was a kid," his sister said. "He was at Flamingo Park from morning until 10 at night. But his avocation became his vocation. If you get paid for what you want to do, then you're one of the luckiest people on earth."

In 1970, the young Coach Bertman won his first championship as Miami Beach High beat Tampa's Leto High, 4-0, to win the state title at Al Lopez Field in Tampa on May 23. Bertman was 32 at the time.

* * * * *

"If you played for Skip and paid attention, you'd get a knowledge of the game," said Nelson Ferreira, a catcher for Bertman's Miami Beach High team. "Skip not only touched you as a player. He touched you as a person."

This is why Catholic High of Baton Rouge baseball coach Jerry Garidel, who sent such players as Patrick Coogan and Kurt Ainsworth to LSU over the years, asked Bertman to give his son Jamin Garidel a chance as a catcher in 1997.

"He can catch in the bullpen. He can do anything," Garidel said.

"Well, I keep a lot of guys, Jerry, but I don't think he's good enough to play," Bertman said, brutally honest as usual.

"I don't care," Garidel said. "I just want him to be around Skip Bertman for five years."

And he was, earning a National Championship ring in '97 as a redshirt freshman and another one in 2000 on Bertman's last National Championship team. Then he batted .400 (4-for-10) in a career-high 11 games on Bertman's last team in 2001.

"He still leads the nation in home runs per at bats in a season," Bertman noted.

Garidel homered against Southern on March 4, 1998, in his only at-bat of the season.

Infielder Luis Garcia, who was on the top of the pile in Omaha after Bertman's first LSU national title, on June 8, 1991, knew what Garidel felt.

"One of the greatest decisions I made was going to LSU," Garcia said, looking back 30 years. "I could've played more somewhere else. But as much as I'm embarrassed to tell you I under-performed as a player, I'm happy to tell you I'm a better human being because I spent three years learning and living with Skip Bertman. I still visualize success. It works. And it is amazing how lucky you get when you're super-prepared."

During the celebration of that Miami Beach High School state title in Tampa back in 1970, Bertman said hello to a former classmate, who had been in a popular, local rock 'n' roll band during their high school days. The musician just happened to be at the big game. Dressed in a coat and tie, he walked up to Bertman, who recognized him immediately. They shook hands.

Musician: "Congratulations, I see you achieved what you wanted to achieve."

Bertman: "Yes. How about you? What happened with the band?"

Musician: "Well, it was great for a year or two. Then I had to drop out. Other kids in the band dropped out. It was taking too much time. I'm a lawyer here now."

Bertman: "Great. How's it going?"

Musician: "Very well. But it's not like playing in a band. I really miss that."

"And he just turned and walked away," Bertman said 50 years later. "You can't make that up. It means try to follow your dream. I never worked a job in my life, but I worked all the time. I wanted to be a baseball coach ever since I can remember."

Many times during his coaching years at LSU, while giving motivational talks to his players, Bertman would use the story of his 1970 chance encounter with his musician-classmate.

"Guys, this is the time of your life. There's nothing like being in a band or playing baseball. Now, go play like hell," he would often say before big games.

"And when it's all over," Bertman said 20 years after his last game, "maybe people will say, 'Skip was a hell of a guy and helped LSU. He was good with the community, funny, taught guys how to play, won some games, and had a good time.'"

Appendix 1

Living proof of the Bertman touch

On a typical summer night in 2001, 16 former LSU Tigers were playing in Major League ballparks – a testament to the Bertman touch that was felt throughout Skip's tenure as LSU's head baseball coach, 1984 to 2001.

Pitcher Kurt Ainsworth (1997-99) made his MLB debut with San Francisco in 2001. Pitcher Paul Byrd (1989-91) was with Philadelphia. Pitcher Mark Guthrie, who was on Bertman's first LSU team in 1984 and first two College World Series teams in 1986 and '87, was pitching for Oakland. Infielder Russ Johnson (1992-94) was with Tampa Bay, and pitcher Randy Keisler (1998) was with the New York Yankees.

Infielder Brandon Larson (1997), second baseman Todd Walker (1992-94) and pitcher Eddie Yarnall (1994-96) were with Cincinnati. Pitcher Curtis Leskanic (1988-89) was with Milwaukee, and outfielder Lyle Mouton (1990-91) was with Florida. Catcher Keith Osik (1988-90), second baseman Warren Morris (1993-96), and outfielder Armando Rios (1991-93) were in Pittsburgh.

Infielder Jeff Reboulet (1985-86) was a Los Angeles Dodger. Infielder Andy Sheets (1991-92) was with Tampa Bay, and pitcher Russ Springer (1987-89) was with Arizona.

Five other LSU players had finished their MLB careers in 2000 – outfielder Albert Belle (1985-87) with Baltimore, pitcher Rick Greene (1990-92) with Minnesota, pitcher Brett Laxton (1993-96) with Kansas City, pitcher Chad Ogea (1989-91) with Tampa Bay, and pitcher Mike Sirotka (1990-93) with the Chicago White Sox.

LSU's annual alumni game, on Feb. 3, 2001, shortly before the regular season opener and MLB spring training, was a star-studded event with many of the above players in a reunion of present and future Major Leaguers like nothing else anywhere.

Timeline

The life and times of Skip Bertman,
former LSU baseball coach and athletic director

1938

May 23	Stanley Bertman is born in Detroit, Michigan, to Louis and Cele Bertman.
	Soon, Mrs. Bertman starts calling her son Skipper and Skip.

1942

Summer	The Bertmans move to Miami Beach by train, as part of a major Jewish migration to the area in the 1940s.
	Soon, Skip is a fixture at Flamingo Park, where he plays, watches and learns baseball.

1948

Summer	Skip plays for the first Little League team in Miami Beach.

1953

Summer	At 15, Skip begins coaching 11- and 12-year-olds in youth league baseball under his mentor, Max Sapper. A former pro baseball player, Sapper was Director of Baseball for the Miami Beach Recreation Department.

1956

April 5	Skip hits two home runs and drives in four runs to lead Miami Beach High over defending Class AA state champion Key West High, 4-2, at Flamingo Park in Miami Beach.
May 9	Skip – a three-year football letterman as a lineman and a four-year baseball letterman as a catcher at Miami Beach High – wins the Miami Junior Chamber of Commerce top athlete-scholar award.
May 20	Skip is named to *Miami Herald's* All-City team at catcher. He hits over .300 with power as he is intentionally walked 22 times out of 66 plate appearances.
May 27	Skip graduates from Miami Beach High and decides to go to the University of Miami – despite an offer of $4,000 to play minor league ball in the Milwaukee Braves organization.

1956-57

Skip plays freshmen baseball at the University of Miami as a catcher and serves in U.S. Army at Fort Jackson in Columbia, S.C.

1958-60

Skip plays catcher and is one of Miami's top players.

A shoulder and arm injury hurt Skip's chances at a professional baseball career that could have reached the Majors – but he wanted to coach anyway.

1961

Spring   Skip graduates with a B.A. in Health and Physical Education from the University of Miami. He soon begins teaching elementary school in Miami while coaching youth baseball and working on a master's degree at the University of Miami.

August   Skip meets Brooklyn, N.Y., native Sandy Schwartz, a fellow teacher at Madie Ives Elementary. They are engaged three months later.

1962

Feb. 11   Skip and Sandy get married.

May   Skip becomes an assistant baseball coach at Miami Beach High. He also continues coaching youth baseball at the Miami Recreation Department under Max Sapper.

1963

Spring   Skip's mentor, Max Sapper, dies, and Skip replaces him as Director of Baseball at the Miami Beach Recreation Department.

Also, Skip becomes head baseball coach at Miami Beach High – fulfilling a dream he had since he went to school there.

April 22   The Bertmans' first of four daughters, Jan, is born. Jodi, Lisa and Lori follow over the next several years.

1964

Spring   Skip receives his master's degree in Health and Physical Education from the University of Miami.

1970

May 23   Skip's Miami Beach High team wins the Class AA State Championship – the first in school history.

The players carry Skip off the field just as he had them rehearse the day before the game.

─────────────── **1975** ───────────────

Skip takes a year off from coaching to write *Coaching and Playing Youth League Baseball.*

─────────────── **1976** ───────────────

Skip is hired by University of Miami baseball coach Ron Fraser as an assistant coach/pitching coach.

Soon Skip is made associate head coach as he is running the team while Fraser handles promotions and fundraising.

─────────────── **1982** ───────────────

June 7   The "Grand Illusion" play that Skip developed for his Miami team works like a charm against Wichita State at the College World Series in Omaha.

June 12   Miami beats Wichita State, 9-3, for the Hurricanes' first National Championship.

Skip's reputation as "the greatest associate coach in college baseball" continues to grow.

─────────────── **1983** ───────────────

April 25   LSU introduces Skip Bertman as its new baseball coach.

─────────────── **1984** ───────────────

Feb. 20   The Skip Bertman era at LSU begins with a 7-1, 8-7 doubleheader sweep at Southern Mississippi.

Feb. 22   LSU beats McNeese State, 8-6, in Skip's first game at Alex Box Stadium. The crowd was 645 for a Wednesday 2 p.m. start.

May 6   LSU beats Ole Miss, 9-7, to finish 32-23 overall and 12-12 in the SEC West for third place.

─────────────── **1985** ───────────────

May 5   The Tigers win at Auburn, 4-3, in a 14-inning marathon to win the SEC West and claim LSU's first baseball championship of any kind since taking the SEC in 1975.

May 10-11   LSU is eliminated from the SEC Tournament at Alex Box with losses to Georgia and Florida. But the Tigers set a home attendance record with a 40,762 total over 33 games (1,235 a game) for 14th in the nation.

May 23-24	LSU reaches its first NCAA postseason since 1975, but it loses 11-4 to Houston and 4-3 to Lamar to get eliminated from the NCAA Central Regional in Austin.

—————————————— **1986** ——————————————

May 4	LSU beats Auburn, 4-3, at home to finish 22-5 in the SEC for Skip's first of seven SEC overall titles.
May 25	LSU reaches the College World Series for the first time, beating Tulane 7-6 in Alex Box Stadium in the NCAA South I Regional.
June 5	The Tigers are eliminated after three games in the College World Series in Omaha with a 4-3 loss to Miami.

LSU finishes 55-14 for the best record in school history. |

—————————————— **1987** ——————————————

May 24	LSU beats Cal State Fullerton, 7-3, at UNO in the NCAA South II Regional to reach its second straight College World Series.
June 5	After the Tigers win two of three in Omaha, they fall, 6-5, to Stanford.

—————————————— **1989** ——————————————

May 28	LSU sweeps No. 1 Texas A&M, 13-5 and 5-4, at Texas A&M behind Ben McDonald, Curtis Leskanic and Pat Garrity pitching to win the NCAA Central Regional.

It was one of the greatest days in LSU sports history. |
| June 8 | The Tigers lose, 12-7, to Texas and are eliminated from the World Series after four games. |

—————————————— **1990** ——————————————

May 28	LSU beats USC for the second time in two days, 7-6, to win the NCAA South I Regional at Alex Box and reach the College World Series. (The Tigers would host NCAA Regionals under Skip for the next 11 seasons.)
June 7	LSU loses to Oklahoma State, 14-3, and is eliminated from Omaha after four games.

—————————————— **1991** ——————————————

June 8	LSU wins its first National Championship in baseball, 6-3, over Wichita State at Rosenblatt Stadium in Omaha.

1993

June 12   LSU wins its second National Championship in three years, 8-0, over Wichita State at Rosenblatt Stadium in Omaha.

1994

Dec. 17   Skip is inducted into the University of Miami Sports Hall of Fame.

1996

June 8   Warren Morris hits one of the most famous home runs in the history of baseball – college or pro – in the bottom of the ninth, beating Miami 9-8 for the National Championship at Rosenblatt Stadium in Omaha.

Aug. 2   The U.S. Olympic baseball team, coached by Skip Bertman, beats Nicaragua, 10-3, to win the Bronze Medal in front of 41,002 at Atlanta-Fulton County Stadium.

1997

June 7   LSU wins its fourth National Championship in seven years, 13-6 over Alabama, at Rosenblatt Stadium in Omaha.

Also, the team sets an NCAA season record for home runs not likely to ever be broken at 188. The Tigers also set the school record for wins and winning percentage at 57-13 and .814.

2000

June 17   LSU beats Stanford, 5-4, on a walk-off single by Brad Cresse in the ninth, winning the fifth National Championship under Skip Bertman.

July 5   Skip tells the Baton Rouge *Advocate* the 2001 season will be his last, and he plans to stay at LSU as a speaker and fundraiser.

Dec. 31   LSU Chancellor Mark Emmert meets with Skip and offers him the athletic director's job. Bertman accepts and will officially start on July 1 after his final season as coach.

Former Bertman assistant Ray "Smoke" Laval leaves the head coaching job at Northeast Louisiana to be a coach-in-waiting at LSU for a season under Bertman in 2001, to take over in 2002.

2001

Spring   South Stadium Drive between River Road and Nicholson Drive – where Alex Box Stadium sat until 2009 – is renamed Skip Bertman Drive. And Bertman's No. 15 is retired.

June 3   LSU falls, 7-1, to Tulane on a Sunday afternoon at Zephyr Field in Metairie, losing the NCAA Super Regional, two games to one, and ending Skip Bertman's coaching career. Bertman then huddles with Tulane's players to motivate them for their first trip to the College World Series.

Skip bows out with one more record as 11,870 showed for his last stand, breaking the record for largest attendance at an outdoor baseball game in Louisiana.

Skip finishes with the highest NCAA baseball postseason winning percentage in history at .743 with a 90-31 mark from 1985-2001.

2002

June 18   Skip Bertman is inducted into the Louisiana Sports Hall of Fame in Natchitoches, La.

July 24   LSU third baseman/outfielder Wally Pontiff, a freshman on Skip's last National Championship team of 2000, dies in his sleep of an abnormal heart condition at age 21.

Skip gives one of the eulogies at Wally's funeral days later, calling him, "Everybody's All-American."

2003

January 4   Skip is inducted into the American Baseball Coaches Association Hall of Fame.

August 13   In his capacity as LSU Athletic Director, Skip unveils a state-of-the-art, but expensive, football season ticket licensing plan – the first of its kind at LSU. The plan is set to go into effect with the 2004 football season to raise money for football and other Athletic Department projects.

2004

Jan. 4   The "Bertman Football Season Ticket Doctrine" proves timely as coach Nick Saban's team wins LSU's first football National Championship since 1958 with a 21-14 victory over Oklahoma.

Two weeks later, invoices are mailed to season ticketholders, and Tiger Stadium has continued to be regularly sold out with waiting lists.

July 23   Athletic Director Skip Bertman promotes men's and women's assistant track coach, Dennis Shaver, to head coach to replace Pat Henry, who became Texas A&M's coach.

2005

Jan. 1	Skip announces the hiring of new football coach Les Miles, formerly the coach at Oklahoma State, to replace Nick Saban, who became coach of the Miami Dolphins.
July 16	Skip hires Chuck Winstead as men's golf coach.
	Ten years later, Winstead's team wins LSU's first National Championship in golf since 1955.

2006

March 25	LSU men's basketball team, coached by John Brady, beats No. 9 Texas, 70-60, in overtime to reach its first Final Four since 1986.
June 28	Skip announces the hiring of new baseball coach Paul Mainieri, formerly Notre Dame's coach.
July 4	Skip is inducted into the inaugural class of the National College Baseball Hall of Fame in Lubbock, Texas.

2007

April 12	Skip hires Van Chancellor, a four-time WNBA champion head coach, as women's basketball coach.
Spring	LSU sets a school record with 12 teams in various sports finishing ranked in the top 25.

2008

Jan. 8	LSU football team wins the National Championship, 38-24, over Ohio State at the Superdome in New Orleans. Thus, Les Miles becomes the first of four coaches hired by Skip to win it all.
March 31	LSU women's basketball, under coach Van Chancellor, beats North Carolina, 56-50, at New Orleans Arena to reach the Final Four.
June 14	LSU track coach Dennis Shaver's women's outdoor team wins the National Championship at Drake Stadium in Des Moines, Iowa.
June 30	Skip works his last day as athletic director and transitions to athletic director emeritus through 2010. Joe Alleva, Duke's former athletic director, replaces him.

2009

Feb. 20   The new 9,200-seat Alex Box Stadium opens. Skip oversaw the $38 million project as athletic director and had been working on it since he was coaching in the late 1990s and early 2000s. (Most of the construction cost was paid for by Skip's football season ticket licensing plan.)

A crowd of 9,054, including the Bertmans, sitting to the left of the LSU dugout, watched the Tigers beat Villanova, 12-3.

June 24   Paul Mainieri's baseball Tigers win the first National Championship for LSU without Skip as coach, 11-4 over Texas, taking the best-of-three series at Rosenblatt Stadium in Omaha. In doing so, Mainieri becomes the third Skip Bertman hire to win a national title.

2011

Sept. 9   Skip Bertman is inducted in the LSU Athletics Hall of Fame.

2013

May 17   The field at Alex Box Stadium is named Skip Bertman Field.

2019

Sept. 13   A 9-foot, 3,500-pound granite and bronze statue of Skip Bertman leaning on a dugout railing is unveiled outside Alex Box Stadium as hundreds of family, friends and former players look on.

2021

March 23   Premier showing of "Hold The Rope," an ESPN/SEC Network documentary on the life and career of Skip Bertman. The film, by Marc Kinderman, was shown at L'Auberge Casino and Hotel outside Baton Rouge.

Appendix 3

Skip Bertman's original check list

(Things-to-do to improve LSU baseball facilities in 1983, the year Skip arrived in Baton Rouge)

Campus Correspondence   LOUISIANA STATE UNIVERSITY

From: Skip Bertman   Date: November 14, 1983

To: Bill McClure

Here is the list of items either in the process of being completed or not yet
started upon that Bob, Ray, Bill and you talked about to be fixed up at the
baseball stadium or practice field. I realize that nothing can be started of course
until after you have finished in the football stadium next week.

1. 100 permanent seats.
2. Aluminum from the tennis center
3. Telephones
4. Paint bathroom floors and add (tile substitute rec by Bill Ferguson)
5. Some type of water proof tile (or substitute) for the walls of bathrooms
   and showers
6. Tile for the training room floor (no substitute)
7. Shower heads and soap dishes
8. Shelves for the equipment room in the lounge
9. Shelves for the lounge are (decorative)
10. 2 benches from Ray Heber
11. 5 planters from Ray
12. New Scale for lockerroom
13. Wood platforms for scale and water fountain in lockerroom
14. Lights for batting cage area and for bullpens
15. New toilet for coaches showerroom
16. All wood boundaries (treated 2 X 4's) for out of play areas
17. Bottom rail on fences placed in and secured
18. Paint scoreboard
19. Protective cover on fence ?
20. Artificial surface for on deck, coaches boxes and walk way to batter's box
21. Top rail of all fancing painted gold
22. Outside stadium foliage attended to
23. Stadium wash blasted
24. Signs for stadium office needed (praices, etc.
25. Concession stands repainted and fixed up
26. Turnstyle and ticket entrance needed
27. Paint box lockerroom floor (we have artist)
28. Professional signs (I have the signs) placed up on staium, locations TBA
29. Windows outside lockerroom and the training fixed and covered with wood and painted.
30. Paint purple trim on dugout office ledge
31. Fix restrooms (all the way, toilets, urinals and new stalls.)
32. Pinic area (tables for right field)
33. New foliage next to ticket office
34. Bleachers painted and fixed
35. Paint above and below TIGER BOX STADIUM sign in front
36. Lights in parking lot across the street   *People*
37. Walk way to left field area fixed
38. Fence 8 foot for the practice field similar grade to existing chain link
39. Gravel or foliage at main fence
40. Signs 330, 400 and 330 for fence
41. Bleachers at practice field for summer ball
42. Bleachers possible in right field at Alex Box
43. Pa system improved
44. Refinish wood in Grandstand and sand and redo metal supports in all seats
45. Take batting cage down under the stands, general clean up under the stands, general
    painting under the stands

46. House lights in Grandstand
47. Additional attached to present batting cage
48. Cement area from lockerroom to batting cage
49. Poison all weeds, cut all foliage around the fence
50. Replace chicken wire behind home plate
51. Green or purple paint on the top of the grandstand
52. Paint foul poles yellow or fence pole as well as chicken wire
53. Fix scoreboard lights
54. Repair sprinkler system
55. Check candle power, replace necessary light bulbs.
56. Cement in dugout steps, possibly coaching boxes
57. Replace wooden benches dugout and add new turf
58. Chain link railing around backstop area repaired
59. Fence on top of the roof or grandstand
60. Paint poles and other areas inside grandstand

Sources

Books, Magazine Articles, Media Guides and Other Printed Material

"A 1987 Omaha Re-Deaux and Lessons Learned in A Post-Season Miss." Jim Mashek. *Tiger Rag* Magazine, May 2020.

Bertman, Skip. *Youth League Baseball*. Chicago: Masters Press, 1989

"College World Series Records Books." Media Relations Staff, NCAA. 1986-2021.

"The Fifth Time Is a Charm." Jim Mashek. *Tiger Rag* Magazine, May 2020.

"Going Out on Top After 18 Seasons and Five NCAA Titles, LSU Coach Skip Bertman Is Calling It Quits." Tim Crothers. *Sports Illustrated*, May 28, 2001.

"High Noon in College Station." Jim Mashek. *Tiger Rag* Magazine, May 2020.

Honeycutt, Leo. *Skip Bertman, The Mind of a Genius*. (Unpublished manuscript, completed Aug. 14, 2017.)

Hunter, Bruce. *Skip, The Man and The System*. Baton Rouge, La.: Victory Publishing, 1992.

"LSU Baseball Media Guides." Bill Franques. 1989-2021.

"LSU Baseball Media Guides." Sports Information Staff, LSU. 1983-88.

"Nowhere To Go But Up: The Birth of Skip Bertman's LSU Baseball Dynasty." Jim Mashek. *Tiger Rag* Magazine, May 2020.

"Skip Bertman, Architect of a Baseball Dynasty." Glenn Guilbeau. Baton Rouge *Advocate*, March 8, 2001.

Newspapers

Articles published in the following newspapers were used for reference in writing this book. The articles, published over a 38-year period, are too numerous to cite individually, though the authors are listed.

Alexandria *Daily Town Talk* – Glenn Guilbeau; Michael Lough; John Marcase; Jeff Matthews; Jeffery Nixon; Bob Tompkins; Bruce Viergutz. Various articles, 1989-96, 2016, 2021.

Baton Rouge *Advocate* – Smiley Anders; Ryan Broussard; Ted Castillo; Christopher Connell; Ross Dellenger; Carl Dubois; Les East; Lee Feinswog; Bruce Hunter; Sam King; Brad Lambert; Joe Macaluso; Jim Mashek; Michelle Millhollon; Dave Moorman; Scott Rabalais; Risa Robert; Chandler Rome; William Weathers. Various articles, 1983-2021.

Baton Rouge *State-Times* – Howard Arceneaux; Sam King; Joe Macaluso; George Morris. Various articles, 1983-91.

Bryan-College Station *Eagle* – Richard Croome. Various articles, 2013-14.

Fort Lauderdale *Sun-Sentinel* – Darin Klahr, "Stuck on the Pitch," January 14, 1997.

Lake Charles *American-Press* – Scooter Hobbs. Various articles, 1990-2009.

Los Angeles Times – Gary Klein; Jason Reid. Various articles, 1993 and '97.

LSU *Daily Reveille* – Scott Branson, "Man Behind Legendary '96 Home Run Had Rollercoaster Career at LSU," April 4, 2012.

MetroWest *Daily News* (suburban Boston) – Rick Smith, "Whatever Happened To: Holliton's Rich Cordani Won Titles At 2 Levels," June 11, 2016.

Mobile *Press-Register* – Gareth Clary; Glenn Guilbeau; Ben Nolan. Various articles, 1983-98.

New Orleans *Times-Picayune* – Teddy Allen; Charlie Bennett; Jeff Duncan; Peter Finney; Derrick Goold; Jim Kleinpeter; Bob Roesler; Wright Thompson; Brian Allee-Walsh. Various articles, 1983-2019.

Omaha *World-Herald* – Steve Pivovar; Tom Shatel; Gene Schinzel. Various articles, 1991-2001, 2016, 2019.

Shreveport Times – Scott Ferrell. Various articles, 1991-1995.

Tuscaloosa News – Cecil Hurt. Various articles, 1997 and 2021.

Online Sources

Blackwell, Brian. "Fame Didn't Change LSU Star Warren Morris," BaptistMessage.com, Aug. 4, 2006.

Cavadi, Wayne. "The Wild Numbers Behind LSU's Probably Unbreakable Home Run Records," NCAA.com, Jan. 29, 2020.

Guilbeau, Glenn. "Skip Bertman Inducted to Louisiana Sports Hall of Fame," LSUsports.net, June 23, 2002.

Marx, Jeffrey. "Collin Strall an Unexpected Product of '96 Title," LSUsports.net, Feb. 18, 2015.

Sherman, Mitch. "Looking Back on Warren Morris' Historic Home Run," ESPN.com, June 26, 2016.

Williams, Doug. "Warren Morris' Home Run Lifts LSU in '96," ESPN.com, June 15, 2011.

Personal Interviews

The names listed here are those of former LSU players and coaches, unless otherwise indicated. The date at the end of each entry refers to the date when the author conducted the interview.

Verge Ausberry, LSU assistant athletic director, 2019-present; he has worked in the Athletic Department since 2001, when he was hired by Athletic Director Skip Bertman. (Aug. 7, 2019)

Blair Barbier, infielder (1997-2000), quintessential team captain, and a hero of 2000 National Championship game. (Oct. 21, 2021)

Skip Bertman, LSU baseball head coach (1984-2001), won five national championships, reached College World Series 11 times, won seven SEC championships, and served as LSU's Athletic Director, 2001-08. (Multiple interviews Feb. 2019 – Dec. 2021)

Mike Bianco, Ole Miss baseball coach (2001-present), LSU catcher (1988-89), LSU assistant coach (1993-97). He is the only man to play for, coach under, and coach against LSU's Skip Bertman as a head coach. (July 10, 2019)

Pete Bush, first baseman (1987-89). He was co-captain when LSU upset No. 1 Texas A&M in College Station twice to reach the 1989 College World Series. (July 9, 2019)

Paul Byrd, pitcher (1989-91) and key starter on three World Series teams, including LSU's first National Champions in 1991. He held the school record through 2021 for most wins in a season with 17 in 1990. (June 5, 2020)

Dan Canevari, LSU assistant coach (1991-2001), who also pitched for Bertman at University of Miami (1977-79). (Several interviews Feb. 2019 – Dec. 2021.)

John Cohen, Mississippi State Athletic Director (2016-present), Mississippi State baseball coach (2009-16), Northwestern State coach (1998-2001), and Mississippi State player (1987-90). (Oct. 19, 2019)

Patrick Coogan, pitcher (1994-97) and ace of '97 National Champions. He was also an original Bertman youth camper in 1984 and is the son of original Coaches' Committee member Michael Coogan. (Aug. 25, 2021)

Rich Cordani, infielder/outfielder (1990-91), hero of NCAA South I Regional title win over USC, and member of the first National Championship team. (April 9, 2020)

Brad Cresse, catcher (1997-2000), a hero of 2000 national title game, and led the nation in home runs with 30 and RBIs with 106 in 2000. (Nov. 2, 2021)

Pat Cuntz, infielder (1983-85), member of Bertman's first LSU team in 1984. (Aug. 15, 2019)

Bill Dailey, LSU assistant coach (1998-2001), on Bertman's last National Championship staff in 2000. (June 8, 2020)

Charles D'Agnostino, original member of Coaches' Committee in 1983. (June 17, 2020)

Eddie Davis, Long Beach State outfielder in 1993. He was a former Bertman camper from New Orleans whose pinch-hit homer set up 10-8 LSU loss en route to LSU's 1993 National Championship. (Feb. 6, 2021)

Shawn Eddy, LSU baseball trainer (1996-2005), and now men's basketball trainer. (Dec. 10, 2021)

Mark Emmert, NCAA president (2010-present), LSU chancellor (1999-2004), who hired Bertman as Athletic Director in 2000. (July 18, 2019)

Bill Franques, LSU baseball Sports Information Director (1988-present). (March 10, 2020 and numerous times previously)

Craig Faulkner, catcher (1984-87), member of Bertman's first team in 1984, first SEC championship team in 1986, and first two World Series teams in 1986 and '87. (Aug. 4, 2019)

Arnold Fielkow, New Orleans Saints vice-president (1999-2005), who worked with Bertman when Saints played in Tiger Stadium after Hurricane Katrina in 2005. (July 29, 2019)

Luis Garcia, infielder/pitcher (1989-91), member of Bertman's first National Championship team in 1991; part of three World Series teams. (March 28, 2020)

Pat Garrity, third baseman/designated hitter (1989-91), hero of NCAA Central Regional title game in 1989 at No. 1 Texas A&M; part of three World Series teams. (June 20, 2019)

Derrick Goold, St. Louis Cardinals beat writer at St. Louis *Post-Dispatch* (2005-present), and LSU baseball writer at New Orleans *Times-Picayune* in 2000. (Oct. 21, 2021)

Rick Greene, relief pitcher (1990-92), a hero of LSU's first National Championship in 1991. He set the school season record for saves with 14 in '91 that stood until 2009, and finished with school career record 29 saves that lasted two decades. (April 10, 2020)

Mark Guthrie, pitcher (1984-87), key starter for three seasons and a member of Bertman's first team in 1984. He was on the first SEC Championship team in 1986 and first two World Series teams in 1986 and '87. (Aug. 3, 2019)

Cedrick Harris, center fielder (1997-2000), one of top hitters on Bertman's last National Championship team in 2000; he was a three-year starter. (Nov. 6, 2021)

Trey Hodges, pitcher (1999-2000), MVP of 2000 World Series as he picked up two victories in relief, including the national title game. (Nov. 5, 2021)

Stanley Jacobs, former LSU Board of Supervisors member, former LSU basketball player, and friend of Bertman. (May 10, 2019)

Rusty Jenkins, pitcher (1989-90). (Sept. 14, 2019)

Tookie Johnson, second baseman (1988-91), three-year starter and member of first National Championship team in 1991. (June 8, 2020)

Steve Kittrell, South Alabama baseball coach (1984-2011), who took the Jaguars to 18 NCAA Regionals, five of which involved LSU. (May 19, 2019)

Brandon Larson, shortstop (1997), SEC home run king with 40 for Tigers' 1997 National Championship team. He set the pace for LSU's NCAA record 188 homers, likely never to be broken. (Aug. 29, 2021)

Brett Laxton, pitcher (1993-96), national Freshman of the Year in 1993, who set World Series championship game record with 16 strikeouts to beat Wichita State. He was a key starter on the 1996 National Championship team. (July 24, 2020)

Curtis Leskanic, pitcher (1989), a hero of LSU's upset of No. 1 Texas A&M in NCAA Central Regional at College Station, winning three times in relief, including the title game. He set the school record for wins in a season with SEC-high of 15. (Feb. 26, 2020)

Richard Lipsey, Baton Rouge businessman, founder of Tiger Athletic Foundation in 1987, major financial supporter of baseball program, and close friend of Bertman. (Feb. 25, 2019)

Stan Loewer, pitcher (1984-87), key starter on Bertman's first team in 1984, first SEC Championship team in 1986, and first two World Series teams, in 1986 and '87. He won a school record 14 games in 1986. (Feb. 22, 2019)

Ron Maestri, UNO baseball coach (1972-84, 2014-15), who was first Louisiana coach to take a team to the College World Series, in 1983. (May 27, 2019)

Paul Mainieri, LSU baseball coach (2007-21), won the 2009 National Championship, reached 2017 national semifinals, and took Tigers to the World Series five times. He won four SEC titles and six SEC Tournament crowns. (July 20, 2020)

Dr. Ronnie Matthews, orthopedic surgeon in Baton Rouge area, performed hamate bone surgery on LSU second baseman Warren Morris in 1996. (May 25, 2016)

Bhrett McCabe, pitcher (1991-95), part of Bertman's first two National Championship teams, in 1991 and '93. He became a clinical and sports psychologist. (June 24, 2020)

Ben McDonald, pitcher (1987-89), LSU's only Golden Spikes award winner and Baseball America Player of the Year in 1989 after setting SEC strikeouts record with 202 and consecutive scoreless innings with 44 and two-thirds. He was the first overall pick in the 1989 Major League draft. (July 18, 2019)

Wally McMakin, Baton Rouge businessman who was the one-man search "committee" that landed Miami associate head coach/pitching coach Skip Bertman as LSU's head coach. He is also a former LSU third baseman (1973-76). (July 18, 2019)

Chris Moock, third baseman/outfielder (1988, '91-92). After serving as a backup quarterback at LSU (1988-90), he developed into a top player on Bertman's first National Championship team in 1991. (April 11, 2020)

Warren Morris, second baseman/outfielder (1993-96), hit the most famous home run in College World Series history and the only National Championship game walk-off with two outs and one on to beat Miami, 9-8, on June 8, 1996. (April 23, 2016)

Lyle Mouton, outfielder (1990-91), dual sports star who also played basketball. He was a hero of Bertman's first National Championship in 1991 with three home runs in Omaha. (Sept. 14, 2019)

John O'Donoghue, pitcher (1988-90), one of the top pitchers on Bertman's strongest staffs during his time at LSU. (Sept. 14, 2019)

Chad Ogea, pitcher (1989-91), workhorse of the pitching staff during Bertman's first National Championship season, in 1991, finishing 14-5 and getting 6-3 win over Wichita State in the title game. (June 14, 2019)

Keith Osik, shortstop/third baseman (1988-90), three-year starter who played on two World Series teams. (May 13, 2020)

Mike Papajohn, outfielder (1986-87), two-year starter in center field who played on two World Series teams and first SEC championship team in '86. He began a successful acting career as an extra in the 1988 movie "Everybody's All-American," filmed in Baton Rouge. (June, 30, 2018)

Rick Perry, Tiger Athletic Foundation president (2014-21), and LSU Athletic Department employee beginning in early 1980s. (March 2, 2021)

Ron Polk, Mississippi State baseball coach (1976-97, 2002-08), and Georgia coach (2000-01). He was a Miami Dade Junior College South assistant (1968-71) when Skip Bertman was coaching Miami Beach High. (Sept. 23, 2019)

Dan Radakovich, Miami Athletic Director (2021-present), and LSU associate athletic director under Bertman (2001-06). (June 21, 2019)

Ronnie Rantz, pitcher (1991-92), member of Bertman's first National Championship team. Later, he started Jumbo cable network that televised LSU baseball games for a number of years. (June 4, 2020)

Mark Richt, Miami football coach (2016-18), Georgial coach (2001-15), and Miami quarterback (1979-82). He tried out as pitcher when Bertman was associate head coach/pitching coach at Miami. (Jan. 5, 2021)

Armando Rios, outfielder (1991-93), a hero of Bertman's first and third National Championship games. He homered in the '91 title game and made the All-World Series team in '93. (July 26, 2020)

Russell Rome, team manager (1985-91), part of LSU's first SEC championship in '86 and first five trips to the College World Series. (March 3, 2020)

Nick Saban, Alabama football coach (2007-present) and former LSU head coach (2000-04) under Athletic Director Skip Bertman. (May 29, 2019; July 22, 2016; and July 21, 2017)

Scott Schneidewind, outfielder (1988-89), scored in the top of eighth to tie NCAA Central Regional title game, 4-4, at No. 1 Texas A&M, flashing Texas' "Hook 'em Horns" sign as he crossed home. (July 11, 2019)

Jim Schwanke, LSU hitting coach (1996-99), instrumental in developing home run monster "Gorilla Ball" teams, particularly the '97 offense that set an NCAA record with 188 home runs. (Oct. 13, 2021)

Mike Sirotka, pitcher (1990-93), one of LSU's most dominant starters and a key part of Bertman's first two National Championship teams. (July 13, 2020)

Dave Snow, Long Beach State baseball coach (1989-2001), went against LSU in classic postseason games at Alex Box in 1997 and at World Series in 1993. (Feb. 5, 2021)

Jeff "Rooster" Southall, LSU assistant (1988-89) and LSU pitcher (1982-83). (July 15, 2019)

Ted Stickles, LSU game management director for the first NCAA Regionals at Alex Box Stadium. (July 8, 2019)

Ryan Theriot, second baseman/shortstop (1999-2001), a hero of LSU's 2000 National Championship game. (Oct. 22, 2021)

Doug Thompson, pitcher (1997-98), dominant starting pitcher for two seasons. In 1997, he pitched a complete-game win on two days' rest over South Alabama to put LSU in NCAA South I Regional title game. (Sept. 17, 2021)

Herb Vincent, SEC associate commissioner (2013-present), LSU associate athletic director (2002-13), and LSU Sports Information Director (1988-2000). (May 30, 2019)

Todd Walker, second baseman (1992-94), one of greatest hitters in LSU history, led Tigers to '93 national title and earned World Series MVP with three home runs, including a grand slam. He helped lead LSU to the 1994 World Series. He holds the LSU career batting average record at .396 and longest hitting streak with 33 games in 1993. (Feb. 22, 2019 and July 16, 2020)

Jim Wells, Alabama baseball coach (1995-2009), Northwestern State coach (1990-94), and LSU assistant (1987-89). (July 11, 2019)

Scott Woodward, LSU Athletic Director (2019-present), former Texas A&M and Washington Athletic Director, and former LSU director of external affairs (2000-04). (June 19, 2019)

Shane Youman, pitcher (1999-2001), key reliever on Bertman's last National Championship team, in 2000. (Sept. 14, 2019)

Index

Note: Names appearing in **bold** are Tigers baseball team members and personnel.
Page numbers in *italics* refer to photographs and maps.

Abdul-Jabar, Kareem, 149
Acadian Ambulance, 64, 77
Adams, Gary, 136
Ainsworth, Kurt, 130–131, 133, 218, 221
Albright, Eric, 36
Alex Box Stadium
  American Baseball Coaches Association Hall of Fame Tournament at, 62
  as another Tiger Stadium, 53–60
  attendance records, 32, 53–54, 80, 86, 120, 149–150, 154, 169, 224, 227
  in disrepair, xiii, 215
  enhancements, additions to, xiii, 161, 211, 230
  field named Skip Bertman Field, *188*, 229
  as intimidation, intimidating, xi, 36, 87, 135, 191
  loudness of, 55–56, 124
  magic of, 124
  map of, *171*
  name-sake, 26
  and NCAA Regionals, 53–60
  new stadium, xvi, 120, 161, 229
  old trailer office at, 65
  pep rally for 1991 Tigers, 75–76
  photos of, *97, 99, 101–102, 106, 112, 185, 188, 190–192*
  weather and, 55–56, 61, 63–64, 124
Allen, Teddy, vi, 51
Alleva, Joe, 162, 228
Anderson, Matt, 126
Antonini, Adrian, 88–89
Arnsparger, Bill, 23, 196
Ausberry, Verge, 156, 160, 164–165, 168–170, 173–176, 196, 232
averages, law of, 122, 199–201

Bahnsen, Bo, 165
Bailey, "Beetle," 84, *105*, 199
Baird, Hal, 121

Barbier, Blair, 118, 120–126, 130, 132–138, 140–144, 148, 153, 156, *181*, 196, 207, 213–214, 232
Barker, Sean, 149
Barnhart, Mitch, 161–162
Battle, John, 35
Baudin, Jerry, 164–165
Belichick, Bill, 79
belief, believe, believing, ix, xii, xiv, 45, 47, 54, 65, 68, 70, 73, 79, 96, 128, 143–145, 199, 202, 207
Belle, Albert "Joey," 208
Bennett, Phil, 160
Berger, Richard, vi, 217–218
Berkman, Lance, 126
Bernhardt, Tom, 119–121, 126, 128
Berrios, Harry, 87, 199
Bertman, Cele, 222
Bertman, Jan, iv, vi, vii, 25, 157, 210, 223
Bertman, Jodi, vi, vii, xv, 25, 95, 147–148, 210, 223
Bertman, Lisa. *See* Pate, Dr. Lisa Jo (Bertman)
Bertman, Lori. *See* Guirard, Lori (Bertman)
Bertman, Louis, 218, 222
Bertman, Sandy (Schwartz), vi, vii, xv, 25, 27, 29, 31, 69, 77–78, *108*, 114, 147–148, 152, 156, 163, *188*, 210–211, 223
Bertman, Stanley "Skip"
  and Alex Box Stadium
    checklist for improvements to, 230
  as angel on shoulder, 83, 87, 91
  as Athletic Director (AD), v, xvi, 151, 155, 161–165, 167–170, 172–173, 175, *192*, 193, 195, 212, 216–217, 226–229
  and "baseball's like that," 209
  on being star in players' own minds, movie, ix, 65, 133, 145
  and belief, believe, believing, ix, xii, xiv, 45, 47, 54, 65, 68, 70, 73, 79, 96, 128, 143–145, 199, 202, 207

and Bon Jovi (band), 29–33
as clairvoyant, 122
and College World Series (CWS)
  1989, 47–51
  1991, 67–78
  1993, 83–91
  1996, 93–96, 113–115
  1997, 126–128
  2000, 129–145
on competing, competitiveness,
  competition, 71, 90, 121, 153, 167,
  210, 214
and customer service, 174, 212
and daughters, vi, vii, xv, 25, 69, 95,
  147, 156, 210–211, 223
and football
  and motor home, RV parking at
    Tiger Stadium, 173
  ticket licensing plan, xvi, 167–170,
    172, 227, 229
and football mentality, 29, 51
and Gorilla baseball, 69, 117–131
and Grand Illusion (trick), 24, 200,
  224
and hips, hip replacement sugery,
  76–77, *108*
and "Hold the Rope," vi, xi, 71–72,
  95, 144, 215–217, 229
and H.W.A. (How-to-Win
  Awareness), x, 139
and imagery, imagining, ix, 68, 96,
  169
and inspiration, inspiring, xiv, 87, 93,
  155, 211, 213
as junkyard dog, 124
and law of averages, 122, 199–201
legacy, 152, *191*, 193
on mental toughness, preparedness,
  ix, 47, 70, 139, 203
as mentor, 193
and mentor Max Sapper, 205, 210,
  217, 222–223
as Miami Beach High baseball coach,
  vi, 23, 161, 200, 202, 218–219, 223
as Miami Beach Recreation
  Department Director of baseball,
  217–218, 222–223
and mindset, ix, 68, 94, 204
and motivation, motivating, as
  motivator, 40, 42, 70, 125, 127, 132,
  174, 213–214, 217, 219, 227
and Nick Saban, 195–198

and odds, ix, x, 203
as old school, 195
on ownership, ix, x, xi, 30–31, 40, 141
on percentages, 70, 120, 199–201,
  203–204
photos of, *97, 105, 108, 112,
  177–178, 185, 188–192*
on practice, practicing, x, xiv, 23,
  29, 118, 136–137, 199–200, 206,
  209–210
and predictions, ability to predict,
  xvii, 40, 43, 122, 143, 196, 199
on preparation, preparedness, x, 32,
  38, 70–71, 203, 206–207, 209, 219
on pressure, performing under, ix, x,
  37–38, 40, 114, 202, 208–209, 214
as rock star, 150–151, 193
and the Shake Off, 205–206
and Stanky Field, 26
on success, succeeding, v, ix, xi, xii,
  96, 133, 193, 199–214
as Summer Olympics (1996) coach,
  206, 226
and Sunday Speaker Series, 132, 213
and Sunday spiritual guidance, xii
and the system, ix, xii, 68, 70, 118,
  144–145, 196, 202
on tenacity, 145
on tendencies, 70, 203–204
on "That's baseball," 51, 79–81
and thinking, how to think, 35, 79,
  204, 213
as Tigers baseball coach
  *(See also particular subjects in this
  heading)*
and offer, 25–27
and Texas A&M (1989), 35–48
timeline, 222–229
and T.O.B. (Transfer of Blame), x
and trick plays, 23–24, 200, 204–205
and trust, ix, 122, 132, 172–173, 202
videos, use of, 44, 69, 84, 93,
  127–128, 132–133, 140, 145, 200,
  209, 211, 213–214
vision of, xiv, 54, 65, 169, 172
and visualization, visualizing, 65, 72,
  96, 132–133, 144–145, 203, 219
on weights, weightlifting, 118–119
and W.I.N. (What's Important Now),
  xii
and Yellow Book, 204–205
Bethea, Scott, 58

Bianco, Mike, 29–33, 36–37, 40–44,
49–50, 61, 73, *97, 101*, 117–121, 123,
150, 233
Birriel, Felipe, 84–85
blame. See *T.O.B.* (Transfer of Blame)
Blow, Red, xiii
Bon Jovi, Jon, 30
Bon Jovi (band), 29–33
Boniol, Don, viii
Boniol, Mike "Bones," 130
Bonnette, Michael, 195–196
Boone, Brett, 56–58
Bowles, Justin, 94, 206
Box, Alex, 26
Brady, John, xvi, 160, 175, 195, 228
Brady, Tom, 79
Brian, Billy, 148–149
Brodhead, Bob (Athletic Director),
23–25, 159
Brodhead, Mindy, 23
Brown, Dale, 160
Brumfield, Victor, 148
Bryant, Bear, 152, 196
Burke, John, 67–68
Bush, Pete, 29–31, 35, 37–42, 44,
46–47, 50, 73, *99*, 150, 233
Bush, President George H.W., 76–78, *108*
Butcher, Arthur, 49
Byington, John, 36, 41
Byrant, Scott, 49
Byrd, Paul, 39–40, 42, 49–50, 55–56,
60–61, 67–69, 73, 75–76, 84, *107*,
117, 200–201, 204, 214, 221, 233

Cala, Craig, 41–43
Canevari, Dan "Cano," v, 61, 68, 77,
105, 118–120, 131, 134, 143, 148–
149, *185*, 202, 206, 209, 211–212, 233
Cannizaro, Andy, 155
Cannon, Billy, 76
Carlin, George, 136
Carruth, Maria, 170, 172
Carter, Joe, 93
Carter, Mark, 152
Centala, Scott, 42–43
Chamberlain, Wilt, 218
Chancellor, Van, xvi, 176, 228
Chandler, Tom, 38
Chatman, Pokey, 176
Childress, Rob, 45
Cirillo, Rick, 56
clairvoyance, 122
Clemente, Roberto, 84

Coaches Committee, xiii, xvi, 74, 149,
169, 211, 233
Cohen, John, 151, 233
College World Series (CWS)
1989, 47–51
1991, 67–74
1993, 83–91
1996, 93–96, 113–115
1997, 126–128
2000, 129–145
competing, competitiveness,
competition, 71, 90, *99*, 121, 153,
167, *184, 191*, 210, 214
Coogan, Patrick, 95, 114, 117, 119,
122–124, 126–129, 156, *178*,
201–202, 205, 207, 209, 218, 233
Cooley, Chad, 119
Cora, Alex, 95
Corcoran, Roy, 149
Cordani, Rich, 53, 56–57, 60–61, 64,
70–71, *102*, 233
Cox, Bobby, 214
Craig, Dameyune, 35
Cresse, Brad, xv, 118, 129–130, 132,
134, 136, 141–144, 147–148, 153,
156–157, *181*, 226, 233
Cross, Augie, 24
Crowe, Russell, 132
Cuntz, Casey, 119–120
Cuntz, Pat, 216, 233
customer service, 174, 212
CWS. *See* College World Series (CWS)

Dailey, Bill, 134, 138, *185*, 233
Dalton, Josh, 130
Daniel, Michael, 127–128
David, Brad, 149
Davis, Eddie, 88–89, 233
Davis, Randy, 40, 85
Davis, Wes, 118, 120, 124–126,
128–130
Dean, Joe (Athletic Director), 54, 59,
159–161, 167–168
DeBriyn, Norm, 152
Dedeaux, Rod, xv, 55
Demouy, Chris, 117, 126, 156
DiMaggio, Joe, 76–77, 133, 213
DiNardo, Gerry, 159–160
Dreifort, Darren, 71, 89–90
Dressendorfer, Kirk, 48
Dugas, Marvin "Big Ragoo," 55, 58
Dunn, Nathan, 95

Earnhart, **Clint,** 129–130
Easley, Mike, 36, 40, 43
Eddy, Shawn, 138, 233
Elsey, Justin, 201
Emmert, Mark (Chancellor), 160–164,
    167–169, 172, 193, 226, 233
envisioning. *See* visualization,
    visualizing (seeing)
Espinosa, Phil, 43–44
Ewing, Mark, 164–165

Fans, fan support, fan experience, v,
    xiii, 37, 54–56, 58–60, 74–76, 80, 86,
    120, 124, 135–136, 139, 142, 151,
    155, 160, 167, 172–174, 212
Faulk, Kevin, 35
Faulkner, Craig, 234
Favre, Brett, 159
Ferdinand, Marie, 156–157
Ferreira, Nelson, vi, 218
Fielkow, Arnold, 234
Finney, Joan, 76
Fisher, Cole, 35
Fisher, Jimbo, 35
Fisher, Pop, xiii
Fontenot, Mike, 134, 137, 140–141,
    143, 148–149
football
    (*See also* Tiger Stadium)
    football mentality, 29, 51
Foote, Kevin, 79
Francona, Terry, 214
Franques, Bill, vi, xv, 53–55, 58–59,
    62–63, 85, 113, 125, 131–132,
    163–164, 211, 233
Fraser, Ron, vi, 23, 25–27, 211, 224
Frick, Matt, 128
Furniss, Eddy, 90, 118, 120–123,
    125–126, 129, *179,* 206, 208

Galy, **Andy,** 73
Garcia, Luis, 42, 60–61, 63, 72–74,
    219, 234
Garidel, Jamin, 156, 218–219
Garidel, Jerry, 218
Garrido, Augie, xv, 79, 81, 136
Garrity, Pat, 35–38, 41, 43–45, 60–61,
    68, 71, 75, *101,* 210, 225, 234
Geautreau, Jake, 155
Gibson, Debbie, 32
Gibson, Mel, 132
Gill, Richard, 160, 197

Gillespie, Mike, 53, 55, 59
Gomez, Hunter, 133, 135, 202
Gomez, Rudy, 95
Gonzales, Izzy, 124
Gorilla Baseball, 69, 117–131, 136, 236
Grahe, Joe, 47
Grand Illusion (trick), 24, 200, 224
Greely, Jim, 86–87, 91
Green, Tyler, 69–71, 90
Greene, Rick, 57, 60–62, 69–72, 80–81,
    86, 91, *105,* 203–204, 221, 234
Grisham, Wes, 41–42, 73
Groff, Matt, 154
Gruver, Matt, 41
Guidry, Weylin, 133, 137, 149, 156,
    208–209
Guilbeau, Glenn, v, 246
Guirard, Lori (Bertman), vi, vii, xv, 25,
    147–148, 210, 223
Guirard, Sophie, 148
Gumbel, Greg, 142
Gustafson, Cliff, 50
Guthrie, Mark, xiv, 73, 117, 221, 234

Hale, Beau, 136–137
Hallman, Curley, 159–160
Harris, Cedric, Jr., 156
Harris, Cedrick, 129–130, 134,
    137–143, 148, 153, 156, *184,* 234
Harris, Marie Ferdinand, 156–157
Hawpe, Brad, 134, 137, 140–141, 148,
    153
Hawthorne, Jim, 113, 124, 131
Hayes, Louie, vi, 217
Heath, Matt, 149
Helton, Todd, 51
Herry, David, 63
Hester, Kurt, 119
Hetzel, Eric, 73
Higgins, Danny, 118, 120, 125,
    127–129
Hill, Aaron, 149
Hobbs, Kenneth "Scooter," vi, 25
Hodges, Trey, 133–135, 137–140, 143,
    148, 153, *185,* 203, 214, 234
"Hold the Rope," vi, xi, 71–72, 95, 144,
    215–217, 229
"Hold the Rope" (documentary), vi, 216,
    229
holy oil, 68, *104*
Honeycutt, Leo, v, 246
Horton, Conan, 122

Howard, Chris, 165
Huffman, Ryan, 86
Huizenga, Wayne, 196–198
Hurriane Katrina, 196, 234
H.W.A. (How-to-Win Awareness), x, 139
Hymel, Gary, 60–61, 64, 69, 73–74, *102*

Imagery, imagining, ix, 68, 96, 169
inspiration, inspiring, xiv, 87, 93, 155, 211, 213
intimidation, intimidating, xi, 36, 87, 135, *191*

Jackson, Kenny, 86–87
Jacobs, Stanley, xiii, 160–162, 167, 170, 172, 193, 234
Jenkins, Rusty, 234
Johnson, Jay, 217
Johnson, Mark, 38, 45–46
Johnson, Michael, 213
Johnson, Russ, 79, 85, 87–89, 91, *109*, 208, 221
Johnson, Tookie, 41, 44, 60–62, 64, 67–68, 70–71, 73, *98*, 234
Jones, Bob, 42–43
Jones, Greg, 176
Jones, Lance, 49
Jones, Rick, 150, 155
Jorgensen, Ryan, 148

Kaizen, 59–60
Karp, Josh, 136
Kasprzak, Mike, 24
Katrina, Hurricane, 196, 234
Keisler, Randy, 156, 221
Kelly, Jim, 27
Khoury, Tony, 80
Kiffin, Lane, 118
Kindall, Jerry, 143
Kinderman, Marc, vi, 229
Kite, Dan, 117
Kittrell, Steve, 59, 86, 234
Knoblauch, Chuck, 36
Koerner, Mike, 118, 120–122, 125–128, 206
Koufax, Sandy, 133
Kragthorpe, Steve, 35

Lamabe, Jack, 24–25
Lane, Eric, vi, 213
Langston, Keith, 38, 41

Lanier, Tim, 93–96, *177*
LaRosa, Mark, 39, 41, 56–58, 60–61
Larson, Brandon, 117–121, 123–128, *179*, 221, 234
Laval, Ray "Smoke," xiv, 30, 40, 135, 148, 175, 216, 226
law of averages, 122, 199–201
Laxton, Brett, 85, 87, 90–91, *110*, 117, 153, 208, 221, 234
Leary, Rob, 73
Leaumont, Jeff, 156
LeMond, Greg, 213
Leskanic, Curtis, 39–40, 42–45, 48–51, 117, 204, 221, 225, 235
Levin, Marlene, vi, 215, 217–218
Lim, Ron, 41
Linden, Todd, 149, 152
Lipsey, Richard, xiii, xvi, 149, 160, 162–163, 216, 235
Loewer, Stan, xiv, 73, 117, 216, 235

Macaluso, Joe, vi, 43, 68
Maddon, Joe, 214
Maestri, Ron, 152, 235
Mainieri, Paul, xvi, 175–176, *192*, 216–217, 228–229, 235
Maker, representing, xvii, 33, 127
Mallios, Harry, 25
Manuel, Barry, 73, 91, 117
Mathews, Dr. Ronnie, 114–115, 235
Matuszak, John, 213
Mazeroski, Bill, 93
McCabe, Bhrett, 216, 235
McClure, Bill, 212
McClure, Trey, 118, 120–122, 129, 131, 156
McDonald, Ben, 29, 35–36, 39–41, 43–51, 73, *97, 100*, 117, 134, 204, 225, 235
McDougal, Scott, 123
McMakin, Wally, xvi, 235
McMurray, Heath, 148, 208
Melius, Barth, 154
mental toughness, preparedness, ix, 47, 70, 139, 203
Mestepey, Lane, 149, 151, 154
Miles, Les, xvi, 175, 228
Milli Vanilli, 32
mindset, ix, 68, 94, 204
Misler, Joel, vi
Moock, Chris, 61, 72–73, 75, 80, *107*, 140, 235

Moore, Bryan, 149, 152
Moreau, Doug, 162
Morris, Jim, 114
Morris, Julie, 115
Morris, Wally, 113
Morris, Warren, vii–xii, 14, 93–96,
 113–115, 128, 139, 148, *180*, 206,
 209, 221, 226, 235
Morris, William, viii
Morrison, Robbie, 93–96, 113–114
motivation, motivating, 40, 42, 70, 125,
 127, 132, 142, 174, 213–214, 217,
 219, 227
Mouton, Lyle, 56, 60–61, 64, 68–69,
 71, 74, *104*, 129, 221, 235
movie, star of your own movie, ix, 133,
 145
Musial, Stan, 218

National Championships. *See* College
 World Series (CWS)
Neal, Mike, 87
New Orleans Saints, vi, 75, 79
Nickell, Jackie, 53, 56
Nola, Aaron, 134
Nugent, Tim, 149
Nunez, Eddie, 165

Odds, ix, x, 203
O'Donoghue, John, 50, 56, 117, 204,
 236
Ogea, Chad, 31, 38–39, 44, 49–50,
 60–62, 64, 68–69, 71, 84, *99*, 117,
 153, 199, 203–204, 221, 236
Olympics, Summer, 50, 95, *105*, 115,
 206, 213, 226
Osik, Keith, 53, 56–58, 73, 221, 236
owning, ownership, ix, x, xi, 30–31, 40,
 141

Page, Phillip, 39
Painich, Joey, 122
Papajohn, Mike, 236
Parker, Clay, 73, 199
Pate, Dr. Lisa Jo (Bertman), vi, vii, 25,
 147, 156, 210, 223
Patterson, Gregg, 117
Payton, Sean, 79
Peever, Lloyd, 79
Penn, Wes, 156
percentages, 70, 120, 199–201, 203–204

Perry, Herbert, 68
Petrosian, Ara, 123–124
Pettit, Bo, 134, 149, 208–209
Polk, Ron, 32, 149–150, 153, 236
Pontiff, Wally, 134, 138, 141–142,
 147–149, 154–156, *186*, 208, 227
practice, practicing, x, xiv, 23, 29, 118,
 136–137, 199–200, 206, 209–210
predictions, xvii, 40, 43, 60, 122, 143,
 196, 199
preparation, preparedness, x, 32, 38,
 70–71, 203, 206–207, 209, 219
pressure, performing under, ix, x, 37–38,
 40, 114, 202, 208–209, 214
Prior, Mark, 137

Radakovich, Dan, 164–165, 169–170,
 172–174, 236
Rantz, Ronnie, 62, 73–74, 77–78,
 80–81, *106*, 236
Raymer, Dave, 148, 154
Reboulet, Jeff, 73, 221
Renfroe, Steve, 152
representing, representation, xvii, 33,
 127
Rhine, Jack, 24
Richard, Ron, 169
Richt, Mark, 27, 160, 236
Rios, Armando, 61–62, 70–72, 76–78,
 83–85, 87–91, *106*, 145, 221, 236
Rodgers, Ben, 216
Roemer, Governor Buddy, 76
Rome, Russell, 36, 236
Ruth, Babe, 121
Rutledge, Trey, 140
 (*See also* Hodges, Trey "Rutledge")

Saban, Nick, xviii, 31, 118, 141, 160,
 162, 170, 175, 195–198, 227–228, 236
Saints, New Orleans, vi, 75, 79
Sapper, Max, 205, 211, 217–218,
 222–223
Saxon, Ben, 134
Schneidewind, Scott, 31, 42, 236
Schnellenberger, Howard, 23, 26–27
Schwanke, Jim, 118–119, 122–124, 236
Schwartz, Sandy. *See* Bertman, Sandy
 (Schwartz)
Scioscia, Mike, 214
Scobie, Jason, 149
seeing. *See* visualization, visualizing
 (seeing)

Sexton, Jimmy, 160
Shake Off, 205–206
Shaver, Dennis, xvi, 175–176, 227
Sheets, Andy, 61, 71–72, 221
Shipp, Kevin, 114, 117, *177*
Shultz, Scott, 85
Sirotka, Mike, 60–61, 69, 84–91, *103*,
    153, 203–204, 208, 221, 237
Smith, Dean, 67, 73
Smith, Jim, 25–26
Smith, Mark, 58
Smith, Robbie, 73, 216
Snow, Dave, 207, 237
Southall, Jeff, 30–32, 237
Southard, Judy, 164
Springer, Russell, 29–30, 39–42,
    48–50, *98*, 117, 204, 221
Stallings, Gene, 159
Stanky, Eddie, 25–26
Stanky Field, 26
star
    in your own mind, 65
    of your own movie, ix, 133, 145
Steiner, Ron, 26
Stephenson, Gene, 73
Stephenson, Phil, 24
Stocco, Mark, 89
Storin, Ed, 217
success, succeeding, v, viii, ix, xi, xii,
    96, 133, 193, 199–214, 219
Sugarcanes, 24
Summer Olympics, 50, 95, *105*, 115,
    206, 213, 226
Sunday Speaker Series, 132, 213
Symank, John, 64
system, ix, xii, 68, 70, 118, 144–145,
    196, 202

TAF. *See* Tiger Athletic Foundation
    (TAF)
tailgating, 53, 55, 135–136
taking ownership. *See* owning,
    ownership
Tallet, Brian, 133–135, 137–140, 148,
    153
Tarantino, Quentin, 38
Taylor, Terry, 36
Team USA (baseball), 95, 115
Tellechea, Johnny, 56, 60–61, *103*
tenacity, 145
tendencies, 70, 203–204
Texas A&M (1989), 35–48

"That's baseball," 51, 79–81
Theriot, Ryan, 131, 134, 137–138, 141,
    143–145, 148–149, 153, 155, *184*, 237
Thibodeaux, Johnnie, 118, 130, 148,
    154, 156
thinking, how to think, 35, 79, 204, 213
Thomas, "Turtle," 134, 149
Thompson, Craig, 139
Thompson, Doug, 121–128, 156, 196,
    201–202, 205, 210, 214, 237
Thompson, Kirk, 43–44
Thomson, Bobby, 93
Tiger Athletic Foundation (TAF), xiii,
    160–161, 164, 169, 197, 235–236
Tiger Stadium
    motor home, RV parking at, 173
    ticket licensing plan, xvi, 167–170,
        172, 227, 229
Tigers baseball
    and College World Series (CWS)
        1989, 47–51
        1991, 67–78
        1993, 83–91
        1996, 93–96, 113–115
        1997, 126–128
        2000, 129–145
    and competing, competitiveness,
        competition, 71, 90, *99,* 121, 153,
        167, *184, 191,* 210, 214
    and Gorilla baseball, 69, 117–131,
        136, 236
    and "Hold the Rope," vi, xi, 71–72,
        95, 144, 215–217, 229
    and inspiration, inspiring, xiv, 87, 93,
        155, 211, 213
    as Major League players, 221
    and mental toughness, preparedness,
        ix, 47, 70, 139, 203
    and mindset, ix, 68, 94, 204
    and motivation, motivating, 40, 42,
        70, 125, 127, 132, 142, 174,
        213–214, 217, 219
    and NCAA Regionals, 53–60
    and pitching lab, 201–204
    and practice, practicing, x, xiv, 23,
        29, 118, 136–137, 199–200, 206,
        209–210
    and preparation, preparedness, x, 32,
        38, 70–71, 203, 206–207, 209, 219
    and pressure, performing under, ix, x,
        37–38, 40, 114, 202, 208–209, 214
    and SEC Tournament (1991), 61–65

and the Shake Off, 205–206
and Skip's farewell 2001 season,
  147–157
and success, succeeding, v, viii, ix,
  xi, xii, 96, 133, 193, 199–214, 219
and Sunday Speaker Series, 132, 213
and Sunday spiritual guidance, xii
and the system, ix, xii, 68, 70, 118,
  144–145, 196, 202
and tenacity, 145
and tendencies, 70, 203–204
and Texas A&M (1989), 35–48
and "That's baseball," 51, 79–81
and thinking, how to think, 35, 79,
  204, 213
and trick plays, 23–24, 200, 204–205
and trust, ix, 122, 132, 172–173, 202
videos, use of, 44, 69, 84, 93,
  127–128, 132–133, 140, 145, 200,
  209, 211, 213–214
and visualization, visualizing, 65, 72,
  96, 132–133, 144–145, 203, 219
and weights, weightlifting, xiv, 30,
  118–119
at the White House, 76–78, *108*
and W.I.N. (What's Important Now),
  xii
and the Yellow Book, 204–205
Tilma, Tommy, 71
T.O.B. (Transfer of Blame), x
Tollison, David, 49
trick plays, 23–24, 200, 204–205
trust, ix, 122, 132, 172–173, 202

Utley, Chase, 136

Vaz, Roberto, 122, 127
Vincent, Herb, 80, 124, 160–161, 165,
  167–170, 173–174, 237

vision, xiv, 54, 65, 169, 172
visualization, visualizing (seeing), 65,
  72, 96, 132–133, 144–145, 203, 219

Wagner, Kevin, 132, 211
Walker, Todd, xvii, 79–81, 83–91, *109*,
  206, 221, 237
Wall, Jason, 40
Wayne, Justin, 138, 140–142, 145
Weems, Charles, 160
weights, weightlifting, xiv, 30, 118–119
Wells, Jim, 38, 42, 122, 126–127,
  151–152, 237
White, Jason, 72
Wiles, Randy, 134
Williams, Jason, 86–87, 89, 95, *110*
Williams, Ted, 76–77, 133, 213, 218
Wilson, Brad, xii, 94
Wilson, Brian, 149, 154
W.I.N. (What's Important Now), xii
Winstead, Chuck, xvi, 175–176, 228
Witten, Jeremy, 124, 126, 134, 138,
  141–142, 148
Wooden, John, xvi, xvii, 152, 196, 217
Woodward, Scott, 162, 164, 167, 170,
  172, 175, 193, 237
Wright, Ray, 138–139, 141–142, 148
Wrona, Bill, 24

Yarnall, Eddie, 117, 221
Ybarra, Jamie, 86
Yellow Book, 204–205
Youman, Shane, 149, 204, 208–209,
  237
Young, Jason, 138

Zinsman, Zeph, 149

About the Author...

GLENN GUILBEAU has been a sportswriter since graduating in journalism from the University of Missouri in 1983. He has been an SEC columnist at OutKick.com/FOX News since 2021.

He's covered LSU sports for *USA TODAY*/Louisiana (2004-21), the Baton Rouge *Advocate* (1998-2004), the Alexandria *Town Talk* (1987-93) and *Tiger Rag* magazine (1983-85). He arrived in Baton Rouge in 1983, near the same time when Skip Bertman was named LSU's baseball coach. A New Orleans native, Guilbeau covered the SEC at the Montgomery (Alabama) *Advertiser* (1985-86) and Mobile *Press-Register* (1993-98).

He and his wife, the former Michelle Millhollon of Thibodaux, met at the Baton Rouge *Advocate* and live in Baton Rouge.

LEO HONEYCUTT, winner of the Louisiana Literary Award for his biography of Governor Edwin Edwards, is also an award-winning 30-year television journalist with credits at CBS News, ABC's *Good Morning America*, NBC's *Today Show*, and CNN.

He wrote the biography of Baton Rouge businessman Gerry Lane, one of General Motors' top dealers. He won New York's Axiom Business Book award for *The Clarke Williams Story*, about the founder of Louisiana's CenturyLink, America's third-largest telecom.

Intriguing Books
from
Acadian House Publishing

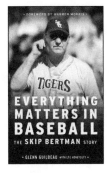

Everything Matters in Baseball
The Skip Bertman Story
A 248-page hardcover biography of legendary LSU baseball coach Skip Bertman, one of America's most successful college coaches. The book reveals Bertman's "Secrets to Success" and gives detailed reports on his five National Championships. It portrays him as a true master of the positive mental attitude, a staunch advocate of hard work, and a stickler for detail. It also describes his stint as LSU's Athletic Director. Foreword by baseball superstar Warren Morris. Illustrated with 32 pages of photos. (Author: Glenn Guilbeau. ISBN: 1-7352641-4-8. Price: $30.00)

Tiger Beat
Covering LSU sports for 35 years

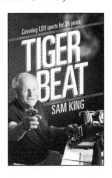

A 240-page hardcover book by a veteran sportswriter who covered LSU football and basketball for Baton Rouge, La., newspapers for 35 years. It features the head coaches over a 50-year span, starting in the mid-1950s, as well as big games and top athletes, including the "Chinese Bandits," Billy Cannon, "Pistol Pete" Maravich, Chris Jackson and Shaquille O'Neal. (Author: Sam King. ISBN: 0-925417-85-8. Price $22.95)

From Bags to Riches
How the New Orleans Saints and the people of their hometown rose from the depths together
The inspiring story of the New Orleans Saints' 2009-2010 football season that culminated with the winning of the Super Bowl. The book explains how the struggling NFL team and the storm-weary people of New Orleans and the Gulf Coast lifted one another's spirits – and fortunes – in the post-Hurricane Katrina years, 2006 – 2010. The narrative is a study in contrasting moods, ranging from the depression and despair that come with being victims of the worst natural disaster in U.S. history, to the euphoria that accompanies the winning of the Super Bowl after 43 years of mostly losing seasons. (Author: Jeff Duncan ISBN: 0-925417-68-8. Price: $24.95)

Getting Over The Four Hurdles of Life

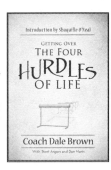

A 160-page book that shows us ways to get past the obstacles, or hurdles, that block our path to success, happiness and peace of mind. Four of the most common hurdles are "I can't / You can't," past failures or fear of failure, handicaps, and lack of self-knowledge. This inspiring book – by one of the top motivational speakers in the U.S. – is brought to life by intriguing stories of various people who overcame life's hurdles. Introduction by former LSU and NBA star Shaquille O'Neal. (Author: Coach Dale Brown. ISBN: 0-925417-72-6. Price: $14.95)

Leadership in the New Normal

A 184-page softcover book on how to be an effective leader in the 21st century. It describes modern leadership principles and techniques and illustrates them with stories from the author's life experiences. He emerged as a national hero and one of the U.S.'s best-known military leaders in 2005 after spearheading the post-Hurricane Katrina search-and-rescue mission in New Orleans. (Author: General Russel Honore. ISBN: 0-925417-75-0. Price $16.00)

Who's Your Mama, Are You Catholic, and Can You Make A Roux? (Book 1)

A 160-page hardcover book containing more than 200 Cajun and Creole recipes, plus old photos and interesting stories about the author's growing up in the Cajun country of south Louisiana. Recipes include Pain Perdu, Couche Couche, Chicken Fricassée, Stuffed Mirliton, Shrimp Stew, Grillades, Red Beans & Rice, Shrimp Creole, Bouillabaisse, Pralines. (Author: Marcelle Bienvenu. ISBN 0-925417-55-6. Price: $22.95)

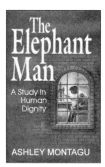

The Elephant Man
A Study in Human Dignity

The Elephant Man is a 138-page softcover book whose first edition inspired the movie and the Tony Award-winning play by the same name. This fascinating story, which has touched the hearts of readers throughout the world for over a century, is now complete with the publication of this, the Third Edition. Illustrated with photos and drawings of The Elephant Man. (Author: Ashley Montagu. ISBN: 0-925417-41-6. Price: $14.95.)

The Forgotten Hero of My Lai
The Hugh Thompson Story (Revised Edition)

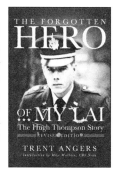

The 272-page hardcover book that tells the story of the U.S. Army helicopter pilot who risked his life to rescue South Vietnamese civilians and to put a stop to the My Lai massacre during the Vietnam War in 1968. Revised Edition shows President Nixon initiated the effort to sabotage the My Lai massacre trials so no U.S. soldier would be convicted of a war crime. (Author: Trent Angers. ISBN: 0-925417-90-4. Price: $22.95)

TO ORDER, list the books you wish to purchase along with the corresponding cost of each. Add $4 for the first book and $1 per book thereafter for shipping. Louisiana residents add 8% tax to the cost of the books. Mail your order and check or credit card authorization (VISA/MC/AmEx) to: Acadian House Publishing, P.O. Box 52247, Lafayette, LA 70505. Or call (800) 850-8851. To order online, go to www.acadianhouse.com.